OBSEQUIUM

By

Victor Blaine

Library and Archives Canada Cataloguing in Publication

Blaine, Victor, 1957-
Obsequium / Victor Blaine.

ISBN 978-0-9868316-0-7

I. Title.

PS8603.L2998O38 2011 C813'.6 C2011-900976-5

Jane Hansen finished adjusting her hair and stepped down the ladder from the executive jet. The number one reporter for the News World Network was ready for her live report. Her cameraman, Nick Farrow, had set up the satellite equipment on the grass next to their parking spot off a side runway.

"Ready when you are," he said stepping from the shade of the jet's wing.

She nodded and took her place in front of the camera. Nick was dripping perspiration from the heat. Jane was cool as a cucumber. She reread her notes then gave her trademark smile to the camera, signaling she was ready.

"Five four three two," said Nick pointing at her.

"Yesterday at dawn, armed men tried to seize key government strong points in Caracas as part of an apparent coup attempt. President Rodriguez, speaking from the heavily reinforced presidential palace, is claiming the CIA is behind this uprising in an attempt to assert American control of the rich oil fields of Venezuela. Civilians are staying indoors. There is no sign of a popular uprising and the army has remained loyal to the president. General Gonzalez, supreme army commander, has assured me that he is in control of the capitol and has driven the rebels back to the harbor where they began their attack. Because most of the rebels arrived by boat, these events are being compared to the Bay of Pigs invasion of Cuba years ago. All indications are that this invasion is just as much a failure. Military sources are predicting that all rebels will have been either killed or captured by this evening. This is Jane Hansen, News World Network, Caracas, Venezuela," said Jane.

As she finished speaking, three air force jets took off behind her.

"Perfect touch those jets in the background. I couldn't have timed it better if they were taking off for our benefit," said Nick.

Jane turned to watch as the jets climbed then turned toward the harbor.

"I wouldn't want to be them," said Nick.

"Who," she asked.

"The rebels. They have only one place to go. Out to sea in any boat they can steal. Once out there they will be cut down by those jets and any armed ship the General has," said Nick.

Jane shrugged her shoulders and returned to the jet. Inside, her assistant, Emily, waited with the telephone.

"It's him" she said raising her eyebrows. This meant only one man.

"Hello, William, what's up," asked Jane.

"Jane darling, I need you in Paris. How soon can you wrap up there and get here?" he asked.

"It's all over but the shouting as they say. We can load up and take off in thirty minutes. What's the scoop?" she asked eagerly.

"More EU-Muslim troubles. Only this time it is not just in France, it's all across Europe. I need you here to be the pretty face and the sexy voice of the network," said William.

Jane smiled. Her boss, William Hamadi, never stopped complimenting her. She had been annoyed by his manner at first, but now she'd come to like it.

"Sure thing boss, keep your pants on until I get there." said Jane.

"OK, if I have to. Rene will meet you at Orly Field. Out," said William.

"Well?" asked Emily.

"Paris, ASAP," she answered heading back outside.

*****

Professor Tom Hansen looked at the clock in his office. Thirty minutes until his class, History 412, the Decline and Fall of Ancient Civilizations, began. The old fashioned rotary phone on his desk began to ring.

"Hello?" he asked.

"You Tarzan, me Jane," said Jane giggling.

Tom kicked his office door shut.

"How are you, sweetie?" he asked. "Where are you?"

"Outside Caracas, at the military air field. There was a coup attempt but it's all over now," she replied.

Tom could hear an explosion in the background. He knew the sound of artillery when he heard it.

"According to who?" asked Tom.

"General Gonzalez," said Jane.

"Right, and if you had interviewed the rebels they would have told you it was all over also. Be careful. You know how much I worry about you," said Tom.

"You shouldn't have married a reporter then, you big dope, " said Jane.

"I couldn't help it. I fell head over heels for you. Nothing could have stopped me," said Tom.

"Really?" asked Jane coyly.

"Could a guy say that if he didn't mean it? So when are you coming home?" he asked.

"I don't know. I just got a call from the boss to scoot over to Paris. Seems the network can't do anything without me. You know how that is," said Jane.

"Only too well, at least in your case. I have a roast thawing. It will be roast beef sandwiches for a week," said Tom.

"Can you forgive me?" asked Jane.

"As long as you don't run off with another man, I can forgive you anything. You know that. I just miss you. A husband likes to ravage his wife on occasion. That's hard to do when she's thousands of miles away."

"You are so romantic in a crude sort of way. I'll make it up to you as soon as possible. Only right now there is so much happening in the world. Like a pot about to boil over. I don't actually see a break coming in the near future," said Jane.

Tom paused.

"I understand. Call as often as you can. I'm not going any where," he said.

"I don't deserve you, sweetie. I'll call again tomorrow. Bye Tarzan," said Jane.

Tom put down the phone slowly. Oh well. Marry the future star reporter of NWN and separation was inevitable. He looked at the clock. Time for class.

*****

Hansen looked around the classroom. The usual characters were asleep in the back row. Others were doodling or studying for other classes. Half seemed to be listening.

"The history of the human race is one of conflict. There are records, stories, and myths of violent acts going all the way back to Cain and Abel. Heroes stepped forward with sword, bow, or sling into legend. So I ask you, where does conflict come from. Why does it happen. Why does it start? Can we learn enough from history to predict it. Maybe even prevent it. Prevent wars?" asked Tom.

5

"Strong leaders have started wars of conquest. Julius Caesar, Napoleon, and Hitler come to mind. But there are other sources of conflict. Like changing demographics. Whether it leads to public debate or open warfare, a demographic shift is guaranteed to to start something. Some examples are the Saxon invasion of England and Christopher Columbus leading the wave of Europeans to the new world. More recently, Lebanese Christians falling from fifty five percent to thirty five percent of the population leading to civil war."

"The largest example of demographic conflict is Africa. In the distant past, African tribes lived securely inside their own territories. Of course, they had the occasional border war when neighbors made trouble. But in general the fighting was sporadic and not ongoing. During colonialism, African nation states were formed for the convenience of Europeans and placed different tribes together inside national borders. A recipe for conflicts that are still being fought today. Everyone blames the Europeans for harming Africa by creating nations containing different cultures. And with hindsight, it is clear that the critics were right."

"Now let's consider the West, where immigration has brought about the same condition. Again, people of different cultures are living together inside national borders. In the past, the larger culture forced the new arrivals to join the mainstream. This is what is called the melting pot. Recently, a new philosophy called multiculturalism espoused the idea that immigrants should retain their languages and cultures even though they have moved to a new country. Multiculturalism opposes the idea that immigrants must conform to the culture of the host country."

"The multiculturalists tell us that different cultures in one country is a bad thing when they talk about Africa. Usually with their hands out for donation money. But then they turn around and say it is a good thing when they talk about the West. Which is it? Good or bad? What are your thoughts? Anyone?"

Hansen looked around the room. Silence. No hands were raised.

"You students are going to answer this question first hand because uncontrolled immigration into the West will play out in your lifetimes," said Tom. "What are your thoughts?"

Hansen looked over the apathetic students. Many avoided his stare.

"Do you care?"

Again silence. This apathy made Hansen question his teaching ability. Were his lectures boring or had the students changed since he was young? Where were the intellectually curious or the

6

annoying kids who argued against every idea? Or had he broken a taboo by bringing up immigration?

"What about America today? Are there any issues that you students feel passionately about?"

More silence.

"The founders of this country pledged to risk their lives, their property, and their sacred honor for the freedom you enjoy today. How many of you would fight for our system of government? Our way of life? Cultural values? Anyone? Does anyone care?"

He paused again. The lack of engagement was frustrating.

"Consider the more recent collapse of the Soviet Union. Bolshevism, communism. The society as a whole had already given up on it. Then came Gorbachev. He didn't like it either. He wanted to improve it, change it, but not discard it. The older bosses knew that even a small change would upset the apple cart. When the possibility for real change happened, the Soviet Union was gone in about a month. A handful of people fought for control of Russia in Moscow after the fall. Nobody else cared enough to fight over it. In part because generations were taught not to get involved in politics on penalty of death. Go back seventy years to the rise of the Bolsheviks and it was a different story. It took a full fledged war to remove the political structure of the Czar. The leadership class fought to keep their land, their wealth, and what they viewed as their country. They didn't give up without a fight."

"Do any of you care enough for our way of life to fight for it? In World War Two there were stories of young men who killed themselves because the army wouldn't take them. They were overwhelmed by shame. Presidents Eisenhower, Kennedy, Nixon, Ford, and George H W Bush served in the war. Reagan served in the army film corp. Carter served in the Navy after the war. More recently we have had two presidents who avoided going to war. It suggests to me that there has been a change in the leadership attitudes of the elites during my lifetime. Let those those poor dumb farm kids die for my country, not me, or my kids."

"Civilizations have come and gone. They grow when they believe in themselves. They die when they stop believing in themselves. Peoples who won't fight for what they have, lose everything. Both as individuals and nations. I see the signs of decline all around us. A certain lack of enthusiasm for our way of life. Have we already passed into the lethargy that signals the end of our civilization?"

7

This is the BBC, Maria Baker reporting from London. Oil prices rose again on world markets today as news of an explosion on the North Sea oil rig, Ocean Conqueror, circulated. The damage was extensive. Twelve men are known dead and twenty two are missing. This is the third North sea rig to stop production this year due to accident. The combination of steadily declining North sea production, which peaked in 1999, and oil rig failures, have dramatically reduced British oil production this year. Home Secretary, Malcom Switch, has said ongoing problems in the North Sea could cancel the GDP growth predicted for this year.

*****

The dark skinned customs official returned Jane's passport respectfully. Jane tucked it into her coat as she hurried past the jet to the waiting news satelite truck. Nick followed with his gear.

"I think the best background shot would be the Obelisk or the Arc de Triomphe," said Rene Matin, Paris producer for NWN. "It would show the traffic jam best."

"Make it the Eiffel Tower. We need to identify our location and to most of the world, the Eiffel Tower is France," replied Jane getting into the truck.

"OK. OK. But we don't have much time. Paris will have total gridlock in about 45 minutes," said Rene.

"Total or just bad," asked Nick.

"Total. It's crazy!" said Rene.

"Not crazy. News. I've been studying your reports during the flight. I think I have the outline of what I'm going to say ready. Now I just need to understand the emotional angle. How is the government reacting? What about the man in the street?" asked Jane.

"It's too soon to know what to think. It is catastrophe!" said Rene.

Jane nodded knowingly and began writing in her travel note book.

"Would you say there is widespread surprise and shock? Have you moved to outrage or violence yet?" she asked.

"Yes then no. We are a civilized people. The knee jerk reaction of you English is not our way," he replied.

Nick looked out the window at the slow moving traffic. So it was bad, real bad. Had to be to get the cynical French so agitated.

"And the government?" asked Jane.

"Nothing to report. They say everything is under control. Not to worry. I don't think they have any idea of what to do. Nobody does," said Rene in resignation.

"Except Norway. Do you have the tape interview ready? I want it to be spliced in just behind my bit. Then my sign off as the men stand up. Got it?" said Jane.

"William told me not to argue. But don't forget I'm the boss here," said Rene firmly.

Not for long apparently. Jane looked out the window of the speeding van at the traffic. Not a white face in sight. She returned to her notes and began to write.

*****

As the voice of the Imam echoed off the Eiffel Tower, Jane faced Nick and his video camera. He began waving his arms.

"What Nick? We need to go now!" She said curtly.

"It's the kids. They're blocking the background shot."

"Rene! Get the little shits out of my shot! Vit! Vit!" she cried as Rene and two of his assistants shooed the rag tag crowd of African and Chinese children out of the way.

"Hit it," said Jane.

Nick gave her the thumbs up.

"Cities all over the world have traffic problems and we've all been trapped in them. But here in Paris, daily life, as well as the traffic, has come to a complete stop. The Muslim faithful have taken their political demands to the streets literally. Starting yesterday, Muslims have been putting their prayer rugs in the streets when they pray, shutting down the transportation systems. Even the subways are coming to a stop because the mostly Muslim work force refuses to work during the prayers. And other immigrant and refugee groups have joined with them. Loudspeakers have recently been placed all around Paris, bringing the voice of the Imam to the city. When you close your eyes you feel that the city of light has become an Arabian capitol."

"For years now, the Muslim Directorate has presented three non-negotiable demands to the EU. First, that Muslims are not subject to the laws and courts of the EU but will instead be accountable to separate Sharia courts. Second, American style affirmative action employment requirements will be implemented for all immigrants and refugees, to force access to all levels of society. And third, recognition of Arabic as an official EU language required of all EU government employees."

"The EU has negotiated the first two points but the third is causing dissension among EU members. Norwegian ambassador Ele Egstrom had this to say," said Jane turning back to her notes as the tape was played.

Ele Egstrom stood outside the EU general assembly hall talking to the press.

"The requirement that all EU officials speak Arabic is simply not acceptable. So few Europeans speak Arabic that this will result in a de facto take over of the EU bureaucracy by non Europeans. We have supported the needs of immigrants and refugees at least as well as any other EU member. We have supported all the demands of the Muslim Directorate and other groups in the interest of cooperation and peaceful relations. But we have now reached an impasse. Norway still remembers being taken over by the Nazi's in the last war. We cannot now voluntarily agree to a cultural take over by the Muslim Directorate. We reluctantly joined the EU after the financial crisis. Now we must consider leaving the EU to preserve our culture and heritage".

Nick signaled Jane to start again.

"Mainstream Muslims across the world have expressed outrage at Mohammed being compared to Hitler. Ambassador Egstrom is being blamed for the widespread rioting and killings of Christians in the Arab world that followed his speech. The EU press is also blaming him for the gridlock that now extends from Lisbon to Helsinki. Egstrom was recalled to Oslo, but is being held in Brussels pending an investigation by the EU Commission of Truth and Justice on charges of racism and inciting murder."

"So far there has been no response from the EU or the other member state governments to the gridlock. There is the sense that something will happen. But what and when, nobody knows. This is Jane Hansen, NWN news, Paris."

Rene quickly lit another cigarette as the children swarmed

around Nick and Jane.

"There is one odd benefit from this strike if you could call it that," said Nick.

"What's that?" asked Jane.

"Except for the Imam, it's quiet. Really quiet,"said Nick.

"Next you'll claim the air quality has improved," smiled Jane.

"Maybe the Muslim Directorate is onto something," laughed Nick.

Rene looked on, smoking his cigarette angrily.

This is the BBC, Elizabeth Barkley reporting from London. The recent uprising in Venezuela has been put down and order restored. Captured rebels are saying they were controlled by the American CIA in the coup attempt. Venezuelan officials close to president Rodriguez say he is shocked by this news. He has called for a meeting of the Organization of American States to discuss sanctions against the Americans. The White House has refused to comment on this, leading experts to conclude that the claims are true.

Meanwhile, Americans are lining up at their filling stations again as fuel shortages grip the nation after many years of reliable but expensive supplies. Mexico stopped selling fuel to the States after the congress voted to limit the number of citizenship amnesties granted each year to Mexican illegals. Experts warn that if Venezuela joins with Mexico in this embargo, the United States will face the possibility of fuel rationing and serious economic fall out.

*****

Tom winked at Tiffany as he approached the Dean of History's office. She smiled back self consciously and motioned him into Dawayne Jackson's office. Always blonde, aren't they.

Dawayne looked up, gathering his thoughts about what he had to say.

"Sit down, Tom, we have some serious things to discuss," said Dawayne.

"This is a nice office. Not the largest. But it has the best view," said Tom sitting in the tall leather chair opposite Dawayne's desk.

Dawayne paused and played with his pen.

"You wish to talk about your new job, I presume?" asked Tom innocently.

"Of course you know about the new federal funding rules

requiring every university to have proportional employment equal to each racial group. That means dropping from seventy five to forty five percent white. Department heads like me count as three, saving the jobs of two white professors, maybe your own. Until that law was passed, you were going to be department head. I want to get past any resentment you feel toward me and get back to the good working relationship we've always had," said Dawayne expectantly.

"I don't feel any resentment. Being dean is more work for little extra pay. Everyone thought I would be the next dean. So did I. But I didn't seek it. Did you?" asked Tom.

"Yes. I always wanted the job," said Dawayne.

"Can I ask why?" asked Tom.

"I have the power to hire and fire. Over time, with personnel changes, I will take this department in the direction I feel is right for the future," said Dawayne.

"You sound like a revolutionary on the ramparts, cursing the system, and pledging to break all traditions," said Tom.

"Tradition would have put you in this chair instead of me. The law broke that tradition and put a new one in it's place. But it's a lot more than an act of congress. It's the result of African American organization and struggle. In concert with other minority groups. These changes don't occur by accident. We are organized. We march, we picket, we vote, we write our congressmen. We focus our political clout where it will do us the most good. Unlike you people," said Dawayne.

"Our traditions have worked pretty well for America. Everyone can have a good life here and that's no accident," said Tom.

"That attitude is why African American culture is ascendant and white culture is in decline. Your myths are holding you back," said Dawayne.

"You mean the one about George Washington and the cherry tree?" said Tom grinning

"Ha Ha. I mean the myth of the individual. You people think that's the answer to everything. It might have been valid when whites fanned out across a wilderness to grab the Native American's land. Small groups of settlers were on their own. That isn't useful anymore. America is a land of competing groups. White, Black, Hispanic, Asian, Arab, Native American, East Indian, mixed heritage, gays, and women. It takes organization and focus of large groups of people to be effective in this political reality. I just don't see white people being effective at getting it together anymore. And that's a shame because I'm not happy about singing the national anthem in Spanish at the football games," said Dawayne wistfully.

"Another broken tradition. Changed at least. I see your argument. But if we abandon the guiding concept of the individual, group identity will replace national identity. This United States will cease to be united in any sense. You will have an endless fight on your hands for every aspect of political power from President to dog catcher. You won't be the favored sons. The Hispanics out number you and they're learning your techniques fast," replied Tom.

"But an official language? I might have to pass a Spanish exam in the future to keep my job! If you people won't stand up for American culture, who will?" asked Dawayne.

"The time for that fight came and went. Nothing was done while there was still time. Now, in my judgment, it's too late," said Tom.

"I don't like what I'm hearing. But you people are really just lazy. Organize," said Dawayne. "And get to it before I lose my land!"

"Your land?" asked Tom, surprised..

"You know how we refer to the native Americans as indian nations? Now they want to be separate nations in fact. They have petitioned the United Nations for recognition of independent sovereignty and they are claiming half the country including the neighborhood I'm living in. If they win, I'll lose the quarter acre I thought no one could take away from me," said Dawayne.

"It's probably just an opening negotiating position. You can look at this as a demographics issue. Their numbers shrank when we took over the continent. Now their numbers are up and they want a larger share of power. White people aren't your solution. Every nation is the sum of the people living there. At one time that was European settlers and Indians. Then black slaves were brought in. Then Chinese railroad workers. But America maintained its WASP political culture through the sixties. World population kept growing and soon people were coming into the country with and without permission by the millions. The wall across the southern border was never completed and the flood never controlled. Now a foreign country, Mexico, has an unprecedented political influence in America. No one can openly challenge the Hispanic lobby. They learned how to march and protest from you. Citizens and illegals together. Whites are no longer the majority. We don't control the political process like we once did."

"I have studied world history as well as current events. Unless human beings have evolved significantly in the last few years,

14

then history will repeat itself in one of two directions. Firstly, nations are formed around cultures. America is now in the process of developing a new culture. This is a slow process that can be difficult but generally peaceful. Since whites won't fight for their culture, it's between the rest of you," said Tom.

"Are you saying that whites are a bunch of pushovers? Our black representatives have been careful not to push too hard to avoid a backlash. Now you imply that isn't going to happen?" asked Dawayne.

"No, not now. Public schools teach the kids that whites are responsible for all the world's problems. Past, present, and future. Who wants to carry all that guilt? So now everywhere you go you see piercings. They aren't a traditional European style except for the ears. Self mutilation is a badge of shame. A sign that reads; I look white, but I'm not, so don't blame me," said Tom.

"And the second course?" asked Dawayne.

"Civil war. If one of the competing groups can't wait for a slow evolution to take its course, a fight could break out. Violence with racial overtones. Picture the burning of Atlanta across the whole country. There would be a shift in political power based on numbers. Whites would continue to control the north. Blacks in the southeast. Hispanics in the southwest and Florida," said Tom.

"Well I hope I don't live to see it. I'm content with things the way they are right now," said Dawayne.

"So am I. In such a future we would be on different sides. We wouldn't have these illuminating discussions any more. At least, not until the fighting stopped," said Tom.

"We agree completely on that score," said Dawayne. "You always were a passionate lecturer. Must be why you are so popular with the students," said Dawayne. "But I pegged you for an idealist. You sound a little cynical to me."

"I was an idealist when I joined the marines. Now my only politics is the politics of me. Do I benefit from new legislation or other changes? If yes, I support it. If no, I fight it," said Hansen.

Dawayne drummed his pen on the desk.

"There is another subject I want to bring up. It's a favor actually," he said.

"Shoot. You can count on me," said Tom.

"I'm relieved that our friendship is intact. That would have been a heavy price to pay for promotion. But a lot of the other faculty members are resentful. You were the chosen one, so to speak. To get past this delicate period of readjustment, I'm asking you to take a sabbatical," said Dawayne.

"I understand. You want me gone while you consolidate your power. You don't have to ask me twice to take a vacation. When and how long?" asked Tom.

"I have a substitute waiting to take over your class. If you continue through your Friday lecture, everything will go smoothly. And say, at least until winter quarter. Longer if you would like it. A year off is the standard thing," said Dawayne.

"I'll pass the word that I support your promotion. No extra charge. I've wanted to take a long trip for some time. Now I don't have any excuses," said Tom.

"I appreciate that, Tom. Any idea where you will go? Australia to visit your relatives?" asked Dawayne.

"No. I've been wanting to live my romantic fantasy about the European explorers. I've been planning to sail my boat to the Mediterranean. Retrace the voyages of Ulysses and Nelson. Christopher Columbus in reverse. And the timing is good," said Tom.

"Why is that?" asked Dawayne.

"You know what the travel agencies are saying. See Europe before it's gone!" said Tom.

"This is the BBC, Maria Herrera reporting from London. The meeting of OPEC oil ministers in Abu Dhabi has ended with a declaration of support for the struggle of Muslims in Europe. Effective immediately, oil supplies to Europe will be cut back twenty percent, to encourage a more flexible position by EU member states toward the demands of the Muslim Directorate. OPEC ministers will meet again next month in Valencia to review the situation in Europe and make further cut backs if required.

*****

Tom Hansen lifted the forward hatch up and onto the new hinge. Saltwater and metal. A never ending battle with oxidation. He finished the assembly and picked up the old corroded hinge. He stood and looked down the length of his forty seven foot Vagabond he had named 'The Christopher'. The sailboat was looking better than it had in years. Ready for a real voyage of discovery. It was a fiberglass boat but the teak deck coverings and the broad stern windows had captured his imagination from the start.

"Tom, I'm sorry. It's all my fault really." said Bob Thomas.

Tom looked up with a start. Bob towered over him on the flying bridge of his forty foot power cruiser in the next slip. They had been moored together for years and as fellow 'yachtees', they had become friends.

"I forgive you, Captain Bligh. Now what am I forgiving?" asked Tom grinning.

"I signed you up to run the club's rummage sale. It was down to you or me. And I knew you were on sabbatical," replied the black naval officer.

Tom flinched in mock pain.

"Drafted again. I hope this ends better than the last time," said Tom.

"No need to make fun of me. Somebody had to do it and I

won't be here. So what's with your boat? It's looking good. Are you selling?" asked Bob, concerned.

"No. I'm actually going on a long voyage for a change. I'm going to sail across the ocean and discover Europe. Find my roots and all that. Want to go?" asked Tom.

"Love to. But I won't have that much time off until I retire. Besides I'm leaving on maneuvers soon. We're going to be playing cat and mouse with a new French submarine. They evade. We find. It's the last chance they will have to test themselves against us as NATO allies. The alliance ends on December thirty first. The European Defense Force takes over. We're concerned about their new design. Now that we won't be allies we have to test every threat. We'll have a few tricks up our sleeves, of course," said Bob.

Tom covered his ears.

"Loose lips sink ships, sir," mocked Tom.

"I'm not worried about you. All the marines I know are trust worthy. Dumb but trustworthy," chuckled Bob.

"Thank you sir, may I please have another," said Tom.

"You're lucky I'm here. Navy and marines go together. The other members think you are a little crazy," said Bob.

"That's the price you pay being a college professor. But I've learned to live with it," said Tom smugly.

"You know it's not that. It's the rumors about you going crazy in Africa. Swinging from vines and screaming like Tarzan. I've always respected your privacy, but I've been dying to know if it was true," said Bob.

"It's all true. I was a sniper assassin. A bad job turned into a long evasion. I used my survival training to go deep into the jungle. One day I decided not to go back. I needed a vacation anyway. I was crazy by normal standards at that moment. It wasn't all bad, though. A young reporter from Australia heard the stories about me and went into the jungle to do a story. She tamed my savage heart and brought me back to civilization. I was really dumb in one sense. I let years pass before chasing her down and marrying her," said Tom.

"That was Jane?" asked Bob.

"Yeah, Jane Bedford, News World Network reporter, before she was famous," said Tom staring into the distance. "We plan to meet when I arrive at the Canaries. She promised me a long slow cruise but her job is keeping her busy right now," said Tom.

"Can't you put your foot down? Don't you wear the pants in the family?" asked Bob.

"She was a reporter before we met. It's who she is and I can't change her. Wouldn't want to," said Tom.

Bob nodded.

"Watch yourself when you get there. Europe isn't like it used to be. For me, people used to stare because I was black. Now they stare because I'm an American serviceman. We're not as popular as we used to be," said Bob.

"I'm not worried. The bottom line is that I'm white. Europe is the homeland of my ancestors. Maybe I need to change my fashion a little but other than that I'm just like the rest of them. I'll fit right in," said Tom.

"Maybe. If you wear a keffiyeh," said Bob.

"My keffiyeh. Right. I promise I won't leave home without it," laughed Tom.

"Looks like you have company. You up for dinner later?" asked Bob stepping back to the cabin.

"You got it," said Tom turning to look behind him.

Grad student, Brent Swain, stood by the gangway. He looked at his shoes. Nervous. His hands in his pockets. Something was up.

"Come aboard, matey," said Tom smiling.

Brent reluctantly walked up, stopped in the cockpit, and stood silently.

"The boat is almost ready to go. And I'm almost ready to go. Something tells me that you are not almost ready to go," said Tom. "Or am I wrong?"

"Well, there's this girl," said Brent slowly.

Tom waited for him to continue.

"She's going to England and wants me to go with her. I know I promised to sail with you but I want to go with her. Now I don't know what to do," said Brent.

"You just answered your own question. You want to go with her. So go with her," said Tom.

"Is it OK with you? I feel bad about leaving you on such short notice," said Brent.

"There's a lot of cliches just for this situation. One is 'a man's got to do what a man's got to do'. Do you love her?" asked Tom.

"Yeah, I guess. I mean, yes I do," said Brent standing taller.

"Then by all means go with her. The right woman is everything you and every other man needs. If she's the one, hold on with both hands and never let her go," said Tom.

Brent smiled sheepishly.

"I thought you'd be pissed," said Brent.

"I could never stand in the way of true love. We'll manage without you. Or change plans. Or whatever. This trip is my

19

dream and I don't expect anyone to buy into it the way I have. I may still have time to find another deck hand. If not, that's life. What's her name, by the way?" asked Tom.

"Lorrie Martin. She's the prettiest girl I've ever met. So smart and cheerful and exciting ..."

"OK Romeo, I get the picture. I wish you the best of luck," said Tom holding out his hand.

Brent shook his hand vigorously, relieved.

"Your cruise brought us together. She really only flirted with me until I told her I was leaving for a few months. Then I found out her true feelings for me," beamed Brent.

"Really?" asked Tom.

"Yeah. She said she needed me. Especially since she wanted to go to England but was afraid to go by herself," said Brent.

"So now she has her own knight errant to protect her," replied Tom.

"Um yeah, I guess. Anyway, I want to. Protect her. You know," said Brent.

"Yeah, I know. Well, good luck with that. I hope it turns out for you," said Tom.

"Thanks, I can't wait to tell her," said Brent turning down the gangway.

He stopped to wave once, then walked up the pier with a big smile on his face.

"Young love," sighed Tom to himself. "So much hope, so unlikely to last."

This is the BBC, Mary Campbell reporting from London. After a brief cabinet meeting, Prime Minister Stanley announced that fuel rationing will start as soon as ration books are distributed. Meanwhile, petrol stations will be closed on Tuesdays, Thursdays, and Sundays with immediate affect. Industry will also be rationed but details are still being debated. Parliament has already confirmed support for the plan given the need for quick and effective action.

*****

Captain Bob Thomas examined the walls and ceiling of the dining room. The room had a sense of opulence and taste that he never saw in America. It was old, too. He sat in his chair near the head of the table. Admirals to his left, captains in the middle, and execs to his right. All the players in the exercises to begin in three days time. His gaze passed down the table. White faces. He was the only black senior officer present. He was used to that.

For him this was normal. He was constantly surrounded by white officers and was comfortable in their company. They knew what it took to make captain and gave him the respect he had earned. There was just one other face that stood out. An exec sitting opposite his own. Clearly an Arab. But with the airs of French aristocracy. The confidence verging on arrogance. There was something else he couldn't put his finger on. Their eyes met. The French exec held his glance for a moment then turned back to his own conversation. Bob had seen that look before, but he couldn't place it.

Admiral LaFollete tapped on his glass for silence.

"I want to welcome all of you from America to our humble lunch room," said the Admiral.

There were a few chuckles as he continued.

"For three hundred years, French naval officers have enjoyed the pleasure of a good meal in this hall before a voyage. German officers also during the last war, but that is behind us. As you know, the NATO alliance that has defined European politics and military affairs, will end on December thirty first of this year. Europe, through the European defense force, will stand on its own feet once again, proud and strong. On behalf of Europe let me say thank you for standing firm in the face of aggression when Europe was on its knees after the last war," said the Admiral.

There was a light applause from the French officers.

"I am also very glad you chose not to use the nuclear weapon on Paris or Berlin. Too bad for the Japanese since they couldn't fight back, eh?" said the Admiral pausing for effect.

The American officers stared at him in silence.

"But before you leave us for good, I want to thank you for coming to take part in this exercise. We have built our best nuclear submarine ever, the Marseilles. But to know just how good she is, we need to test ourselves against the best. And we all know the best is the United States Navy," said the Admiral.

He paused for the light applause.

"We will send the Marseilles out into the Atlantic with your three submarine chasers and play hide and seek. Each scenario will be more difficult and when we finish we will know just how close we have come to your standards," said Admiral Lafollete.

He turned to his American counterpart, Admiral Messman.

"Which are your captains?" he asked.

"Steele, Beecher, and Thomas," replied the Admiral.

"I would like to raise a toast to the fox, Captain Rochambeau, of the Marseilles," said Lafollete.

All eyes turned to Rochambeau amid a chorus of good wishes.

"And another toast to the hounds, Captains Steele, Beecher, and Thomas," said Lafollete.

Another chorus of congratulations followed.

"Now gentlemen, let's be seated. I am hungry and can not wait to enjoy the best food in all of France!" said Lafollette.

*****

Captain Thomas took his coat from the clerk and turned to his exec, Charles Hampton.

"Nice dinner," said Thomas.

"Between you and me, I'd rather have a hamburger and fries. French fries but of course," said Hampton putting on a French accent.

"Ahhh, Captain Thomas, let me bid you bon chance. And I

extend the offer to tour my boat before we sail, to you as I have the other captains," said Rochambeau extending his hand.

They shook hands.

"She is not as lovely as this," said Rochambeau waving toward the hotel. "But still in my eyes it is a beauty."

"I feel the same about my ship, captain," said Thomas.

His gaze moved to the exec with the dark features who stood at Rochambeau's elbow.

"Let me present my executive officer, Commander Bery," said Rochambeau.

They shook hands.

"Commander Bery comes from one of our finest naval families. One with a glorious history of service to France. He will take my place one of these days I am sure," said Rochambeau.

Thomas watched Bery's eyes move from his to Rochambeau's. There was a hint of a smile on his face. Obedient yet condescending.

"My duties prevent me from enjoying you tour tomorrow. Possibly after the exercise?" said Thomas.

"Of course, if schedules allow, eh?" said Rochambeau moving to the door. "Good night to you."

"And you," replied Thomas.

Again the look from Bery. Condescension. Now he recognized that expression. He'd seen it among his own people back home. The look of a house nigger about to get even with his master.

This is the BBC, Mary Coles reporting from London. A large crowd gathered at the recently reopened Masjid Taiba mosque in Hamburg. Saying the closure was another sad example of xenophobic racism, EU Commissioner of Justice, Freedom, and Security, Ahmoud Antilier, apologized to the crowd and joined the applause after the unveiling of the statue dedicated to the martyrs of 9/11. This mosque, then known as the al-Quds, was where many of the 9/11 terrorists were recruited.

*****

Captain Bob Thomas stood by the door to the sonar room.

"Report," said Thomas.

"Nothing. A few random reflections but nothing we can say is the Marseilles," replied Chief Yablonski.

"A creditable effort. But the Marseilles, she is the best, no?" beamed Lieutenant Emile Blanc. "According to the test plan, the Marseilles was to cross through the search grid ten times over five days. It's a win for us, I think. You haven't caught her even once?"

Thomas eyed the French liaison officer calmly. He knew the French liked to crow like roosters when they got something over us. It was more important to them to beat the Americans than to beat any of their real enemies.

"Beecher says he got one firm reflection two days ago," said Thomas.

"My colleague, Lieutenant Tassini, who was there, says this report is exaggerated," replied Blanc.

The sonar crew looked annoyed. They would be glad when this outsider was removed from their otherwise compatible team.

"The test is over in two hours. I want everyone to stay on their toes right to the last minute. No slacking off. Carry on," said Thomas.

The sonar team returned their focus to their equipment.

"Lieutenant Blanc, I am returning to the bridge. Would you like to observe the last of the exercise from there?" asked Thomas.

"My place is here for now. In two hours I would happily give you my report in person if that is acceptable," said Blanc.

"Good, I'll expect you," said Thomas.

He nodded to the Frenchman and left the sonar station. Back toward the bridge. Right turn. Backtrack. Down four decks. Through a number of hatches to a door guarded by two marines. They came to attention and knocked five times on the door. The door opened and Thomas entered a large maintenance room over crowded by the nine men in blue maintenance coveralls. Civilians. Most of the space was filled with electronics loaded just before leaving port and assembled during the voyage.

"Your timing is good, Captain," said Ralph Moeller, project leader from Griffin Dynamics Corp. "The Marseilles is traveling at eleven knots, depth nine hundred and thirty feet, course thirty six degrees. She's about six thousand yards away in terms of a surface view. Look at these."

Moeller led Thomas to a bank of computer screens.

"Here we are shown in green. The Marseilles is in red. Over here is the 3D view," said Moeller using the mouse to turn the display screen to a number of different viewing angles.

Another man handed Thomas a spare set of headphones.

"That's the raw reflection pattern," said Moeller holding out a second headphone. "And this is the filtered data from our latest modifications."

Thomas listened to one then the other. Grid arrays used to collect and combine wave energy were nothing new. The relentless pursuit of improvements had led to the equipment hidden in this room. It was the latest directional grid array technology with state of the art interpretation software. Dialed in during the Marseilles first pass.

"So how has it worked?" asked Thomas.

"We are ten for ten. This is the last pass going on right now. How is the old stuff working?" asked Moeller.

Old stuff. The regular sonar equipment was the best in the American navy. Until now.

"Oh for ten," replied Thomas.

The other technicians looked at each other proudly.

"Carry on," said Thomas leaving the room.

The marines snapped to attention and closed the door behind him. Technically he was cheating. They had promised to use their best equipment against the Marseilles. On the other hand, this was experimental gear, jury rigged to the hull. Barely installed in time for the test. Thomas hadn't planned on checking in on the new stuff until the French Lieutenant had left the ship. Blanc had gotten under his skin a bit. Thomas had the last laugh now.

This is the BBC, Anjela Singh reporting from London. The mayor of New York City officiated at the grand opening of the Sevilla mosque across from the site of the former World Trade Center. When negotiations to rebuild the St. Nicholas Greek orthodox church broke down, the port authority offered the site to the mosque developers. The Saudi ambassador and foreign minister were also on hand to tour the one hundred million dollar, thirteen story masterpiece of architecture.

A protest group of 9/11 survivors tried to march from Battery Park to the site but were held in the park by a strong police presence.

*****

Claude Bery stepped onto the bus. He could see the respect and trust in the eyes of the other passengers that his uniform brought him every where he went. Tradition, order, glory. People saw what they wanted to see in him and in others who wore the uniform of France.

Two stops later a young man dressed like an Arab got on and made his way to the seat opposite his own. The other passengers looked on this new arrival with nervous expectancy. Suspicion, loathing, contempt. He turned to look out the window. That could be me over there. But for the luck of the draw.

His mind wondered back to graduation day at the naval academy. Dress uniforms, parades, speeches. All the grandeur that France could muster for its future heroes. His mother and grandparents were there in the stands somewhere behind him. Then it was over and the graduates went to greet their families. It was then he noticed the well dressed Arab man in spectacles. The man smiled at Bery like a proud father. Claude looked around to see which graduate the man was greeting. When he looked back, the man was gone. On to the kisses from his mother and grandmother and the hug from his grandfather. The usual happy words then the separation to go off to the real celebrations with his class mates. As he was leaving the parade ground the Arab man was suddenly at his side. This time holding his elbow firmly. He was about to shove the man away when the tears in the man's eyes made Claude hesitate.

"If you want to know more about your father, call this phone number," said the man pressing a business card into his hand. The man backed away then turned and walked toward the car park.

It was months before curiosity got the best of him. He called the phone number and arranged a meeting with the man who had given him the card. The whole story came out. Hard to believe at first but it all made sense.

His mother was a very white daughter of the aristocracy from the old naval family of the Berys. She joined the youth rebellion of her day and struck out to change her world. Her form of rebellion was to marry an Arab college professor to the shock and horror of her family. She left her family for his, proudly calling herself a new woman and cursing the bourgeoisie. But after many years and two children, their marriage reached an impasse.

Her husband, Wahid Zahir, insisted that she convert to Islam. His wife, Angelique, balked at this. Finally she realized that she was not so much a new woman as to abandon her family and the faith of her ancestors. French law and her family would see that she got custody of both children. Zahir's culture demanded that he get custody of both children. They agreed to split up the children and raise them separately. But they could not choose. How could a parent choose one child over the other? They had drawn lots. Claude would go with his mother. Kazim would go with his father. They agreed to never see each other again. Claude knew little of his father until he had broken the agreement. Then so much became clear. Why the family treated him differently. Why he had always felt like an outsider. Then he met his brother, Kazim. Strange is fate. Kazim looked like his mother. Claude looked like his father. How much easier for everyone if their positions had been reversed. He visited his father and his father's family often. He felt like he had found his home. At last.

Claude looked across the bus at the young Arab. Kazim raised one eyebrow in acknowledgment.

*****

"You are sure you won't be missed?" asked Kazim.

"I'm sure. Only a declaration of war would recall me right now," replied Bery.

The two brothers entered a nondescript building in the Arab quarter. Kazim knocked and spoke quietly to the man behind the door. The brothers entered and were escorted into a crowded meeting room.

"You young fools! I have been getting small bits of information from here and there that add up to the direction you are taking. Let me make this clear! I forbid you, and the whole Muslim Directorate forbids you, to carry forward with your plans," said Mansoor Wadi, director of the Muslim Directorate in France. "You don't know what you are doing. How dangerous this is!"

The sixteen younger men arranged around the room glanced toward their leader, Mustapha Najid. Najid stared back at Wadi with contempt but remained silent.

"All of Europe is ours! Without firing a single shot everything you see around you will be ours. The cities, the factories, the land itself. All ours. We will create the Caliphate. We will have millions of Djimmis to serve us! All you have to do is wait. I am not a young man, but I still expect to see Islam take control of every European country before I die," said Wadi. "All of you will reap the benefits without effort. How can you justify a plan that could upset this inevitable conquest?"

"The time is right. We don't need to wait any longer," replied Mustapha Najid.

"You don't know what you are risking! What do you know of violence? You have lived in peaceful Europe your whole lives. Others have lost their homes, their families, seen their children die in their arms. This kind of tragedy must not happen here. Let the wombs of our women lead the way. Our numbers grow steadily every year while the European's numbers decrease. Let them wallow in their decadent sterile life styles. Time will wash them away like the soil on their hillsides. What is left will be a very fertile plain for us and our descendants," said Wadi angrily.

"Mansoor, it is precisely because we have lived our whole lives in Europe that we know that now is the time to strike," said Najid slapping the table. "They have no leaders to oppose us. They have no laws to oppose us. They have no will to oppose us. Every demand we make, they give in. Even sheep have spines. Europeans have less than that. We have men in key positions in every country. There are very few who could organize anything in the way of resistance. A quick strike to remove these few, coupled with control of the media, and it will be over before most Europeans figure out anything but a crime wave has happened.

We mop up a few loose ends and we have a fete acompli," said Najid firmly.

"You forget about the Americans? They have the power to intervene anywhere they feel like," replied Wadi.

"And get into another occupation? They learned their lesson in Iraq, Afghanistan, Libya, Syria, and Lebannon. They have no desire to lose more soldiers so soon. They have the power but with the end of NATO, they have no obligation. They do not concern me. They are almost gone from these shores. The only thing that concerns me is you. And the Muslim Directorate. I need your leadership and guidance. You have the name recognition, the status, the wisdom to lead a new political future. Yes, I am the radical. The innam will fear me. You are the moderate. If you are offered as the alternative to lead the new Europe, the innam will embrace you. We will have everything that we desire," said Najid.

"Will you? Every General who has survived a war admits that when the shooting started, events did not go according to plan. You are walking into a dark room and don't know what you will find there!" said Wadi.

"We have a card up our sleeves that cannot be trumped. Not even by the Americans," said Najid nodding to Bery.

"What are you talking about?" demanded Wadi.

"That will have to remain my secret. Will you change your position? Support me?" asked Najid.

"I am a realist. There is some flexibility here. I will bring up your ideas with members of the Directorate that I trust with my life. Maybe a new consensus will be made. Until I can do this, I need your promise that you will do nothing without speaking with me first. Can you do this?" asked Wadi.

"You have my word. I will not start anything without meeting with you first," replied Najid.

"Good. May Allah watch over you," said Wadi standing and moving to the door.

"And you," replied Najid.

Wadi and his body guards left the room. When he heard the outer door close, Ahmoud Antilier turned to Najid.

"How do you know the Americans won't intervene. And what about the Russians?"

"The Saudis are close to the Americans. They say the new president wants to change their policy to one that is less Euro-centric and more worldly. He has much more interest in Africa and Asia than his predecessors. The Americans have strongly hinted that oil supplies are more important than events in

Europe. That's diplomatic talk for they won't intervene. Unless Russia gets involved. Then they will shake their nukes at each other. Either way, nothing will happen to stop us," replied Najid.

He waved Claude and Kazim to the meeting table.

"We have the pleasure of meeting the distinguished executive officer of France's newest nuclear submarine, the Marseilles," said Najid.

Claude made his way around the table shaking hands while Kazim looked on. Then Claude sat opposite Najid.

"What can you tell us," asked Najid.

"The Americans were unable to detect us. We can hide and strike at will. The only limitation is that we will have to be near the surface to deploy the antenna. And this will only be done at night and when the American satellites are not above us," replied Claude.

"Can you take the ship without sounding the alarm?" asked Ahmoud.

"Yes. One third of the boat is already with us. I have a picked crew waiting to go aboard. It is safe to estimate that we can keep things quiet three days before the usual American satellites notice that we have left. Without NATO, it will take longer for them to know what has happened. We will be safely hidden before that," replied Claude.

"The Marseilles is the hidden card that I spoke of. Commander Bery will report directly to me while the rest of the command structure slowly falls into our hands. The Russians will think twice before crossing the border when they know what we have sitting off shore. So will the Americans. Now does anyone see trouble in securing his assigned nation?" asked Najid.

Anwar Saidi motioned with his hand.

"What troubles you about England, Anwar," asked Najid.

"They have a lot of military tradition. We have not penetrated their old school to the degree that I would like. Also, they are the most connected to the Americans and other places like Australia. I can take half the country right away. Another quarter in two weeks. What happens after that cannot be foreseen," replied Saidi.

"If you have many obstacles to remove, go swiftly and boldly. Kill as many as you need to, as fast as possible. It will get easier as you go, not harder," said Najid.

He turned to the others.

"We must be swift and certain. Our men will replace the old guard and few will be the wiser. The old Europe will disappear so long as we don't allow resistance to grow to the point that

Europeans rally around someone or someplace. Speaking of which, Ahmoud, what news do you have about General Salazar?" asked Najib.

"Nothing new. He is speaking out against us but no one in Spain or anywhere else listens. We are watching and waiting. For now," replied Antilier.

"He is trouble, Asim. Make him one of the first when the time comes," said Najid.

Khalil Asim nodded.

"The last two men who tried to conquer Europe failed. Do you know why? England and Russia. Napoleon was going to invade England but couldn't get across the channel. In frustration he turned to the east and was broken on the steppes of Russia. Then he was finished off by the British at Waterloo. Hitler, same mistake. Couldn't get across the channel. He was also broken on the steppes of Russia. Then finished off by the British and Americans. We won't make the same mistakes. Our people are already across the channel waiting for us to give the word. We will conquer England. We will not attack Russia. We will prevail," said Najid confidently.

"But what if England is uncontrollable?" asked Saidi.

"You sound like a frightened woman. There is nothing left of the England that dominated the world but a few old movies and museums. As a last resort, we will use the Marseilles to destroy England. See that we don't have to, Anwar. I own property there," said Najid.

This is the BBC, Indra Suvarti reporting from London. Muslim Directorate spokesman, Mansoor Hamdar, confirmed that the rate of European Christians converting to Islam more than tripled right after the World Trade Center terrorist attacks. And doubled again after the Madrid train bombings. Mr. Hamdar points out that it is always a good time to embrace the prophet and suggests that these conversions were a coincidence.

*****

Brent followed Lorrie and Hamjid Bassa down the sidewalk into London's Arab quarter. As they laughed and giggled exuberantly, Brent began to wonder what was going on. Lorrie did not act like his girlfriend. If Hamjid kept touching her he would have to say something.

The music blared out of the night club. Hamjid waved to the bouncer and pointed at Lorrie and Brent. The bouncer nodded and Hamjid led them inside. He pointed at a booth along the wall and the occupants scattered to other tables.

"You will like this place. Rock and roll Arab style. The band is from Quatar. They are very famous," said Hamjid.

Lorrie smiled contentedly. Her big eyes never leaving his face.

Brent studied his surroundings. They could actually be in Quatar for all he could tell. No punk rockers, fish and chips, or Guinness here. A barmaid stood by. She wore a head scarf, with nothing but her face showing. How disappointing. Hamjid leaned over to touch Brent's arm.

"Don't worry, beer is served here. We are quite liberal," he said with a devilish wink. "We'll take three pints."

Hamjid leaned in close to Lorrie.

"I must make a phone call. Don't go anywhere, my beauty," he said reaching down to squeeze her knee.

She nodded, entranced.

Lorrie was already a little drunk from the last place. The place where they had met Hamjid. He had swept her off her feet right in front of him. She had ignored his protests, but this was too much.

"This would be a good time to leave. It's late. I don't like it here," said Brent sliding next to Lorrie.

"Don't crowd me," she replied moving away.

"I don't like this place. It makes me uneasy," said Brent.

"You're such a baby. What could happen here? This is London, silly," said Lorrie. "Really, you are more of a disappointment every day."

"You're my girlfriend and I have to put my foot down," he said moving back to the end of the booth.

"Yeah, right. Your girlfriend? Are you really that stupid? Man, I picked a ripe one didn't I," she said slurring a little.

"Why are you talking like this?" asked Brent.

"I said you were my boyfriend, but I lied," she giggled drunkenly. "Daddy would never let me go anywhere fun. Not even this boring country. Especially after all those girls were murdered on spring break last year. I couldn't visit India, Africa, or Arabia but I could visit all three here in London. All I needed was a boy that Daddy liked to be my ticket to adventure."

"You don't love me?" asked Brent dreading to hear the answer.

"Of course not, silly," she laughed.

"Never?" he asked.

"Never. But I knew Daddy would. And here I am. Why don't you go and have an adventure of your own? There must be something you want to see here. And maybe you'll get lucky and find a girl as boring as you are," she hiccuped.

"Your father took me aside and made me promise that I wouldn't leave your side. Not under any circumstances. Your lack of feeling for me doesn't break that promise," said Brent angrily.

"I don't believe it. You're getting angry. I didn't think you had it in you," she said downing her beer.

Hamjid returned with two tough looking friends. He slid in next to Lorrie and gave her a squeeze around her waist.

"Great news, my beauty. Friends of mine are having a party. I want you to meet them. They will love you," he smiled.

"OK," she answered looking at Brent.

"Your guard dog can come also," laughed Hamjid touching Brent's arm lightly.

Brent looked down at his arm with irritation.

"Woof, woof," said Hamjid playfully and Lorrie burst into laughter.

Hamjid took her hand and escorted her to the door. Brent

followed. Hamjid's buddies flanked him.

Brent was the third wheel. Not wanted and not wanting to be there, but yes, following along like a dog. What about these silent friends? They gave him the creeps. Was there some danger he couldn't put his finger on or was this just the inbred racism that his school teachers said whites must learn to control?

Four young men emerged from the alley ahead. Now this wasn't good. He was certain of it. Just then one of Hamjid's buddies stepped on his heel. His shoe fell off and as he stooped to put it back on, he saw Lorrie and Hamjid pass the four toughs from the alley without trouble.

"Good one, bozo," he said turning to the one who had stepped on his heel. Hamjid's two friends had stopped behind him and stood silently.

"Lorrie, wait," Brent shouted as she and Hamjid entered the intersection and turned left down the side street.

She didn't respond to him. Captivated by Hamjid's attention, no doubt. He made to pass between the four young men but two of them put out their hands and shoved him back.

"Hey, what is this?" Brent asked in surprise.

One of Hamdar's buddies buckled Brent's knees from behind and he collapsed. As he struggled to get up he was kicked repeatedly. Instead of trying to stand he rolled suddenly to one side. Momentarily clear, he stood and raced to the corner, six hoodlums in pursuit. He turned left and raced ahead of his pursuers.

"Lorrie!" he shouted. "Lorrie!"

He sprinted on to the next intersection. There was no sign of them. They had vanished. What the hell? He stopped and faced his pursuers as they surrounded him again. Now what?

"Go back," said one of them pointing back the way they had come.

"No," he said trying to break out of the circle.

Both arms were pinned behind him as one of them punched him repeatedly. He gasped for breath as he slid to his knees on the sidewalk.

"Go back, now!" said the first one.

He looked around the empty street. He had lost her. The six men laughed and jeered as he walked unsteadily back the way he had come.

This is the BBC, Mary Campbell reporting from London. Lia Hirsiyaan, ex Dutch parliament member, was shot to death in the streets of Washington today. A lone gunman approached as she pedaled her bicycle to her job at the American Enterprise Institute. The gunman, identified as Mohammed Bougatti, was the same man who gunned down Theo van Roth in the streets of Amsterdam many years ago. Dutch sources said he was recently released from prison after a successful rehabilitation program. Witnesses said he shot her once then began screaming at her in Arabic. He then shot her again and stabbed her twelve times. When she tried to crawl away, he shot her repeatedly and stabbed her twenty seven more times before slitting her throat and pinning a letter to her chest with a 14 inch dagger. Police arrived as he was reloading his weapon and called upon him to surrender. When he raised his pistol the police opened fire, shooting him fifty three times. He died at the scene. The Muslim Directorate of America is calling this police action an atrocity of excessive force and is demanding an investigation and the dismissal of all the officers involved.

*****

"I can't understand why she would dump a great catch like you," said the female officer rolling her eyes. "But that is not a police matter."

"But she never came back to the hotel. I know she's in some kind of trouble!" said Brent.

"All you know is that she left you and went off with another boy. At worst another American college girl run wild. It happens every day," said the officer.

"I was attacked!" replied Brent.

"Assaulted. Witnesses?" asked the officer.

"No," replied Brent.

"You don't know who they were. How are we supposed to

begin? Where do we start? We could ask around but you don't know where you were last night. And you admit to drinking so just how reliable is your story anyway? If there was a fight, who started it? Them? Or you? It would waste my time to take such a report," she said.

"But you have to do something!" said Brent.

"What? What do we have to do? Other than a few bruises that you probably earned, there is no evidence of a crime here," she replied sliding Lorrie's photo back across the desk. "Come back in two days and I'll fill out a missing persons report. Until then you wait back at the hotel until she shows up."

"What fucking good are you people?" said Brent tucking the photo into his jacket.

"Watch your language, Mr. Swain. I didn't lose the girl, you did," replied the officer acidly.

"What ever," said Brent storming from the room.

The constable shook her head. If these American girls could learn to keep their legs crossed, her job would be a lot easier.

*****

Brent called the hotel again. Nothing. He would retrace his steps and maybe with a lot of luck they would cross paths. He looked at the crowds walking in every direction as far as he could see. OK, maybe it would take a miracle. Shouting in the distance caught his attention. He moved through the crowds toward the sound.

The park was full of angry men waving their fists. Thousands of them. A few bobbies looked on from a discrete distance. As if this was just an average normal day in London.

"Death to the west, death to the west, death to the west!" they shouted.

Over and over they shouted, taking short breaks when their leaders shouted a few other words Brent didn't understand. Then back to the chorus.

"What the hell?" Brent said to himself.

He crossed the street and stood in the outskirts of the crowd. The Arabs who surrounded him eyed him suspiciously, but Brent didn't care. He walked around the outskirts of the crowd then he heard a different voice. One speaking in English. He moved toward the voice and mingled with the Englishmen who had stopped to listen."

"What we have in England today, is a complete failure of leadership!" shouted Oliver Winston Clarke. "Why would I say this? Listen and I will explain. It comes down to two words we all know. Us and them. Have you thought about these words? What makes the difference between us and them? I have thought about this and I will share what I have learned. There can be only one difference between us. I mean it literally. One difference. I see the puzzled looks on your faces. You are waiting for me to tell you what that one difference is. It could be many things. Still puzzled? OK, then. I'll rephrase what I'm saying. Two men can have one significant difference between themselves and still see the other as 'us'. Two Englishmen from Cornwall will see themselves as 'us'. They are very much the same in race, religion, and culture. What about a black man from Cornwall? If he dresses, talks, and acts like the rest of Cornwall, he can be one of 'us' even though he looks quite different. That is what I mean by one difference. He is different in skin color but the same in every other way. He is an 'us'. We can make assumptions about his behavior that will be true. We overlook his one difference. For the sake of conversation, lets call this the one difference law of social behavior."

"What if this man has two differences? The answer is no. He is not one of us. We can no longer make assumptions about his behavior that falls within our expectations of normal or typical. We must first learn what the differences are, then negotiate through what we hold in common to achieve what ever social or business transaction we are trying to complete. As this other man becomes less like us, we have less and less common ground to work with. Everything has to be communicated and negotiated, nothing can be assumed to be in common. This lack of common ground changes a man from an 'us' to a 'them'."

"The nation states that we live in today were formed by groups of 'us'. Our commonality brought us together. Race, language, culture, and religion. People who are the same in these four ways will almost always be living in the same country. These binding factors were only disrupted in the distant past by invasion. An army attacks you and forces the people to change or die. Colonization was a form of invasion. Culture, language, and religion were brought in that were different than what was there before. And of course, the mixing of races leads to a new variety of children in the land. Colonization was an invasion at the top of society. Slavery is also an invasion, but from the bottom of society. Again, a new race, religion, and culture was brought to a land where it didn't exist before. Not by an army but by very unwilling participants. The colonial period has ended. Slavery as well, at least in the civilized world. We now face a new type of invasion. Immigration. Before world war two, there was little immigration except to the new world. Now it has grown to be a large problem. Our airports and harbors are filling with a new wave of immigration that we in Europe have never seen since the Mongol invasions of the twelfth century. World population continues to increase. Global warming is expected to reduce food production. The pressures driving this new invasion will continue to increase not decrease. What will happen to the world we were raised in? In a word. Gone. Gone completely. Gone for all time."

"Every nation is the sum of the people living in it. Change the makeup of the population and you fundamentally change the nation as a whole. Colonial invaders ruling from the top can be driven out and the previous culture restored. But when the invasion comes from the bottom, in great numbers, it is permanent. The new immigrants, who start at the bottom of the economic ladder, will not be leaving. Ever. They are fundamentally changing our society, our nation. Permanently."

"No one wants to hear this. What a mean spirited man I am. How can I want to hurt the little darlings who only want a better life? So do we accept this change because we see the brown people of the world like lost little puppies that need nurturing? The compassion for others that has helped make the West the greatest civilization in history, is now working against us. Some argue that the immigrants will be just like us in the long run. This is an appealing argument. What if it is wrong? Can you live with that? Apparently, yes, most of you can. And those with another opinion are ignored or denigrated."

"What about those immigrants who have no intention of assimilating in any way. People who have no interest in the proud traditions that we hold dear. Who further more, insist that you adopt their way of life. Who will pursue this objective by any means necessary. How does the assimilation argument hold up under these conditions? They don't. They won't. They never will."

"You have only to look at the men behind me to see what I am talking about. The followers of Islam. They want their own language, not ours. They want their own courts and laws, not ours. They wish to maintain their own culture, not ours. They maintain their own dress codes, not ours. They insist on their own schools, not ours. They don't respect our ways at all. This is an invasion of both the old and new sort. Islam is not secular. It is the fusion of church and state. And as such is fundamentally incompatible with Western values. They wish to force us to adopt their ways like a conquering army. At the same time, they will be here permanently, in large and growing numbers, like an underclass invasion. Islam is a religion for people who can't handle freedom. And they can't allow others to be free lest they lose control of their own members."

Brent looked around the growing crowd of white faces. A few bold souls began to cheer and applaud while most looked on nervously. They knew that what wasn't supposed to be said was being said right in front of them. And they could be found guilty by association. But they remained.

"In their small numbers and short time amongst us, they have challenged every political institution in Europe. As their numbers grow this challenge will only strengthen. In fifty years we have gone from an almost homogeneous nation to one with a growing cancer inside. A cancer that will grow and lead in only one direction. The end of England as we know it. Will the future bring the Islamic Republic of England, Scotland, and Wales? Or will there be a destructive civil war along the lines of what has devastated Lebanon? It doesn't have to be either of these. And so I have come a long way around to my first statement. There has been a complete failure in leadership all across the West. One that will lead to the destruction of our way of life. Of who we are. And it doesn't need to happen. We are bringing this disaster upon ourselves by our failure to act now while we can still prevent it. We see the iceberg ahead but no one will change the course. And you know what happened to the common men and women locked below decks while the elites got away on the life boats."

*****

Anwar Saidi turned to consider the growing crowd of Englishmen. He studied the speaker. Oh yes. Oliver Clarke. This irritating man always turned up to cause trouble. He nodded to his right hand man, Farouk Aziz.

Farouk followed Saidi's glance toward Clarke. He had written Clarke's name down on a special list long ago. And just because Farouk and his allies were here enjoying their right to free speech, that didn't mean he would let Clarke enjoy the same privilege.

Farouk would have liked to kill the man now. Here. End the irritation. But it could wait. Clarke would be dealt with properly later. For now, he would just have a little sport.

"Stand still, Abdul," he said to one of his body guards.

Farouk was a very good shot. Still, it was easier to rest the

40

pistol against something solid. And Abdul was like a rock. He nodded to the other body guards who momentarily divided the crowd, leaving a clear line of fire to Clarke's back. He squeezed the trigger.

*****

Brent heard the shot as Clarke crumpled onto the ground. A gasp of shock went through the crowd. They looked around fearfully and then began to scatter. Brent looked in the direction of the shot but saw only the backs of the protesters.

"Death to the west, death to the west, death to the west!" they chanted.

Brent was alone as he ran toward the stricken figure on the ground.

*****

The bobbies did nothing. Hadn't they heard or were they afraid to take action? Farouk watched discretely as Clarke's little crowd ran from the park. Except one. One young man ran toward Clarke. This was not expected. He raised the pistol as he studied the young man. He put away the gun. Clearly an American. They were always getting involved in things that didn't concern them. It took courage to aid another man when at any time he could be shot. Simple courage. Which is why he believed the Europeans despised Americans so much. Americans still had courage, Europeans had none. But he had no quarrel with America. They were leaving Europe. Conquering the great Satan would fall to the next generation.

*****

"Are you OK?" asked Brent looking down at Clarke, then at the hostile crowd.

"Death to the west, death to the west, death to the west!" they shouted on and on.

Clarke held his right calf and grimaced with pain.

"Get back to the road! It isn't safe for you here," said Clarke.

"Give me your arm," said Brent pulling the man up off the ground.

Brent placed Clarke's arm across his shoulder.

"Where to?" asked Brent as Clarke hobbled along side.

"My place, get a taxi," replied Clarke reaching the street.

Brent waved from the sidewalk as the taxis passed. Ten went by without stopping.

"There was a time when the taxis wouldn't stop for foreigners. Now they won't stop for us," said Clarke, grimacing. "This really is starting to hurt!"

Clarke sat heavily on a bench as Brent removed his undershirt and tied it around the wound. Passers by looked at the pair with fascination, like they were watching the evening news on the tele. Then they averted their eyes and went on down the sidewalk like they had seen nothing.

"Stay here," said Brent.

He jumped in front of the next cab. Forcing it to stop with the screech of brakes. Brent held the door while Clarke hobbled over.

"You can't get into my cab. You will make a mess! I won't take you!" screamed the cabbie.

Brent grabbed him by the collar.

"Shut the fuck up and do what I say!" ordered Brent.

"Americans. OK. That's different. But you must not dirty my cab! I have nowhere close by to clean it," said the cabbie.

Brent let go of the driver. Clarke gave an address and they sped away.

"What a fucked up country," said Brent to himself.

*****

Clarke lay on his dinning room table with the brightest lights in the house aimed at his calf. Brent looked on as the dark skinned surgeon, Ranjit Amapurti, tightened the last suture, closing the wound.

"The wound will hurt when the local wears off. The muscle is damaged but will heal. Stay off your feet as much as possible for a week," said Ranjit. "You are lucky my friend. You could have been killed today."

"I disagree. I think it was a very good shot and not a miss. He got me where it would have the most affect with the least damage. Very sporting of him, really," said Clarke, wincing as he moved his leg.

"Still, you are in great danger. As is anyone who speaks out against the Muslim Directorate," said Ranjit packing his medical bag.

"As long as I believe in what I'm doing and have friends like you, I'll continue. Somebody has to do it and unfortunately," said Clarke motioning to his leg. "there isn't anybody else."

"I have to get back to the hospital. Take care," said Ranjit.

"I'll keep in touch," said Clarke.

Ranjit nodded to Brent then closed the door on the way out.

"Be a good chap and tidy up that table will you? Thanks," said Clarke as he hobbled to his easy chair.

Brent set to work.

"Can you help me, then?" asked Brent.

"About your girl? Yes, of course. I owe you that much. I have contacts over there that can at least tell me where she went," said Clarke pausing. "You have to brace yourself for the possibility that she will never be coming back."

"What are you talking about?" asked Brent.

"Just what I said. This kind of thing has happened before. If Hamjid is working for who I think he is, Lorrie is it, yes, well, she has been kidnapped," said Clarke.

Brent looked relieved.

"So we will get a ransom note. Then the cops can swoop in and rescue her," said Brent hopefully.

"If we're lucky," said Clarke closing his eyes.

There were three sharp raps on the front door. Then it opened admitting an immaculately dressed Russian man. His tailored suit said money to burn.

"I came as soon as I heard the news," said Ivan Borovich clasping Clarke's hand. "No don't ask me how. Then I would have to kill you."

Ivan went to the cabinet and poured two glasses of vodka. Keeping the bottle for himself. He turned to Brent.

"And who is this? Let me see. Good teeth. Over fed. With a child like innocence. An American I see. I can spot you from miles away!" said Ivan shaking Brent's hand.

"This is Brent. He came to my aid when I was shot," said Clarke.

"Good man," said Ivan kissing Brent's cheeks. "Courage under fire is rare. Apparently Englishmen no longer have any since all the others ran away."

"Brent, this is Ivan Borovich, Russian military attache at the embassy," said Clarke. "He's known as Ivan the terrible across London."

"All the ambassadors call me Ivan the terrible. And all their wives call me Ivan the wonderful!" Ivan laughed. "But seriously, did you see who shot you?"

"No, I was facing the other way," replied Clarke.

Ivan turned to Brent.

"I looked when I heard the shot, but the protesters were all facing in the other direction," said Brent.

"I happen to know that our friend Saidi is back from Paris. He and his enforcer, Farouk Aziz, were in the park when you were shot," said Ivan. "My sources say that something big is coming."

"Oil crisis, grid lock, demands from the Muslim Directorate, and a paralyzed and worthless EU assembly giving itself death penalty power," said Clarke. "Everybody feels like something big is coming, but nobody knows what."

"True. I have other news as well. I have been recalled to Moscow," said Ivan.

"It's the gulag for you at last. It's about time," said Clarke smiling.

"The gulag. Ha ha. You are so funny even in this time of pain," laughed Ivan. "No. I am to take command of a tank division on the border. Normal rotation. Keeping an eye on our Polish and Ukrainian neighbors. It will be boring but another step up the ladder."

"Are you coming back to England?" said Clarke.

"Not soon. But I will return. Like your MacArthur," said Ivan turning to Brent. "Why not come with me. Brave men are always of value. It would be good for you to spend some time with real men. Russian men."

"I have to stay in London right now," replied Brent.

"Ah, well, to bad for you," said Ivan. "Get well, Oliver. I will keep in touch. You are a very important man in this struggle."

"Struggle? What Struggle?" asked Brent.

Ivan put down the vodka bottle. "Ask Oliver. He knows. Well, cherio old chap. Tally ho and I'm off!"

With a flourish and a bow, Ivan was gone.

Clarke waved off Brent's inquisitive look.

"It's a complicated story. I'll fill you in later. Right now I want to rest," said Clarke.

Brent didn't move.

"I'll make calls like I promised. Come back tomorrow at four o'clock. I should have something for you by then," said Clarke.

Brent nodded and went out.

"For many years now, Lyon in the autumn meant riots, fires, and destruction. Minority populations going out of control for almost a month each year, burning cars and buildings. But this year in Lyon, as well as other places, all is quiet. Commissioner, how do you explain this?" asked Jane Hansen holding the microphone.

"Misunderstandings have plagued the relationship between French and new French populations. My department, the Commission for Equality and Justice, has worked to spread understanding between French and immigrant populations. Our policy of accommodation toward Islam is now paying off in the form of the peaceful streets you see around you," replied the EU Commissioner smugly.

"Your critics insist that your policies are not accommodation but appeasement. That you give in to every demand of every group. That as a result, this city and other immigrant neighborhoods are no longer French territory. Instead they have become small parts of Africa, Asia, and Arabia," said Jane.

"That view is held only by a very small minority of racists and extremists. Rational Europeans don't hold these views. No. In fact, I believe that these immigrants are best viewed as a spice added to the normally bland affair we call Europe. And we all benefit from their being here," replied the Commissioner smiling confidently. "Now I must leave for the renaming ceremony."

"Who requested the name change for the city. French or new French citizens?" asked Jane.

The Commissioner frowned, his left eye twitched in irritation. He ignored the question.

"The city will now be know as Kubri al Bukra. In Arabic letters of course. With the roman letter version in small print underneath," said the Commissioner with satisfaction.

"Bridge to Tomorrow. A tomorrow where Arabic supersedes French?" asked Jane.

"The winds of change are blowing through this continent.

Whether we like it or not, this growth of Islamic consciousness is a political fact," said the Commissioner firmly, indicating the interview was over.

"Thank you, Commissioner," said Jane.

The Commissioner nodded and moved on with his entourage to the next reporter. Jane turned to Nick.

"What do you think about the lack of rioting?" asked Jane.

"Less rioting is always good. Did changing the name make people more peaceful?" replied Nick. "Maybe. Something changed."

"Maybe Muslims have more of a stake in their city now," said Jane.

"Their city," said Nick. "Sums up the situation, doesn't it."

*****

"I can tell you what I know so far, after you down that scotch that you thought was for me," said Clarke.

Brent continued to hold out the drink to Clarke.

"Just do as I say, lad," said Clarke firmly.

Brent downed the small glass.

"Now sit here," said Clarke pointing to the easy chair opposite.

"Do you remember when the Soviet Union broke up?" asked Clarke.

"Yes," said Brent.

"Well, when the small republics were freed they opened up their borders to people who were previously controlled or excluded. The barn doors were left open, so to speak," said Clarke.

"What has that to do with me?" asked Brent.

"I'm getting to that. Anyway, this sudden freedom to travel resulted in some tragic events that were unforeseen," said Clarke.

Brent started to feel the scotch.

"Women had the freedom to pursue a better life abroad. A few were able to get modeling contracts, good jobs, and marriages to wealthy men. These stories spread quickly and soon most of the young women dreamed of the same success. They had their guards down as they rushed from the country with high expectations," said Clarke.

"Good for them," said Brent dryly.

"Good girls were lured from their homes by pimps and swindlers. They were home one day and the next they were sex slaves in the middle east and other lawless places. Remember when Yugoslavia broke up? Lots of girls ended up around the

46

outskirts of the fighting to service the troops. There is a slave trade around the world in women," said Clarke.

"Too bad," said Brent.

"Yes it is. Europe has always had prostitutes but they worked in their own countries. Now that the EU has ended its traditional border checks, it's easier for all manner of crime to move from place to place. There is a slow drain of women from Europe just like their Ukrainian and Moldovan counterparts before them. White women are the most desired and hence valuable. American girls most valuable of all. It makes sense. It's foolish to take out your anger on a company of well armed marines. Much more pleasant to take out your anger on a young American girl," said Clarke.

Brent slumped in his chair and covered his face with his hands.

"Are you suggesting Lorrie has been kidnapped by slave traders? In this day and age? In London?" asked Brent.

"It's happening everywhere now. Even the States. And yes, that's exactly what happened. My source tells me that she was taken out of the country last night," said Clarke.

"I can't believe this. What kind of fucked up country is this anyway?" asked Brent. "You have to be wrong about this."

"I wish I was, but my information is solid," said Clarke.

"Is there any hope of getting her back?" asked Brent.

"There is always hope. The kidnappers could foul up or an accident could bring her to the notice of the police. You must brace yourself for the possibility that you will never see her again," said Clarke.

Clarke waited silently. Brent sagged in his chair.

"Oh god, what will I tell her Dad? I promised him that I would protect her. She apparently didn't love me but I loved her," said Brent wiping a tear from his eye.

"Call him from here tomorrow. I'll explain what I know about the matter. I am still sending out inquiries and maybe we will pull a rabbit out of the hat," said Clarke.

"What can I do?" asked Brent.

"Sit tight and pray. Prayer has actually achieved things that can't be explained in any other way," asked Clarke rubbing his eyes.

Clarke looked around the room, but Brent had gone.

*****

Brent made for the door of the pub.

"You there! You can't take that pint outside," shouted the barman angrily. The bad news was that he had probably lost a good mug. The good news was that the sour faced yank had left.

Brent took another drink of ale as his surroundings began to spin. He collected himself and made off slowly down the sidewalk.

He saw a Muslim woman approaching. Black cloak, hood, and face covering. When she was close enough to see he was drunk, she started to change course to avoid him. He took two steps to block her path.

"You bastards take my girl so I'm going to take one of yours! Take that shit off!" he shouted.

Brent yanked off her hijab and veil with one hand and hurled his ale into her face with the other. Then he just stared with his mouth open.

As her hijab flew off, a wave of silvery blond hair cascaded down around her pale face. Deep blue eyes looked back in anger. She reared back and slapped him hard with one hand, then the other. She punched him in the stomach for good measure. Brent fell to one knee trying to find the air that had been knocked out of him.

"You stupid prick! God damned wanker! Who the hell do you think you are! My brothers taught me to fight and now I'm going to make you sorry you were ever born," she shouted in a thick accent.

She stomped on his foot and grabbed his hair. Brent came to his senses and stood up, dragging the girl up off the ground.

"I'm sorry," he said.

She was about to spit in his face but could feel the genuine shame in his demeanor. She let go and slid down his chest to the ground. Brent picked up her scarf and held it out.

"Here," he offered.

"You drunken bastard," she hissed snatching it from his grasp. "You've made a right mess of it, haven't you."

"I apologize," said Brent.

"What the hell am I supposed to do with this, hey?" she asked holding out the torn scarf. "And this fucking ale. I can't go home smelling like beer you stupid sod. Drinking is forbidden."

"My room is across the street," said Brent pointing. "You can get cleaned up there."

She looked across the street and eyed him suspiciously.

"No funny business or I'll break you in half," she said.

Brent nodded.

Celia Banks wrung out her clothing over the tub. Then she arranged her wet things over the registers and turned the heat up all the way. Brent watched her go about the room in her bra and blue jeans. He couldn't keep his mind off the funny business she had warned him against.

"There. This is going to take a while," she said.

"I can take them to a laundry. They should dry quicker," said Brent.

"There isn't one close. Besides, I can't walk the streets without these. It isn't proper. And if anyone saw me here with you I'd be disgraced as an unfaithful woman," she replied.

Brent grabbed a blanket and handed it to her.

"You seem like a decent chap now. What the hell got into you back there?" she asked, settling into a chair and wrapping the blanket around herself.

Brent gave her the story as sleep began to overtake him.

"You were a fool. It's obvious that she used you from the start. But what do you expect from sluts anyway. Promiscuity always leads to trouble. That's the good news that Islam has brought to Europe. Good news for girls like me, anyway," she said.

"Huh?" said Brent.

"Huh, huh, huh!? she repeated, making fun of him. "You Americans should learn to speak English some day. I'm a woman who wants a man to love me. I want to be married. I want to be the mother of a large pack of children. When I say this out loud everyone makes fun of me. The men who are really boys want to have sex with me without giving anything in return. They ridicule marriage. They don't want children because they're afraid of the responsibility that comes with them. Then the feminist bitches say that marriage is how men enslave women and take their power away whatever that is about. They say that by wanting marriage I'm part of the conspiracy holding women down. So their sorry empty lives are my fault! And the pretty girls don't want birth to change their skinny bodies so they aren't having babies at all. Which is fine for them, but they also put down women who do. So my life was shit until I met Farouk. He agreed with everything I believed. I converted to Islam and live by its good word. Any day now he's going to ask me to marry him and it will be just too damn bad for all the boys who missed their chance to have a wife like me!"

"That's sounds nice," said Brent dreaming about having a wife like her. His head fell forward onto his chest.

"This is the BBC, Mellisa Bains reporting from London. The defense minister, John Simpson, has been sacked by the Prime Minister over the Military Fuel scandal that has gripped the nation. Three days ago, an inventory of military fuel reserves uncovered a huge shortfall and with it, a network of black market fuel sales that have been going on for more than a year. With the fuel shortage worsening, black market prices have reached as much as twenty pounds per liter. While the amount of fuel stolen from the reserve has been classified as secret by the military, unofficial sources say that more than half of the reserve is missing. It is also reported that two Colonels in charge of fuel supplies are missing along with their families. They are assumed to have left the country with a tremendous amount of cash. New defense minster, Omar Asouf, has sworn to bring those responsible to justice quickly."

*****

Tom liked the early watch. Dark and then the dawn. It was a beautiful sight he never grew tired of. He flipped on the radar for a moment. The ocean looked empty in every direction but it was good to check anyway. No surprises that way. And why have radar at all if he wasn't going to use it. Nothing. Switch off. The eastern sky had a touch of color in it. A new day was coming. He sat back under his blanket and drifted into a light sleep.

"I'm living in the best of all possible worlds!"

Tom opened his eyes with a start.

"What the hell? Was I dreaming or am I hearing voices?" said Tom to himself. He turned. Was there something in the water slowly drifting astern?

He reached down and flicked the GPS position recorder then tugged on the lines releasing the sails. He turned the wheel as the motor came to life. Back to the GPS coordinates. He sounded the horn and heard a commotion from below. Stan shot out of the hatch with life jacket in hand.

"What's up?" he asked scanning the horizon.

"I heard a voice coming from the water," replied Tom. "Go forward and man the spotlight."

Stan looked relieved and then more concerned as Jim joined him.

"If I've gone crazy, don't worry. We're only a couple of days from the Canaries," said Tom.

Stan shone the spotlight back and forth as the eastern glow increased.

"I've got something" he shouted. "Port twenty."

Tom throttled back and steered for the face bobbing in the water. Jim stood on the hanging ladder and reached out as they drifted close. The black man's eyes opened as Jim grabbed him. Waiting arms pulled him onto the deck where he lay without moving. A ragged shirt, pants, and a belt was all he wore.

Stan pushed on the man with his foot. No reaction. "Now what?"

Tom went below for some water and a blanket. He poured water slowly into the man's mouth.

"It's the best of all possible worlds," the man whispered then fell into an exhausted sleep.

The three men watched silently. All thoughts of sleep gone as the first rays of the sun hit the top of the mast.

"He's too weak to be trouble. But I'll tie his hands just in case," said Tom.

Stan and Jim looked relieved. Jim chuckled to himself.

"What?" asked Stan.

"Today is Friday."

"Huh? Oh."

The three men laughed.

"OK, Robinson, let's get back on course," said Tom.

*****

The man slept all day. He stirred in the evening while the others were eating dinner. He made to sit up and noticed his hands were tied. He looked surprised.

"Why?" he asked simply.

"We were being careful. Until we know you better," replied Tom.

"But I am an American like you," he replied with a slight French accent.

"Yeah right," retorted Stan from the wheel.

"I was not born there like you. I am American in my heart," he replied.

"What are you doing out here?" asked Tom.

"It is a long tale. Could I have something to eat?" he asked.

"OK," Tom reached around and untied him.

When he had his food he began to speak.

"My name is Wisdom Achebe. I was born in a village in central Chad. I was surrounded by my family. We had enough to eat. Life was good. I had started school at the mission but one day an airplane came and bombed my school. Many children and teachers were killed. Grandfather took over teaching the children of our village. Islamic rebels from the north and mercenaries from Sudan kept attacking my people. Grandfather gathered what we could and took me to a refugee camp. It was there I discovered America. I helped American refugee workers as much as I could. They taught me many things. I remember they would say they were living in the best of all possible worlds then all laugh. I didn't understand it but I knew it must have been a joke only Americans can understand. Rebels attacked the camp one day and all the Americans left."

"That day I decided to go to America. Grandfather said it was a good dream but he died in the camp. I walked to Nigeria just as the war started there. I was captured by the Mahdi rebels and forced to join their army. I fought for a long time and learned Arabic. I kept moving west. Sometimes a soldier, sometime a slave laborer. I moved on when I could escape. In every country Islam fought to gain power. I hid when I could, fought when I had to. Finally, in Dakar, I joined a boat of refugees heading for the Canary Islands. Our boat sank and we had to swim. I was the last alive and near the end when you arrived. From certain death to rescue. It was then I knew I was living in the best of all possible worlds. A world that gave me hope."

The crew was silent as Wisdom finished eating.

"I'm short a crew member. Would you like to sign on with us? If not, I could drop you at the Canaries. It's our destination," said Tom.

"Could you take me to America?" asked Wisdom.

"Do a good job on this boat and I will take you to America," replied Tom.

"Then I will be your best crewman," he said smiling.

Tom went below and brought back some papers and a pen. He handed them to Wisdom.

"Sign your name on the bottom line and you will be officially part of my crew," said Tom.

Wisdom paused to read the document.

"What is an extended warranty? If it has to do with sailing, I am happy to sign it," said Wisdom.

"You can read English, then?" asked Tom.

"The Americans in the camp taught me," replied Wisdom.

"Making you sign your name was purely symbolic. English language skills are better. After all, it's the only thing holding America together anymore. Or was," said Tom. "Wisdom, I want you to know Jim Berman and Stan Metcoff.

They shook hands.

"Stan, take Wisdom below and set him up in Brent's bunk. You'll be part of the regular watch starting tomorrow," said Tom.

"Yes sir," replied Wisdom following Stan below.

*****

It was hot in the office. Comandante Santiago Cabrera pointed to the chairs in front of his desk.

"I know who you are Jane Hansen. What do you want from me?" he asked.

"I have some questions for my story about the constant influx of Africans to your shores. Especially in light of the news from Madrid. Sources there tell me that the islands of Lanzarote and Fuerteventura have been completely overwhelmed by boat people. That you have lost control of those islands and are on the verge of losing control of others as well," said Jane.

"No cameras in here!" said Cabrera acidly.

Nick lowered the camera and flipped the off switch.

"We have not lost control of anything. You have heard wrong. Things are a little unsettled right now but that is expected when desperate frightened people arrive. A settling time is required. Nothing to be concerned about," he said evenly.

"Then explain the attacks on the aid workers bringing food relief. Five killed, twenty beaten, a supply ship looted, then set on fire. You call that control?" asked Jane.

"There was some trouble. But when you consider the big picture, this is a small thing," said Cabrera.

"Not to those aid workers," said Jane.

"But who are the real victims? The Africans have nothing to look forward to. No chance for a decent life. They risk their lives to come here. I admire their courage. Besides, Europe is responsible for the troubles in Africa. We deserve this," said Cabrera.

"You deserve an invasion? Stealing, burning, looting, and

destroying like pirate raiders of old? You would have defended yourselves in the past. Now you do nothing to protect yourselves. Why?" asked Jane.

Cabrera stared at Jane coldly.

"Be very careful Jane Hansen. You are taking this conversation in the direction of racism and xenophobia. These concepts are clear violations of EU and Spanish penal codes," said Cabrera firmly.

"This is all part of the story, law or no law," said Jane.

"Consider the progress we have made," said Cabrera changing course. "Everyday hundreds of refugees wash up on our shores. We take them to the camps on each island where they are fed and taken care of. We behave with great humanity. Especially in light of the fact that the refugees now outnumber the Spanish people ten to one. Our resources are strained beyond limit with little complaint from us."

"Hasn't that ruined the tourist trade? I have heard that only Tenerife and Gran Canaria can be visited safely," said Jane.

"We are handling a humanitarian tragedy of immense scale. A few less tourists is a small thing compared to the big picture. We are providing hope for the hopeless. We process each arrival for skills and aptitudes. And yes, they must wait for years, but then we bring them to the transportation camp outside of Guimar. From there they take ship for camps in Europe where they will begin new lives. We can do no less for them," said Cabrera.

"I want to visit the camp at Guimar. Get some film for the network. Do a few interviews," said Jane.

"No. That will not be allowed. You media people are trouble makers. I recommend that you get back on your plane and fly away," said Cabrera.

"Well, I respect your honesty. OK then. We'll take some tourist photos instead, then go back to Paris. Does that work for you?" asked Jane.

"Just stay away from the camps. Now I have other matters to attend," said Cabrera firmly.

Cabrera stood up. He might not like Jane, but good manners were important.

"Thank you, Comandante," said Jane shaking his hand.

*****

Nick drove the Land rover across the plain toward Guimar.

"I thought you said we wouldn't go there?" asked Nick.

"That was then. This is now. We aren't going to knock on the front gate. We will be two tourists out exploring the countryside. Is it our fault if we stumble across a refugee camp containing three hundred thousand people? Imagine spending years waiting to get to Europe. Finally you arrive at the last camp before going to Europe. A better future is assured so long as you behave. We can't get to the other islands. This is the only camp we can visit. And I want to get the human angle for the story," said Jane.

"Right. You never quit, do you," said Nick.

"Not when there's a story to tell," said Jane.

Nick pulled the Rover onto a dirt side road and drove far enough to be out of sight from the highway. He looked at the map.

"Shouldn't be far from here," he said.

They slowly picked their way through the bush. A clearing opened up. Across it was a long fence. Eight vertical feet of wire. On the other side, roughly three hundred thousand refugees. Tents stretched into the distance. A light breeze carried the stench of humanity crowded into a small area with insufficient infrastructure. No guards in sight. They crossed the clearing to the fence. Black faces eyed them curiously. A few children approached.

"I want all the dirt on life in the camp. What they expect to happen. Camera ready?" asked Jane.

"When you are," said Nick.

The children stood looking back at them.

"English? Speak English? Anyone?" asked Jane.

One of the children ran back to the camp and pulled on the arms of some adults. They approached.

"Hello, I'm Jane Hansen, News World Network. I'm here to do a story about your lives. I have a few questions for you," she said.

The three African men looked back suspiciously. Caution in their eyes.

"It's OK. Television," said Jane pointing to the camera. "Now Nick. How long have you been on the Canaries?"

The two men looked at each other. A few other adults drifted over. Bleak lives momentarily diverted by the interview.

"Seven year," said the shorter man.

"And you?" asked Jane.

"Five year," said the other.

"When do you expect to arrive in Europe?" asked Jane.

The shorter man interpreted for the growing crowd. He responded.

"I have my paper," he said smiling. "March I leave camp.

"Meanwhile I study English and Spanish. I talk fine both, yes?"

"You certainly do," said Jane smiling back. "Do you have hope for a better life than this?"

"Yes," he pointed to the crowd. "Last camp. Next going to Europe. Easy life. No worries."

"Do you have a family?" she asked.

"Yes. But keep secret. Single man, better chance. I come back for them later. They know. All know this," he replied.

"How do you react to the news we hear from Madrid?" she asked.

The man shrugged his shoulders looking puzzled.

"The Spanish government is talking about closing this camp," said Jane.

"What you say? Again, say again please?" asked the man concerned.

"This camp will be closed soon. All of you sent back to Africa," said Jane.

Nick grabbed her shoulder and spun her around.

"What the hell are you doing, Jane," said Nick angrily. "The only thing keeping them going was the hope of getting to Europe. Take that away and there's no telling what will happen! Besides that's just a rumor. It's unlikely Madrid will do anything about the burned aid ship."

The crowd of refugees were now shouting at one another. Pointing at Nick and Jane. The small crowd ran back into the camp shouting. A rock bounced off Nick's camera. More followed.

"Why is killing the messenger so popular? We're leaving now," said Nick grabbing Jane's hand and pulling her behind him. "Your mouth is going to get us killed some day. I really hope it's not today."

Jane looked back across the clearing to see a mob growing, pushing on the wire fence as far as she could see. Sections began to fall and refugees fanned out into the clearing. They shouted angrily and pointed at Jane.

No time to consider the sharp branches tearing her shirt and stabbing her face as they dashed for the Land Rover. Nick threw the camera into the back and started the motor as the first refugees arrived. They surrounded the car, shouting. Nick jammed it into reverse and floored it, knocking people aside in his rush to make the highway. The windshield cracked as a barrage of rocks rained down on them.

Nick got to the highway backwards just ahead of the mob. He jammed it into first, and sped away. Jane started to speak.

"Shut it, Jane! We're taking the coast road to the airport. Then we're out of here. If Cabrera finds out what you did back there you'll be in big trouble. Which you deserve. Only problem is I'll be screwed as an accomplice. Just hope the riot you started doesn't spread. Have you considered what three hundred thousand angry people could do to this island?" shouted Nick.

Jane sighed and looked out the window. Too bad Nick hadn't got video of the riot starting. That would have been priceless.

This is the BBC. Angela Unkele reporting from London. All tourist flights into the Canary Islands have been suspended because refugees have left their camps to protest the intolerable living conditions provided by EU aid agencies. Another cause is the length of time taken to process then move new refugees into EU nations. It can take ten years in some cases. Reports of isolated cases of violence has caused the Spanish Interior Minister to recommend tourists return home until these protesters return to their camps.

*****

The sea was calm as the Christopher approached Tenerife Island from the southwest. The diesel propelled them steadily against the headwind.

"It would have been cool to make the island in the day. Like old time sailors making a home coming. I'm dying to walk on dry land for a while. And I'd like to see the old parts of La Oratava and Santa Cruz," said Stan.

"Smell that?" asked Tom.

"Smoke, maybe. Like forest fire smoke," said Stan.

Tom raised his binoculars. He could see the glow of fires along the coast. He tried his cell phone again. Busy signal every time.

"Jim bring up the scanner, would you?"

Jim came up to the deck with the radio.

"What's up? The BBC said there were some protests going on. Didn't sound like much."

Tom screwed in the antenna lead from the mast and turned it on. It began cycling through the channels. It stopped. Voices in Spanish could be heard. Calm voices mixed with shouting. He cycled the stations slowly. Listening to each for awhile then moving on.

"I know some Spanish," said Jim. "Somebody is in trouble. There were orders as well as cries for help. Like police stuff."

"That's battle chatter. Orders out, reports in, casualty figures. I couldn't follow it all. My Spanish isn't that good," said Tom.

"Boat approaching, Captain Tom. Port quarter. I see two boats," shouted Wisdom from the bow.

In the distance, bright searchlights snapped on illuminating a sixty foot motor yacht. Decks crowded with people. Too far away to see clearly. The reflected glare off the yacht illuminated a military patrol boat. Tom watched through his binoculars as a muzzle flash was seen from the yacht. The sound of multiple gun shots reached him as the patrol boat was lit up by return fire. People collapsed to the deck and fell overboard as automatic weapons fire raked the yacht.

"Wisdom, get below and if anyone comes aboard, get into the shelf under my bed. Understand?" said Tom.

"Yes, sir," said Wisdom, disappearing down the ladder.

Tom pushed the transmission into reverse.

In the distance, a boarding party jumped onto the yacht. Soldiers began tossing smoke grenades down the hatches. Smoke billowed out as people came up from below gasping for air and were forced to lie face down on deck. There was a struggle between a soldier and a civilian. The civilian was clubbed down as four others jumped overboard. The soldiers took over quickly. The yacht's running lights were switched on. A cloud of diesel smoke rose from the stack.

The patrol boat began to move again. Heading for the Christopher.

A searchlight snapped on illuminating the bow of the sailboat and moved aft. All the deck guns were manned with additional armed soldiers on deck. All weapons pointing at them.

"Hands on heads, now!" said Tom reaching up.

The light stopped on the crew. Three white faces bright in the glaring light. The patrol boat drew up alongside.

"Quienes son usted! Identifiquese!

"Americanos," shouted Tom.

"Your names and boat 's name.

"Tom Hansen, owner. Crewmen Jim and Stan. This is the Christopher from Virginia," shouted Tom in reply.

"Where have you come from?" demanded the Spaniard.

"We have just made passage across the Atlantic from the United States," said Tom.

"Throw us two lines. We will board your boat now," said the Spaniard.

"Jim, throw the bow line across. Stan, the aft. No sudden moves. Those boys are real nervous," said Tom softly.

Tom dropped the fenders and the the two hulls came together. Four soldiers jumped across, three of whom went below as one kept them covered.

"Clear!" shouted the soldiers from below, one by one. A fifth man crossed to the Christopher as the others stepped back to their own vessel.

"I am Teniente Midano of the Spanish army. Have you landed at any of the islands yet?" he asked.

"No. We just arrived," replied Tom.

"Good we found you first. The refugees have taken most of the pleasure boats on the island. Stay away from any boat you meet. The refugees are very dangerous. The army holds the harbors at Los Christianos and Santa Cruz. You my land there safely and stay until the region is secured. Can you find your way or do you need escort?" asked Midano.

"We'll manage," said Tom.

The Spaniard's shoulder radio crackled to life. Midano jumped back to his boat and turned.

"Welcome to Spain," he shouted as the patrol boat went to full power and sped away into the night.

*****

Tom lowered his nap sack to Wisdom, who waited in the inflatable.

"Stand off shore until I radio you. Make for the harbor at Los Cristianos and wait there if you sense trouble of any kind. Remember. Keeping this boat safe is your top priority. We'll do a radio check when we get to shore. Flash the light twice in reply," said Tom.

"Got it," said Jim a little uneasily.

Stan watched silently as Tom pushed off. Wisdom began to row the inflatable.

"Sure you want to go with me? You could get caught and be put in one of the camps," said Tom.

"That is no problem. I had hoped to be in these camps when I left Africa," replied Wisdom.

They dragged the boat into some brush and covered it. The Christopher flashed twice and Tom returned the hand held to his jacket. He pulled two forty fives and flashlights out of the nap sack. He handed one of each to Wisdom.

"Only use this if you have to. Running away is the best policy," said Tom.

They crossed the deserted beach to the small resort hotel on the headland. It was dark. Ominously quiet. So different from the honeymoon memory he cherished. Tom stopped. Listening for any sound. Wisdom watched from behind.

The front doors stood open. The parking lot was empty except for one burned out car. Tom motioned Wisdom inside and closed the door. He turned on his flashlight. The check-in desk had been ransacked but otherwise the lobby was intact. Wisdom turned on his light and scanned the floor.

"No blood," he whispered.

"Jane was supposed to meet me here. I have to check each room," said Tom.

Wisdom nodded. Understanding. He covered the hall as Tom searched. Fortunately it was a small place.

"Looks like the tourists left in a hurry. But no signs of violence and most of the cars are gone," said Tom relieved.

They headed back to the lobby and turned to the dining room. The view over the ocean was spectacular. But there was a smell. Tom pointed to the kitchen entrance and raised his pistol. With Wisdom on the other side of the door he burst in and flipped on his flashlight. All was quiet. But it was a mess. On the other side of the preparation table a hand lay on the floor. Two bodies, stabbed to death. Were they the owners? Tom couldn't remember and their features were distorted in death.

Wisdom looked on unmoved. He had seen death often. He scanned the empty shelves.

"They took the food and moved on," he said.

*****

Tom and Wisdom crouched in the bushes as the gang of refugees passed. The gang carried a collection of garden implements and clubs. In the distance, the lights of the airfield lit up the sky. Helicopters were taking off and landing in the distance.

"The army's perimeter should be just ahead. Probably why those jokers were coming this way. You stay here. I'll check the airport for news about Jane then I'll be back for you," said Tom handing over his gun and radio. "And remember. Don't get caught with a gun."

The road was clear as Tom headed for the airport. He knew soldiers were ahead but he heard the diesel before he was challenged.

"Parar, manos," shouted the sergeant as his squad emerged from cover.

Tom stopped and raised his hands. A flashlight peered into his face and his pockets were padded down sloppily.

"Turista. Americano," said Tom.

"Where did you come from?" asked another sergeant.

"Punto Verde resort. I saw some trouble while hiking about so I hid until dark," said Tom.

"OK. Go on to the airport. There is shelter," said the second sergeant.

"Will do. How bad is the trouble anyway?" asked Tom.

"Everything is under control," he replied firmly.

Tom nodded and continued on. He passed another army checkpoint at the gate and headed for the terminal. In the distance two military transports were unloading soldiers and their gear. It would likely take three days to restore order and another month to find the last refugees hiding in the bush. Then there would be the other islands. It would be months before this mess was straightened out.

He paused inside the terminal entrance to see the new type of refugee. White faces, lost, confused, angry, afraid. The ticket windows were abandoned. He would learn nothing here.

There were two guards in front of the control tower. He put on his marine officer face.

"Yo soy Major Tom Hansen, ejercito de Estados Unidos. I am reporting here to assist with the air traffic controllers," said Tom pointing upward.

The guards looked at each other, uncertain. They moved aside and Tom entered.

Everyone inside looked worn out. On duty since the trouble began. He walked confidently into the flight office. A captain looked him up and down from behind his desk and chuckled.

"Americano, yes? I can spot you from far away. You shouldn't be here. Tourists are to wait in the terminal for evacuation," he said firmly.

I am Tom Hansen, United States marines. I have one question I need to have answered, soldier to soldier.

The captain paused. Then nodded.

"An NWN news jet was supposed to arrive here three days ago carrying reporter Jane Hansen. I was supposed to meet her. Is the plane still here?" asked Tom.

The captain rubbed his eyes and began typing into his computer.

"An NWN Genstar took off just before the trouble began. Destination Madrid. No passenger records," he replied. "Now get out."

Tom came to attention and saluted. The captain made a lazy salute and turned back to his computer shaking his head.

There was a dark office to the left of the entrance. A telephone visible on the desk. Tom went in without hesitating. The phone had a dial tone. He pulled out a notebook and dialed NWN central switching and Jane's private code.

"Hello, NWN central switchboard," said the operator.

"Hello, this is Tom Hansen, Jane Hansen's husband. I understand she is in Madrid. I need to talk to her right now," said Tom.

"Searching," said the operator.

"She has landed yesterday and checked into the Real Madrid. She left a note. Should I read it?" asked the operator.

"Yes," replied Tom.

"Sorry darling, had to leave suddenly. You know why by now. Call me when it's safe. I'm in Madrid," said the operator.

"Thank you. That's all I needed," said Tom hanging up the phone, relieved.

An officer entered the room throwing his brief case across the desk.

"Madre Dios!" he shouted as he threw himself into the easy chair before noticing Tom.

"Quien es usted!" demanded General Ernesto Salazar.

Tom came to attention.

"Tom Hansen, Sergeant, United States Marines, retired," answered Tom.

Salazar almost smiled.

"I could use a Marine division right now. Are there more of you?" he asked.

"No sir," replied Tom.

Salazar motioned for Tom to relax.

"You are lucky, senor. You will soon be out of this and you have a country to go back to," said Salazar. "I am not so lucky."

"You can't go back?" asked Tom.

"We will see. I was given a small army and ordered to bring order to this chaos by my government in Madrid. Now I have been threatened by two EU Commissioners not to hurt anyone. The Commissioner of Justice, Freedom, and Security as well as the Commissioner for Development and Humanitarian Aid phoned after my arrival saying that refugee casualties will be on my head! I'm supposed to get these rioters back to the camps through dialog only! Dialog! Can you believe it! I have demanded clarification from Madrid. They are ignoring me. At dawn I will proceed with what I know must be done for the good of Spain. If my Government doesn't support me, I will be left to take the blame for those killed before I arrived as well as any in the future. These idiots in Brussels will end my career at the very least," replied Salazar.

Salazar ran his hand through his hair.

"Go to the terminal and you will get transportation out of this. I want to get some rest before dawn," said Salazar placing his feet on the desk.

Tom nodded and went out. He stopped at the Terminal for a drink of water. Fountains didn't work. Toilets were probably plugged by now as well. He looked at the mass of white faces in the dim light. Welcome to the refugee life style.

*****

The sun was over the horizon in the east as the inflatable bumped against the Christopher.

"Well?" asked Jim as Tom and Wisdom climbed aboard.

"She's safe in Madrid," replied Tom. "Secure the inflatable, make sail, and raise the American flag."

"Aye aye Captain. Sails up," said Stan.

The wind had changed.

"Follow the coast to the northeast. Alert me if you spot any other craft. There's nothing for us here. We won't be stopping," said Tom going down the stairs.

Jim stared wistfully at the shore then set to work.

Jane checked her face in her hand mirror then lay her purse at her feet.

"Hit it," she said.

The red light on the camera came on. Nick gave her the countdown.

"EU security forces surrounded the house of General Ernesto Salazar at dawn this morning. After storming the house the security forces found it empty. The general, his family, and his servants were gone. It appears they left suddenly, abandoning their possessions to escape. The EU Commissioner of Justice, Security, and Freedom, Ahmoud Antilier, has charged the general with crimes against humanity for his role as commander of the forces sent to bring order to the Canary Islands. As commanding general, he is being held responsible for up to three thousand refugees who were killed by his troops."

"Spanish government spokesman, Juan Hernandez, says he violated direct orders not to harm any refugees in the Canaries. The EU defense force commander Michel DuMorrier, has confirmed this, saying he said the same thing in a telephone conversation with the General when he arrived on Tenerife. As a result, the Commissioner of Justice, Freedom, and Security, is considering bringing additional charges of insubordination for the willful violation of his oath to the Euroforce Command"

"Only three months ago, the EU assembly voted to restore the death penalty for the most serious crimes. Treason, war crimes, crimes against humanity, and crimes against immigrants. The general will be facing two of the four and finds himself the most wanted man in Europe. Government officials have asked this network to broadcast his photo and ask for the help of all law abiding citizens to bring this criminal to justice. This is Jane Hansen, NWN, Madrid."

Jane walked over to Nick as he shut down the camera.

"You can splice in the photo when we get back to the studio," she said.

"I bet he was tipped off. Soldiers are a tight bunch," said Nick.

"Does it really matter? If he hasn't left Europe, he's toast," replied Jane.

"It's strange really. Yesterday he was a hero of Spain. Today the EU is making an example of him. Notice that there aren't any Spanish police or military people here? It's an EU show," said Nick.

"Nobody has stood up for him either. And they won't unless they want the same treatment," said Jane.

"That sounds familiar," said Nick.

Nick moved his boot, exposing a swastika in the dirt. He brushed it away. Jane shrugged and looked away.

*****

"Let's try here," said Jim finding a table at the open air cafe.

It was a pleasant sunny day. Not warm but pleasant enough to sit outside. There were few other customers.

Stan pulled out his language book and leafed through it.

"It always helps to say something in the local language," said Stan.

Jim shrugged and stared around the square. Tangier. It had looked seedy to him from the moment they had neared the harbor. After resupplying the boat, Tom had let them go off to explore the city. Everywhere they went, men stopped and watched them silently. Like sharks sizing up their next meal.

"It says Arabic and French are both used here. I don't know either of them. I took Spanish in school. How about you," asked Jim.

"Russian," replied Stan staring at the menu."Not much use here."

"Then let me help you," said Mustapha Hajoui.

Stan turned and stared at the Moroccan man in his crisp three piece suit and short dark hair.

"I will just pull up this chair and join you," he said. "I actually like Americans. Unlike many of my friends."

He held out his hand confidently to Stan who stared nervously back at him. They all shook hands then all sat down.

"You are here to have lunch? What were you thinking about?" asked Hajoui picking up a menu. "What food did you want?"

"We want something Moroccan. We are from America and want to experience your country while we're here," said Jim.

"Yes, very wise. Why come to Tangier and have a big mac?" laughed Hajoui.

The waiter approached and Hajoui spoke quickly in Arabic. The waiter nodded and went inside.

"I have ordered tajine for each of us. It's a traditional stew that each restaurant makes in its own way. And of course a side dish of couscous. With a popular tea. And to celebrate your country we will finish with coca-cola," said Hajoui.

"Umm ... Thanks," said Stan.

"So you look like students taking the after graduation trip. Am I right?" asked Hajoui.

"We're graduate students in history. Our prof is making Christopher Columbus's first voyage in reverse. From America back to Spain. We're deck hands," said Jim.

"Across the Atlantic in a boat. How interesting. I hope it is a large one filled with girls in their tiny bikinis," said Hajoui, his eyes flashing knowingly.

"It's a fifty foot sailboat. It's roomy for its size but no girls. We hoped to meet them when we got here. No luck so far," said Jim as two women passed wearing the burqa.

"Yes, well, this isn't the west where your women will have sex with everyone they meet," said Hajoui.

"That's not exactly true. About the west, I mean," said Stan.

"But it is," said Hajoui. "I have been to your country and know this first hand. Do you want to hear a funny story? My father sent me to university in America. He thought that I should absorb the culture of the world's most powerful city, Washington DC. So he sent me to the University of Washington where I became a husky. Bow down to Washington, eh?"

"But that's in Seattle," said Stan.

"Yes, we know that. But he didn't and I never told him. I didn't want to embarrass him. It's better to experience America outside of New York, Washington, and L.A anyway. The big cities are dirty, crowded, and people are too busy to talk to you. You learn more about America in the small places that are still like they were fifty years ago. I can say that I saw the America and the Americans who rose up from a frontier to become the world power for a time," said Hajoui reminiscing.

"We're still the world power," said Stan defensively.

"Yes but for how long? America now reminds me of England. The British dominated the world before you but after world war two their empire was completely gone. They continued to see themselves as powerful long after the facts had changed. They are just another industrialized European country now. Real power takes wealth. Too much of yours goes to foreign oil suppliers and shoddy Chinese merchandise. You haven't balanced your government budgets for decades. How can you be a world power and have to beg money from every country in the world? And your industrial base continues to shrink as a few business owners get rich from outsourcing while the rest of the country becomes poorer. Power requires wealth and a strong vision to guide it. The British don't have either anymore and I see you going down the same road," said Hajoui.

"We have the military power and a lot of nukes," replied Stan.

"Russia does also but they are not called a world power anymore. And what good are nukes if you can't use them," said Hajoui. "Let's leave this subject for now. You are young and are still learning about our world. You chose wisely coming to Tangier. It is a very Moroccan city. More than Casablanca where I live. My city has more tourists and is more Western."

The food arrived and they ate silently for a while.

"Good stuff. Glad you came along," said Jim.

Hajoui nodded lighting up a cigarette. Stan opened his coke and noticed a van stop across the square. Steam blew out from the front. Two men got out and opened the hood. Stan nudged Jim.

"Reminds me of my car back home," chuckled Stan.

Another van appeared and backed up to the first. Men got out, weapons showing when they weren't careful.

"Hey, what's going on over there," asked Stan.

"Nothing. Just some local car trouble," said Hajoui.

"Lot of guns around," said Jim.

"They are from the interior. When you leave the coast a lot of men carry rifles openly. It's like Texas out there," replied Hajoui.

The rear doors of the vans opened and the men began to move their cargo. Three blonds, three brunettes, creamy skin bright in the sunlight. Handed one by one from the first vehicle to the second. The young women stared at the ground not responding to anything but the shoves of the men. Jim had never seen anything like this before.

"Hey, we gotta do something," said Jim rising from his seat.

Hajoui pressed Jim's arm back down to the table and held him there firmly.

"Sit down. Sit down now!" barked Hajoui.

Jim complied slowly.

"This isn't right. Those aren't Arab girls," said Jim.

"Listen to me carefully. There is nothing you can do about this situation. You have no weapons and there is no cavalry to come to the rescue. Go over there and you would only be hurt and nothing would change," said Hajoui.

Jim looked at Hajoui angrily.

"What are they doing here?" asked Stan.

Hajoui shrugged.

"The dregs of Europe. Probably drug users and prostitutes. Girls who won't be missed by anyone. Why do you pretend to care anyway?" said Hajoui.

Jim watched the second van leave the square then slumped into his chair.

"I feel like I failed somehow. But I don't know why," said Jim.

"You didn't fail. The fathers of those girls failed. A good father wouldn't let these tragedies happen. He would teach his daughters to live correctly and intervene when necessary. I know. I have two daughters. You Americans let your young women run wild. Drugs, sex, bad choices. Then you defend your failure as freedom. Freedom. Hah! Look where freedom got those women in the van. Women are the most precious part of every society. You abuse yours through neglect," said Hajoui contemptuously.

Jim and Stan looked at each other. Stan motioned that they should leave.

"You think I am crazy and want to run away, right? Stay and learn something," said Hajoui.

Jim and Stan turned back to Hajoui.

"What is your point?" asked Stan.

"The point is that you will lose your country because you have already lost your women. Your television tells them they will only be happy having sex with criminals from bad neighborhoods. The number of children born out of wedlock grows every year. More children than ever don't know who their father is. This is a social time bomb," said Hajoui snapping his finger. "I don't like the burqa but it shows that we protect our women. And by extension our heritage. And our future!"

"Yeah, well, we're going now," said Stan rising.

"It was, umm, interesting," said Jim.

"Yes, go. Go back to your little boat. Go back to your dying culture. Keep your blinders on. Life is more pleasant that way. Don't listen to me. You say you are history students? Bad ones for sure. You have learned nothing," said Hajoui.

"What ever. We'll get this one," said Jim picking up the bill.

"You are young and powerless. By the time you learn life's truths it will be too late for you. For your country. I am not mad at you. You have my compassion," said Hajoui lighting another cigarette.

Stan followed Jim out of the square.

"Do you think he's right?" asked Stan.

"No way! If he was, we would have seen something about it on television," replied Jim.

Jane Hansen nodded to Nick. The red light came on.

"This morning, EU commissioner for External Relations and European Neighborhood Policy, Benito Chasner, announced his decision to apologize to the Muslim world for the expulsion of Muslims from Malta and Sicily in 1224 A.D. Calling this an embarrassing moment in European history, he stated that the acknowledgment of this injustice is needed for both Christians and Muslims to move on to a more sensitive and forward looking relationship. A vote in the EU assembly is expected to pass almost unanimously. The lone voice of objection comes from Maltese EU representative, Fredo Michealo. Why do you object, Mr. Michealo," asked Jane.

"The expulsion of Muslims from Malta occurred around 1224 after they rose up and tried to seize the island for themselves. Why does the EU legislature spend time apologizing for events from eight hundred years ago when we have more urgent problems to solve for Europe and the world today? I don't feel the need to apologize for what is now ancient history. Malta was conquered by Phoenicians, Carthaginians, Romans, Arabs, Normans, Knights of St. John, Napoleon, and Britain. More recently Italy and Germany tried and failed. Does England, as a Norman kingdom, owe us an apology for the Norman invasion of 1092, or do we owe them an apology for the English soldiers killed here protecting us during World War Two? If the EU assembly devotes its time to apologizing for every battle or injustice that has occurred in recorded history, it will not have time for anything else. Besides, I will never apologize to nations and cultures that have raided our coast for centuries, killing our people, and taking countless others away to slavery."

"Thank you, representative Michealo. This is Jane Hansen, NWN news, Malta."

*****

The Christopher steered toward Cadiz. Tom stood with his old round telescope to view the approaching city. The sun warmed him in the otherwise chill air.

"We're sailing historic waters. The British fleet used to patrol back and forth waiting for the Spanish ships of the line to come out and do battle. Back and forth, back and forth. Occasionally heading to Gibraltar for supplies or back to England with dispatches. What a life," said Tom.

"Why don't we head for Capetown instead? It has history also and it'll be warmer there," said Stan.

"The British used to patrol the channel all winter. Through snow and rain. This is pretty easy sailing compared to that," said Tom ignoring his comment.

Stan shrugged.

"Stand by to take down the sails. We can motor in from here," said Tom.

*****

Jim stepped onto the pier with the bow line and made the boat secure. Two officials approached. The older man was white and the younger man was dark.

"Hello there, welcome to Spain. I am Chief Customs Inspector Balboa. You are Americans?" he asked nodding to the flag.

Tom shook his hand. "Yes, three of us. Wisdom is from Chad originally."

Balboa looked at Wisdom, now dressed in the most collegiate outfit Tom could put together. Balboa looked unconcerned.

"Passports please," said Balboa.

The inspector matched the three passports to their owners, writing down the numbers as he went.

"What about him?" asked Balboa pointing to Wisdom.

"Wisdom has no papers. We found him floating in the Atlantic ocean after his boat sank. He is now a member of our crew," replied Tom.

"If he stays on your boat during your stay I have no problem with this. But don't leave him here, we have too many refugees to deal with already," said Balboa.

"I won't. He's going to America with us when we go home," said Tom.

Balboa turned to his assistant. "Photograph this man and we are done here, Mahmood.

"But sir, you didn't ask the questions. And what about the inspection?" asked Mahmood.

72

"You inspect the boat, I'll ask the questions," replied Balboa sourly.

Mahmood went below deck and the sound of drawers opening and closing was heard from below.

"Are you carrying alcohol or tobacco for resale in Europe?" asked Balboa.

"I wish" said Stan lightly.

Tom gave him a withering stare. "No."

"Firearms, explosive devices, chemicals for such?" asked Balboa.

"No."

"Subversive material, pornography, or religious books?" asked Balboa.

Tom wanted to ask what qualified as subversive or religious but he had the sense that Balboa was a reasonable man willing to look the other way on any minor irregularity. Tom just had to give him the chance.

"No."

"That is all then. How long will you be staying?" asked Balboa.

"Cadiz is very historic. I thought about ...."

"Terrorists!" shouted Mahmood from below.

Mahmood ran up the ladder onto the deck with two books.

"We must get the police, Inspector. These men are terrorists. Look! I have the proof right here!" shouted Mahmood, out of breath.

Balboa took the books and examined them. Trouble. His easy afternoon plans were ruined.

"The Pride and the Rage. The Force of Reason. The books of Oriana Fallaci are banned in the EU. She has been declared anti-Islamist and anti-immigrant. You of course, being ignorant Americans, couldn't possibly know this. Possession of these books are a serious breach of EU law," said Balboa gravely.

"Trouble over two books? We really are ignorant Americans," said Stan sarcastically.

"I'll run for the police!" shouted Mahmood. He turned to go.

"Wait!" said Balboa firmly. "I am in charge here. I will handle this."

Mahmood looked uncertain. "But ..."

"I am still Chief Inspector and you will do as I say," snarled Balboa. "You will photograph these books as evidence then you will remain silent."

Balboa handed over the books and pulled out his notebook. A large fishing boat pulled into the harbor covered from bow to stern with people. They had the desperate look of refugees.

Hungry and tired. A little frightened.

Balboa looked up and followed Tom's gaze. Damnation. More work. Mahmood was eying the boat as well.

"Welcome to Spain," Mahmood shouted to the fishing boat in a somewhat better mood.

"Mahmood, greet that boat and do the inspection. I know you can handle it by yourself. I will finish up here," said Balboa.

"Yes, chief. And I will notify the police on the way," he said.

"No, I will notify them myself," said Balboa firmly.

Mahmood paused uncertain, nodded, then walked down the pier toward the new arrivals.

"Damn refugees. Invaders are what they are," said Balboa to himself.

He handed a citation to Tom.

"You are required to report to the magistrate promptly at eight am tomorrow morning to answer to the charges of terrorist activism for carrying these books. I am sorry. My hands are tied. If I was alone I would drop them into the ocean and forget about it. Mahmood makes this a different thing. He is a Muslim and sensitive to anti-Islamic propaganda," said Balboa. "More sensitive to this than to a boat full of Arabs who will never be Spaniards in their hearts and will never try to be."

"Can't you keep them out?" asked Tom.

"No. EU law requires us to accept refugees. Especially Arab refugees. I have no control over these laws. No one does. It is all decided in Brussels. Far from where this problem is happening. There are fifty thousand people in refugee camps around this city alone. Everywhere along the Mediterranean it is the same story. Refugee camps. Crowding. Boats arriving everyday," said Balboa.

"How long can this go on?" asked Tom.

"No one knows. When all the camps are full, some are sent as far north as Finland and Iceland. It then appears to be a smaller problem and is ignored. But I don't like it. This is no longer the city I grew up in or the Spain I grew up in for that matter. The Muslims are causing trouble at every opportunity. First it was the burqas. Then protection from deportation. They aren't citizens but they are demanding political rights and Arabic as an official language. Arabic will soon be required for members of the customs staff. Real Spaniards like me won't be able to get jobs in this service. It will be all Arab immigrants running the bureau."

"The foxes running the hen house," said Tom.

"Just so. But what can I do? I am getting old. I just want to retire quietly and live in peace. Surely that is not too much to ask?" asked Balboa.

Wisdom shook his head sadly. Peace was clearly not in his future.

Balboa sighed. "It was such a wonderful city."

The Inspector picked up the contraband.

"I will return in one hour with the police. They will chain your boat to the pier and most likely take all of you into custody," said Balboa.

"Can we travel in Europe now? Are we marked men?" asked Tom.

Balboa opened his notebook and tore out the sheet containing the passport numbers. A gust of wind carried the page out into the bay.

"How careless of me. No, not yet. What happens next is up to you," said Balboa walking away.

The crew stood silently.

"We will wait five minutes for the Inspector to get clear then we'll head out," said Tom calmly.

"No shore leave? I wanted to see the old fort. Get some food. Meet those famous 'Ladies of Spain'," complained Stan.

"And then spend who knows how long in jail. I don't want to lose my boat. I'm leaving now. You are free to go ashore and fly back to the states if you wish. Just steer clear of Mahmood and his welcoming committee," replied Tom.

Stan turned from Tom to the shore and back to Tom.

"If those British sailors could stay afloat for six month solid, I guess I can manage a few more days," said Stan.

Tom looked at Jim and Wisdom. They nodded in agreement.

"Good. Jim, untie us. I'll take the wheel," said Tom.

They cleared the harbor wall and set sail to catch a very cold north wind.

"Behind me is the villa where Mansour Wadi and his whole entourage were gunned down in cold blood sometime in the night," said Jane Hansen in her professional voice. "He was the head of the Muslim Directorate of France and his successor, Mustapha Najid, stands next to me. Mr. Najid, what are your thoughts about this crime?"

"He was a great man. A great leader. I admired him and will continue his good work into the future," said Najid. "It is still hard to believe he is gone. I talked to him only yesterday."

Najid leaned closer to Jane and firmly grasped the microphone.

"Why do you Europeans want to kill us? We are legal immigrants who obey the law and live for the day when justice for all is fact instead of a dream," lamented Najid, maintaining his grip.

Jane pulled her microphone free with irritation then focused on the camera.

"EU police spokesmen are saying that this is the work of the most wanted man in Europe, Spanish General Salazar. Why the General had these men killed is not yet known. The entire Muslim Directorate leadership is in town to discuss the current oil crisis with the Saudi and other OPEC foreign ministers. No other delegations have been threatened. Security in town is increasing as hundreds of Euro Force soldiers patrol the city. This is Jane Hansen, News World Network, reporting from Valencia."

Nick gave the countdown.

"I'm at the premiere of the new blockbuster film entitled "The Futility of Mud" and next to me is film star Evan McCullum. Evan, it's so good to see you again. What can you tell us about the film?" asked Jane standing on the red carpet.

"It's a period piece from the Great War. I play Captain Wells, an idealistic young officer seduced by the false ethic of king and country. The true nature of war knocks some reality into his simple mind and by the end he realizes the greatest truth of all," said Evan knowingly.

"And what is that?" asked Jane.

"That there is no cause worth dying for. The only winners of any war are the men still alive when it ends. Heroes die in battle so lesser man can benefit from their sacrifice. What's the point in that?" asked Evan sourly.

"Is that what the character believes at the end?" asked Jane.

"Yes, just before he kills himself. His suicide is an attempt to personally atone for the atrocities committed by his society and rightly so. This is the proper theme of all European art that has any merit. I am proud to say that films such as this one have transcended art and now lead the mainstream culture and even guide government policy," said Evan smugly.

"Is that what you believe personally" asked Jane.

"Absolutely. I might fight to protect my immediate family. Beyond that I wouldn't pick up a gun for any reason. Not ever!"

*****

Tom, Jim, and Wisdom walked along the sea front boulevard. They paused to watch when they heard the sound of the Mullahs calling the faithful. Muslim men stopped what they were doing and took their prayer rugs into the street. All traffic was blocked while they prayed. Tom watched a nearby motorist swearing in his car. When he noticed Tom watching him, he stopped and turned his head to avoid eye contact.

"What scumbags. Stopping traffic like they own the place. If it was me I'd just keep running them over until they wised up," complained Jim.

"That wouldn't stop them. It would make the others more resolute," said Wisdom clearly ill at ease.

"And make the bleeding hearts demand more preferences for them to offset their misplaced guilt," said Tom picking his way among the faithful.

It was an unusually warm day for December. Global warming showed no sign of slowing. They found a table in front of a cafe overlooking the sea front. The owner came out.

"I'm sorry. Service will be a little slow right now. All my staff are in the street. I can serve the soup and the stew but the rest will take some time."

"That's alright. We'll take what you have with beer all around to start with," said Tom.

"Very good."

"So this bullshit is going on all across Europe every day? Blocked streets, no service. What, on religious grounds?" asked Jim.

"It's my way or the highway. And they're controlling the highway," said Tom.

"Shit, what's happened to France? Why don't they stop this?" asked Jim.

"It's not our country. Not our problem. But to answer your question. Nothing has happened to this country. That's the problem. Nobody will do anything. Their leaders are unable to reconcile the idea of who they think they are, and who, in fact, they have become," said Tom.

The owner passed out the lunch. Tom sipped his beer.

"I have seen this before. First the marching, then riots, then fighters," said Wisdom waving his arm toward the faithful. "I have now seen France and I do not like it."

The praying stopped and the faithful cleared the streets. As the restaurant staff returned to their workplace, one young man stared constantly at the Americans. Tom returned his stare without flinching. The young man spoke to his friends in a loud voice. They laughed and looked at Tom.

"He says you are rude for staring at your betters and that you need to be taught manners," said Wisdom.

"Ask him if he intends to do the teaching himself?" said Tom.

Wisdom shrugged and translated. The other men stopped on the terrace to follow the conversation. The young man replied angrily.

"He says that he will not let a Frenchman address him in this way," says Wisdom.

Jim looked nervously at the crowd growing around their table.

"That's fine. I'm not a Frenchman. I am American," said Tom.

Wisdom translated. The young man shouted and then spit on the ground.

"He says he doesn't like your attitude or Americans," said Wisdom.

"Tell him that we're even. I don't like his face," said Tom.

Wisdom translated and the other men grinned and chuckled at his reply. The young man shouted louder still, shook his fist, then walked quickly down the sidewalk. The others fell silent and went back to their jobs.

"No need to translate. I get the idea. He's not used to meeting resistance. He can't figure out what to do," said Tom.

They finished eating in silence.

"So you are the Americans, yes?"

Tom turned to see a Gendarme leaning on the rail separating the cafe from the sidewalk.

"That's us. Why do you ask?" said Tom.

"I'm looking for three trouble makers who I was told are Americans," said the gendarme.

"Well that wouldn't be us. We're tourists enjoying a lovely day. We're not trouble makers," said Tom smiling brightly.

"But you are. The young man you angered is going to find his nasty friends and they'll come back for you," said the Gendarme.

"And?" asked Tom.

"There would be trouble. I might have to get involved. That would be dangerous for everyone in these times. Small incidents get blown out of proportion and big trouble starts. Go back to your hotel and stay out of sight for the rest of the day," said the Gendarme.

"Prisoners instead of tourists then?" asked Jim.

The Gendarme shrugged.

"It's best. I don't want trouble here,"

Tom stood. The others joined him.

"You've got trouble already. You just won't face it," said Tom.

The Gendarme stared blankly as they strolled down the sidewalk.

"I came on this trip to enjoy Europe. When is the enjoyment part going to start exactly?" asked Jim.

Tom laughed. Wisdom trailed the other two, turning every so often to watch behind them.

They returned to the marina where Stan waited in the boat. An old man leaned on the harbor wall staring at the sailboat, now named the 'Constitution'.

"C'est magnifique," said the old man nodding toward the sailboat.

"Yes, I think so. We made it here from America without any trouble and that is good in anyone's book," said Tom.

"So you are Americans?" he asked.

"Yes we are. But don't spread it around. We're not as popular as we used to be," said Jim handing the supplies to Stan.

"America. I dreamed of moving there when I was young," he sighed. "When we are young our futures are unwritten and we have so many possibilities. Then over time our choices are made and our options decrease until we are old and left to quietly pass our final days."

"Yes, well, at least we have choices, at least for a little while," said Tom.

The old man stared out to sea for a moment. Tom enjoyed the silence. Suddenly the old man grabbed Tom's sleeve and pulled himself close. Tom looked at the man carefully and waited.

"Please take me with you! To America. I'll give you everything I have. It's not much but it would pay my way. I want to leave here before I die. I hate this place."

Tears formed in the old man's eyes. He let go of Tom's sleeve, stood back, then collapsed on the nearby bench. He held his head in his hands.

"I'm sorry," he said quietly.

Tom sat next to him.

"Do you have a family? Could you leave them behind?"

"I had a family. A wife and three lovely daughters. Now they are all gone. Stolen from me," he replied.

"Stolen? What do you mean?" asked Tom.

"My eldest met an Arab man. He charmed her. He was so exciting. So much more of a man than the French boys. What could I do? I didn't know any better. I did nothing to stop them. They married and she converted to Islam. We were still civil then. Maxine came home to visit when she wanted and all was well. Before I new it, Yousef had introduced Deva and Francine to some other Arab boys. They spent all they're time together. I was concerned and told them so. They grew angry. Called their own father a racist. It wasn't true. I am tolerant toward foreigners. But what is wrong with French boys I asked? They married these Arab boys. First Deva, then Francie. That's when the trouble started. When they had taken all that I loved, all that mattered to me, they stopped being civil. My daughters were forbidden to even visit me. They were forced to convert, wear the burqa. My daughters wearing the burqa here in France!" shouted the old man, his arms shaking with anger.

"Stella, my wife was allowed to visit them at first. She told me how they were resented by the other Muslim women. Abused. Nothing could be done to save them from this. Their large families would only lie to cover this up. And no officials wanted to get involved with family disputes involving Muslims and their customs. Their customs are sacred I was told. And ours are dirt? Have we no rights anymore? We never saw our grandchildren. They were raised as Muslims and forbidden to meet with us."

The old man took out a handkerchief and wiped his eyes.

"One night Francie, my youngest, came home. She had been beaten for the last time and had run away. I took her in and told her husband and his family to go to hell. She wanted a divorce and I supported her. Her husband and her family took to standing outside the house just waiting for her to come out so they could grab her. They petitioned the court to resolve the matter using Sharia law. The court ruled that she had converted so she had lost her secular rights. They turned the matter over to the new Sharia court. I tried to think of some legal strategy but there was never any chance for us! The Gendarmes watched as her husband and his family dragged her from my house screaming for my help. I ran out to save her. I called on my neighbors to help me. They shuttered their windows and looked away. I fought them until I was beaten down. The police arrested me and I came to my senses in jail. I spent 3 months in jail for assault. My wife died while I was locked up. Francine and her family disappeared. The others threatened me with trouble when I started asking questions. And no one will help me. I've lost my wife, my daughters, and my grandchildren. In a blink of the eye all that I have ever worked for and dreamed about has gone."

The old man stood up and stared out at the sea. No longer aware of Tom sitting on the bench.

"I will go to America like I always dreamed of. I'll start a new life there. Yes, that's what I will do," he muttered as he walked away.

"Their women resent competition from white women. They are not kind to outsiders," said Wisdom. "Would you take that man to America?"

"He's too old to start over. It's too late for him now. Like he said, no more choices," said Tom walking down to the boat.

Mustapha Najid stood looking out the windows of the headquarters of the Muslim Directorate in France. Paris was spread out before him. His city. He was raised in the rough neighborhoods that surrounded the city. He controlled the future of this city now. The future of this nation.

Mansoor Hamdar knocked and entered. Anxious.

"I have news I knew you would want to hear immediately," said Hamdar.

"What is it?" asked Najid from the window.

"It's the new pope. Our sources at the Vatican have seen his Christmas speech," said Hamdar.

"And?" asked Najid.

"He will be calling on EU leadership to expel Turkey, Albania, and Bosnia from the European Union," replied Hamdar.

"They won't expel anyone. The EU leadership is drunk with dreams of expansion. They would bring every country in the world into the EU if they thought they could control them all. No, this is a small thing. For now," said Najid turning to face Hamdar. "There is more?"

"Yes. He will be urging that Arabic not be given full EU language status. He is the first leader to come out against us," said Hamdar.

"That is a surprise," said Najid slowly. "All the previous popes stressed peace and reconciliation at any cost. The last pope was our strongest ally in smoothing the feathers of the few who would have fought against us."

"He is not European. He is from Costa Rica," said Hamdar.

"So he brings the fire of revolution from the new world. Don't be concerned, Hamdar. His influence has decreased along with the church population of Europe. I don't know that enough people will listen to him for it to matter," said Najid.

"I agree that he is harmless on his own. But he carries a power well beyond his station. He has a moral authority that could suddenly empower our enemies. When he comes out against us,

82

he will legitimize those that we have so successfully vilified and marginalized. These other groups may gather new momentum and increase in numbers," said Hamdar.

"I see your point. You are right. If he is planning to start a crusade against us, then we have to take more control of the situation," replied Najid. "All we have to do is intercept the broadcast. Go down to Rome and hire an actor. Get a copy of the speech and remove the parts we don't like and film the result. We'll broadcast our version out to the world and no one will know the difference," said Najid.

"The Vatican will know immediately. They'll call the press, use the internet to get the story out if they have to. What then?" asked Hamdar.

Najid turned to look out at his city. Hamdar waited silently.

"Go to Rome tonight and prepare to record the edited speech. And thank you, Hamdar. You have brought a new clarity to our needs. This may be a sign of god's will. I had planned to wait until the new year to strike. That way NATO would have been fully disbanded and the Americans would have no excuse to intervene. Now I have a good reason to change the time table. Move it up to the day our enemies are most vulnerable. Yes, I see no reason not to do this," said Najid beginning to pace.

"What about NATO? The Americans? Are you sure?" asked Hamdar.

Najid waved him off.

"Not to worry. I met with the Saudi foreign minister last night. He assures me that the Americans have no interest in getting involved. He's certain. They are more interested in oil than anything else," said Najid. "Call our leadership members for a meeting in Rome in three days time. I will stay in Rome and direct operations from there."

"Not from here?" asked Hamdar, surprised.

"France will fall into my hand like a ripe apple. I don't need to be here. I need to be in Rome," replied Najid. "Go. Get started."

Hamdar nodded and walked out. Najid turned to look out at his city. His uncertainties faded. The anxiety was lifted. He felt good, almost joyous. The decision was made. Everything was clear. The takeover would happen as he had foreseen it. It was all in God's hands now.

This is the BBC, Brian Corescu reporting from London. The EU general assembly has voted today to eliminate Latin phrases from all legal and government documents. French member, Zin Ben Ali, argued that this dead language was elitist and discriminated against the common man as well as all immigrants who were already having enough trouble learning the languages of their new countries.

*****

Brent entered the train station and looked around for Oliver Clarke. The station was old but in it's day the ornate fixtures would have been impressive. They still were actually.

He saw Clarke standing near the kiosk talking to another man in an expensively tailored suit. The man took a small package from his coat pocket and handed it to Clarke. He then turned and walked away. When the man noticed Brent staring at him he turned suddenly in the other direction and hurried to the exit.

"Not buying drugs, I hope," said Brent.

"No, of course not," said Clarke putting the package in his pocket.

"Who was that?" asked Brent.

"I don't know his name. He didn't volunteer it and I've learned not to ask. But he was a friend of mine none the less," said Clarke.

"Huh? What are you talking about?" asked Brent.

"He was from the crown prosecutors office. You remember the day I was shot? Of course you do, how could you forget. Well, I was just informed that my speech was recorded by one of our government agencies. The bastards recorded my speech but wouldn't help me when I was shot. That man made a copy for me and warned me that my apartment was about to be stormed by the EU Gestapo. That isn't their official name but it fits. I'm telling you this because if you continue to associate with me, you will also become a target of the intelligence services. Guilt by association. I'm sure you understand," said Clarke.

"You haven't done anything wrong! Why would they do this to you?" asked Brent.

"They have reasons," replied Clarke as they walked toward the platforms. "I have to leave London and it would be best if we parted company."

Clarke stopped at a yellow line painted across the floor. He stepped across the line then stopped Brent from following.

"You are a history major, right? Well, this line is the Rubicon. Do you understand?" asked Clarke.

Brent paused to consider the serious look in Clarke's eye.

"Yes, I do. If I cross, there's no turning back," replied Brent.

"Right. I want you to know that things are becoming more serious by the day. As we speak, my apartment is being ransacked. When the goons leave I'm sure there will be secret cameras and listening devices installed. Phones will be tapped and all financial transactions will be tracked. My mysterious friend believes that my speech will be ruled in breach of the new EU crime of hatred toward immigrants. Which now carries the re-instituted death penalty. If this happens I will be an enemy of the state, of the EU."

"But you're the only one who tried to help me with Lorrie. The only possible link I have to finding her. I'm not about to let you disappear. From now on, I'm your shadow," said Brent stepping across the line. "I pledge my life, my fortune, and my sacred honor to your cause so long as you pledge to help me with mine."

"Good lad. It does my heart good to know that there is some courage left in the West," said Clarke. "We have to hurry to make our train."

"Don't we need tickets?" asked Brent as they hurried down the platform.

"I never buy tickets in advance. I pay on the train. And I never get aboard until the train starts to move," replied Clarke.

"Russians, assassination attempts, surveillance. Are you James Bond or something?" asked Brent.

"The fictional British hero? No dear boy. Not even close. I'm the man who stopped the mosque!" said Clarke jumping up the steps.

"The what?" asked Brent following him onto the moving train.

Clarke passed compartment after compartment filled with women in burqa and their large families. The demise of England was on this train as much as anywhere else. He found an empty compartment two cars down. Brent followed him in and sat

85

opposite saying nothing. Clarke sat peacefully staring out the window.

"You never heard about the man who stopped the mosque?" started Clarke.

"Never," replied Brent.

"As you people say it, it was my fifteen minutes of fame. I crossed the Rubicon back then without even knowing it. I've wanted to cross back and live my life they way it was before, but I can't. I know that now," said Clarke wistfully.

"What happened?" asked Brent.

"I'll start with some history first. I grew up in a small village called Dunhamdale-on-Thwaite. A place so essentially English that I can't describe it properly. Immigration never touched us there so the place hadn't changed in a hundred years. I went to school there and was raised in the England of the old books and movies. I left there for university and a government job in London. At university, I discovered a different England. A new England populated by a new people who weren't English and never would be. My observations on this subject were strictly taboo. I wanted to get along so I learned to go along like everyone else. I was content to wear blinders until I came face to face with an elephant in the tea shop. An elephant which everyone ignored or said didn't exist. But an elephant none the less. I'm talking about the Islamification of Europe. Beyond the flood of Africans, Chinese, and others, are the policies of the Arab states. The mosque in every town policy. Have you heard of this?" asked Clarke.

Brent shook his head.

"The Saudis are the leading members of a coalition of private and government interests who are literally building mosques in every city, town, and village in Europe. Even in places where there are no Muslims. Like Dunhamdale-on-Thwaite. They have money to burn and are spending it to spread their culture around the world. So I was home one holiday and went to a town meeting where a mosque construction proposal was being pushed through the local council without opposition. Something inside me snapped and I stood up in the meeting, went up to the microphone, and said in front of everyone there that I would fight this proposal. The room went silent as I stormed out of the room. I went to the pub and regretted my rude interruption of things which did not concern me. I swore that I would never do anything like that again. But then my phone rang all night. Threats of various kinds. All having to do with the mosque. The next morning I met some of my mates and told them what was happening. They were all on my side. No one in my town nor anywhere near it wanted a mosque built there. But they, like me, had been conditioned since school days to follow and not lead. To keep opinions to ones self. It's no wonder no one is standing up to these events. We're a nation of sheep. I was a local boy so I was able to talk to the whole town. People trusted me enough to say what they really thought. Everyone in town was behind me, but secretly. Everyone was afraid to stand up and be counted. I had tapped into a strong and growing force in England. But so heavily repressed it still shocks me," said Clarke.

"I got everyone in town behind me and we studied every bylaw and rule from the hamlet to the national level. We made no progress because everyone on the council was being bribed. Petitions failed. Marches were meaningless. Public outcry carried no weight. Then the press weighed in. I was called the new Adolph Hitler. The press called for my arrest before I could do more harm to the image of the country. There was enough law left then to protect me. The only way to stop the mosque was to get rid of the council. Luckily, an election was due so my mates and I ran for seats on the council and won in a landslide. The council tried one last time to approve the mosque through an illegal closed meeting, but one council member who will remain my hero for life, warned me. We marched in and caught them in the act. My mates took over the council and elected me mayor. What happened next taught me how bad things really were in England. The press said I was on my way to a Nazi takeover of England. The bribes which were given to the old council were now offered to the new council. I held a secret meeting in the woods. We made a blood oath then and there, like we had done as kids, to stand by each other to the end. The longer we held out, the more money was offered. The church was against me because I was divisive. The foreign office was against me because it embarrassed them in front of their Arab paymasters. The employment ministry said I was keeping good paying construction jobs from the area. Land owners said I was keeping land prices down. The press was against me because they are owned by wealthy enemies of the West. The prime minister said I was trying to make England backward and unjust. Every political organization in the country made threats and offered bribes to me and the city council. As the final vote of the council approached, a representative of the Saudis came to meet me. He offered a very large carrot then hinted at a very nasty stick. It was time for another secret meeting. I decided that we should take every bribe offered. But we would video tape and document every payoff in order to expose the corruption. So we did just that and when we had taken all the money we could, we voted against the mosque proposal. Then we took all the evidence to the press and the prosecutors. We had them, by god. We waited indignantly for heads to roll but nothing happened. The police discovered that all the money had been paid as consulting fees. Nobody got in trouble but me and the council."

"Other government agencies tried to ignore, bypass, or force the mosque to be built against our will. Our war chest of bribe money was enough to stop them at every turn and we did. Along the way, my paychecks from work stopped showing up. No one could explain it. Then my desk disappeared one night. Then every night. I spent each day trying to find my files and do my job. I was fired on performance grounds. They got even. Anyone on the city council or in any way connected to the city government was punished. Parents were denied health benefits or were made to wait ridiculously long times. I can't get an honest job in this country. I no longer try. The council and I cleared half a million Euros each from the bribe money."

"Holy cow! That much for one mosque in a place nobody ever heard of? Why so much?" asked Brent.

"Because we resisted. The mosque didn't mean much. The will to resist was the danger. It had to be contained at any cost. Eventually the media frenzy moved to another story. We have been ignored since then because we never tried to take our politics outside of our little town. A place that doesn't matter," said Clarke.

"If you haven't tried anything since, why did a stranger give you that tape," asked Brent.

"Well, this is the strange part. The press thought they had destroyed my reputation sufficiently to isolate me. The opposite happened. They had put my face before the nation. I'm recognized by many people as I walk down the street. I go to a restaurant and I'm told a stranger has paid my bill. I go to the pub and never have to pay. Other towns people ask me how they can also fight for their rights. Secretly, of course. No one wants to be attacked the way I have. I have concluded that the majority of the nation is behind me but are afraid to stand and be counted. So I began to speak publicly. I don't talk about the mosque. I talk about the future of this country and what is going to happen if we don't change course. Ivan and others took me seriously and began sharing information. Some nasty in the EU has taken notice as well. Things are coming to a head. Some big bumps in the road are coming," said Clarke.

"Yeah, you've said that before," said Brent.

"You can get out of this mess at any time. You can go back to America and I won't blame you," said Clarke looking out the window at the green fields of England.

Jane Hansen jostled with other members of the press to get the background shot she wanted. Behind her was a brown two story house. Most of the windows were broken. Plywood covered most of what was left. Parked by the front door was a moving van surrounded by police who were in turn surrounded by crews of the world media. Beyond them was a boisterous crowd of masked young men, jeering and shouting.

"We are here in the Swedish city of Malmo watching the last Jewish family in the city load their belongings into a moving truck as they prepare to leave the only home they have ever known," said Jane.

A stone hurled from the crowd shattered the last remaining window. The crowd cheered.

"Mr. Mayor, representatives of the Jewish community in Sweden say that violence against them has risen steadily over the last ten years and the authorities do nothing to stop or control it," said Jane.

"That is an obviously false accusation. You can see the police all around us protecting the Kopecki family while they gather their things so they can leave," replied Mayor Khaled Shahir. "I am here personally to see that they leave safely."

"Look at this crowd. It is unmistakably hostile. Clearly anti-semitic," said Jane.

"They are not anti-semitic at all. They are expressing their feelings toward Israel and its policies toward Arab peoples. Policies of racism and genocide. Policies that offend the people of Malmo which is now a majority Muslim city. Really, they are showing remarkable tolerance. No Jews have been murdered in Malmo during my tenure as mayor," said the Mayor proudly.

"What do the policies of Israel have to do with this family? They have lived their entire lives in Sweden and have no ties with Israel," asked Jane.

"A Jew is a Jew whether he lives in Israel or any other land. They are all part of a world wide conspiracy that is responsible for most of the wars of the last four hundred years. Who paid for these wars? The Jews and their banks. No. They are all part of the same problem. All to blame equally," replied the Mayor.

"If I used your logic, then since a few Arabs are to blame for the destruction of the World Trade Center, then I can blame all Arabs equally," said Jane.

"No. That is ridiculous. Only those who actually flew in those planes can take the credit," replied the Mayor, smiling at Jane.

This is the BBC, Ali Ben Said reporting from London. Norwegian Ambassador to the EU, Ele Egstrom, was executed in Brussels this morning by guillotine. Norwegian representatives have worked continuously for weeks to free the man convicted of racism and inciting murder on the basis that he has diplomatic immunity from prosecution. The commission ruled that no one can claim immunity from charges of racism, murder, or treason. The commission further ruled that should Norway try to succeed from the EU, that the entire parliament, called the Storting, would be charged with treason and face the death penalty as well.

*****

Gozo was unseasonably warm as Tom sat comfortably in the sunshine outside the cafe. The Xaghra windmill sat quietly in the still air. The peace and quiet was wonderful and Tom closed his eyes. Then the silence was broken by a large plane passing overhead and turning toward the airfield. He looked up. It looked military. Cargo type. The church bells began to sound. People spilled out onto the streets. They weren't happy. The cafe staff came out onto the street also.

"How could they do this to us?" asked the waiter as he passed.

A second military transport passed overhead. The people pointed and shook their fists. Tom looked around. A young British lieutenant sat nearby reading a newspaper.

"Do you know what's going on?" asked Tom.

The lieutenant tried to ignore him then looked up.

"Is something going on?" asked Lieutenant Edmond Bane absently.

"Isn't it obvious?" asked Tom.

Bane listened to the shouting.

"Something about betrayal. The EU. Peace keepers from Tunisia," replied Bane.

Someone turned up a radio.

"... has been declared a zone of shared sovereignty. As of noon today, peace keepers from Tunisia and Libya, have been given control of the Maltese Islands of Gozo and Cominoto to administer as quarters for the Muslim refugees which have overwhelmed the resources of Malta ...."

"Damn it. That will spoil my holiday. The girls here love a British uniform. I've spent a week with Elizabeta, a week with Nardia, and now I'm invited to stay with Maria. I'll probably have to shift station back to Malta where I'll be competing with the rest of my shipmates," said Bane.

"Sounds like a rough posting," said Tom.

"My ship came originally to patrol the Med for refugees. We'd collect them and take them back where they came from. Then the Muslim Directorate told Parliament they wouldn't stand for this racist policy any longer. So for a year we've honored our EU commitment by stationing a destroyer here. But we never leave port anymore. What's a loyal officer to do?" asked Bane dryly.

Tom pulled out his radio.

"Come in Stan. Come in Jim," said Tom.

"Jim here."

"The local shit has hit the fan. Head back to the boat," said Tom.

"Now?"

"Yes, now. The EU just put this island up for grabs. We don't want to get caught in this. Be on the boat in one hour. Sooner is better. And be careful, there may be trouble," said Tom.

"Again? But we need the rest of the day to finish with the Ggantija Temple plus some Roman ruins."

"Tomorrow. If things are calm," said Tom.

"Alright. One hour. Out."

Bane closed his cell phone.

"These things are useless when anything big happens," said Bane. "Why don't you come with me to Maria's house. It's just up the road and maybe she will know more about what's happened," said Bane.

Tom nodded as two military jeeps pulled into town. One of the soldiers stopped to nail a bulletin to the door of the church. They moved on as a crowd gathered.

"This way," said Bane heading out of the town.

Such a lovely day. The sun was making it almost warm. Panic was starting. Some people were clearly packing their belongings. Others yelled and shook their fists.

"She's just outside of town on the hill up ahead. Hey! What's this about?" asked Bane.

A villa ahead was being guarded by soldiers. Two trucks were parked outside. A flag was being raised. As they approached, the soldiers raised their rifles and shouted in Arabic.

"Damn it! I saw her first!" shouted Bane back at them.

Two shots fired into the air brought three officers out of the villa.

"Smile and back away slowly," said Tom.

"I will not! Not until I know what has happened to Maria," replied Bane hotly.

"She will survive this. But we won't unless we leave now," said Tom pulling on Bane's elbow firmly.

"I hope you bastards burn in hell for this," said Bane smiling broadly.

"That's the idea. More bowing and scraping won't hurt either," said Tom as they backed away.

The Tunisian officers lost interest and went back inside. Another military transport passed overhead. Back in Zaghra the bells had stopped. The crowd around the cathedral was dispersing slowly. Looks of shock on their faces. Bane went to find a pay phone. Tom stopped the waiter at the cafe.

"What's going on?" asked Tom.

"We've been sold out. The EU has given our homes to the Arabs. We will be sent to Malta in exchange for Muslim refugees there. My life," he said waving his hand at the town, "gone."

Bane returned from his phone call.

"Shocking news! My ship was sunk last night! A terrorist bomb went off and it capsized in Valetta harbor. Nobody knew where I was so I was assumed drowned," said Bane. "Most of my shipmates boarded a Norwegian destroyer that was recalled in disgust. Now I'm really stuck," said Bane staring at the windmill.

"Could be worse," said Tom. "What about the Maltese?"

"An exchange. We can take one suitcase of belongings off the island. Same for the locals. They, the Arab peace keepers, will clear each town, one by one, removing the Maltese and replacing them with refugees," said Bane.

The waiter held out two large beers.

"The owner says he would rather give this away than leave it for the invaders," said the waiter.

"Thanks, mate," said Bane chugging the glass down. "If this is my last memory of Gozo, it's a good one. By the way, did you say you had a boat?"

"Yes. At Marsalforn Bay. I'm leaving when I get there. Do you need a ride?" asked Tom.

"I would appreciate it. These bastards might extend privileges to me as a fellow officer," said Bane.

"Or they might still be really pissed off about Iraq and Afghanistan," said Tom.

"Precisely," said Bane.

"I have a good crew and I'm the captain," said Tom.

"I fully understand, sir," said Bane saluting sarcastically.

Tom turned to leave as Bane grabbed all the beer he could carry.

"This is only the first sip, the first bitter foretaste of a bitter cup which will be proffered to us year by year unless by a supreme recovery of moral health and martial vigor, we arise again and take our stand for freedom as in olden times," said Tom as they strolled away.

"There's nothing bitter about this beer, I assure you. Or were you quoting Shakespeare, old chap?" asked Bane.

"You don't recognize Winston Churchill?" asked Tom in surprise.

"You have mistaken me for one of those smart chaps who studies hard in order to get a good job in America or Australia. I tried hard work once but it didn't appeal to me. No, I'm part of the upper crust. I've been well fixed since birth. I leave historical speeches to smart chaps like you," said Bane.

"What happens when the smart chaps decide to turn over your apple cart?" asked Tom.

"Never happen old boy. The little people love things the way they are," said Bane. "Besides, we're not total fools. To prove it I will share a bit of wit that has just struck me. Years of overwhelming immigration has driven us out of Gozo where years of overwhelming German bombing couldn't. It's ironic, isn't it," said Bane.

"Yes, isn't it," said Tom.

*****

Tom scanned the sidewalks with his binoculars. Stan and Jim hadn't arrived yet. The crowd around the harbor was growing.

"I have lots of money to pay you. Take me with you," cried the man holding out a handful of Euros.

The man had three suitcases, a cart full of silver dinnerware, and other valuables. Soon to be lost forever. The man wanted to jump into the Constitution with his belongings but Wisdom stood opposite him, arms crossed.

"You could make a bundle here. Take the richest people away for a share of their loot," said Bane.

Tom looked back at him in disgust.

"Or not," said Bane looking away.

The seafront was becoming full of instant refugees all thinking to get away by boat. Bags and bicycles were packed with whatever they thought was important. The road was solid cars, none able to move.

"We're going to move into the bay," said Tom. "Bane cast off forward."

The growing crowd shouted in dismay as Tom started the motor and slowly moved away from the quay. Shouting and fist fights were breaking out between the other boat owners and the desperate crowd. Unoccupied boats were being stolen.

"Come in Jim, come in Stan," said Tom into the radio.

"Jim here. We've just arrived. It's looking crazy, over," said Jim.

Tom scanned the harbor.

"The seawall is clear of people. Get over there fast. We'll meet you there, over," said Tom.

"Got it. See you in two minutes," said Jim.

"Your crew?" asked Bane.

"Yes. Stand by to pick them up. They will probably have to swim for it," said Tom turning the boat slowly in a circle to hide his destination.

Jim and Stan walked briskly down the seawall alone until Tom swung the Constitution in that direction. Wisdom caught their cameras and knapsacks. The crowd in the Marina picked up their bags and boxes and ran towards them.

"Jump!" shouted Tom.

As soon as his two wet deck hands grabbed hold of the rope ladder, Tom started the boat moving. There was a thud on the deck as a suitcase hit and bounced into the sea. More followed. Some missing, some hitting, some opening in mid air scattering their contents. One man threw a small crate too heavy to go far. It sank instantly. Their owners followed them into the water, pleading and begging for rescue.

"There's a bird on the seawall that is just too good to leave behind," said Bane looking through the binoculars. "I'd go back for her in a moment."

"You are free to do so, if you choose," replied Tom staring at the swimmers. "Dammit. We have room for twelve to fifteen on the short trip to Sicily. Jim, Stan, get ready to pull them into the boat. We're going back."

"Captain Tom," called Wisdom, pointing to the mouth of the bay.

A Tunisian patrol craft was rounding the cape and heading for the bay. Tom hit the throttle and headed out.

"Jim, run up the stars and stripes. They have no business stopping us. But if they do, we won't argue," said Tom angrily.

The American flag flapped in the breeze as the patrol craft moved slowly past. Tom saluted and the man watching from the bridge saluted back then turned his attention toward the harbor.

"Bad show about those swimmers. You gave them hope then left them behind. Worst thing you could have done. Cruel really," said Bane shaking his head.

Tom turned on him.

"One more minute in that harbor and we wouldn't have gotten out! Stan, take Bane below and set up a bunk before I throw him overboard," said Tom angrily.

The Dean of Cultural Studies had a large office and that made Nick Farrow's job easier. He signaled to Jane that he was ready.

"Professor Jensen, over the last thirty years rape in Norway has gone from a rare event to a serious problem. Your recent speech to the EU assembly, calling for reduced sentences for Muslims convicted of rape, has left many surprised if not stunned. Can you explain your position," asked Jane Hansen.

"Of course. First you must understand the view of rape in the Arab world. In their native lands rape is scarcely punished because it is generally believed that it is women who are responsible for rape," said Jensen.

"Why would that idea carry any weight? This is Norway not Arabia. Their ways do not count here," said Jane.

Professor Jensen raised his eyebrows.

"To the contrary, Jane. We now live in a multicultural society. We must all adapt to the new society we live in. Our women must adapt as well. Norwegian women must take their share of responsibility for these rapes because their manner of dress is regarded by Muslim men as inappropriate. So I justified the reduction of penalties for rape by Muslims of our women as a cultural misunderstanding on our part," said Jensen.

"Statistics across Scandinavia show that seventy percent of these crimes were committed by Muslim immigrants. That during one three year period, all rapes in Norway were committed by Muslim immigrants. Doesn't this sound like more that a cultural misunderstanding?" asked Jane.

"I don't follow you," said Jensen.

"The situation across Europe goes beyond the criminal actions of misguided individuals. It has been pointed out that these numbers are so unbalanced that it reflects a new kind of cultural warfare. To intimidate European women and humiliate European men. Muslim men across Europe call themselves part of a conquering army and that all women are war booty. In France, gang rape of white and overly white acting Muslim women even has its own name. Tournade. My turn. Yet you want less punishment, not more. Why?" asked Jane indignantly.

"Why? Because they are from a different culture and we are not allowed to judge them by our standards! This is obvious to Europeans who possess the highest levels of sophistication. A level of sophistication far beyond anything an Australian like you is capable of!" snarled Jensen.

This is the BBC, Hasiwah Nawar reporting from London. The bodies of sixteen members of the Sicilian mafia were found outside the town of Ribera on the island of Sicily this morning. Investigators have discovered that the men killed were part of a smuggling operation that brings North Africans into Europe for money. Unnamed sources tell us that recent immigrants have now stepped in to take over the human smuggling trade for themselves, pushing out the traditional criminal element here. A Carabineiri spokesman is warning Sicilians to prepare for an all out war between the costra nostra and the new arrivals.

*****

Tom scanned the entrance to the Tiber with his binoculars. There were crowds visible on the Ostia Lido, walking in the chill air. It was the knot of small boats by the marina entrance that caught his eye. He would have to pass a gauntlet of watchers before entering.

"Head for the Tiber entrance. We're not going to the marina," said Tom.

Jim turned the wheel.

"Isn't the customs dock there?" asked Bane.

"This is Italy. No one will notice one more small boat," said Tom.

"We had some trouble in Spain . . ., " started Stan.

Tom gave him a silencing glance. Bane looked at everyone.

"OK with me. I'm enjoying my status as missing in action. No need to pop up on anyone's radar screen just yet," said Bane.

"Look at those houses. Looks like fishing nets hanging from their front porches," said Stan as they entered the Tiber. "And look at all the boats."

Boats of all types lined both sides of the river.

"No one will notice us here," said Tom.

"A grain of sand in the desert. Perfectly safe. We can all go

100

ashore. I'll just call Sonya. She has lots of girlfriends. Enough for everybody," said Bane happily.

"Wisdom and I will go ashore. The rest of you will stay on the boat until I radio you and give you further instructions," said Tom.

"What? What is the problem? This is Italy for god's sake. Not some sand heap like Malta," exclaimed Bane.

"My gut tells me something is up. I've learned to listen to these feelings. It's kept me alive," said Tom.

"Good for you, but my feelings tell me that this city is full of girls who need my personal attention. You can't moor the boat next to the shore and expect me to stay put," fumed Bane.

Tom scanned the shore again with his binoculars. Bane threw up his arms in annoyance .

"You've gone nutty, mate, and it's crimping my style," said Bane.

The others waited silently.

"Jim, you are acting captain. Stay a couple of miles off shore tonight. Treat Italy like the Canaries. I"ll take Wisdom with me, armed," said Tom.

Jim nodded.

"What about me?" demanded Bane.

"You're staying on board until I give the all clear. You talk too much and I don't want anyone to know we are here. Not yet anyway," said Tom.

A jet passed overhead.

"The airport is walking distance. You can go there or anywhere else tomorrow," said Tom.

Wisdom handed over a backpack with a radio and a forty five.

"So I am a prisoner?" said Bane.

"No. A security risk," said Tom.

Jim put the Constitution against a pier and Tom and Wisdom stepped off.

"If you don't hear from us by noon tomorrow, you're on your own," said Tom.

"Aye aye, captain," replied Jim.

"I won't forget this," muttered Bane.

Jim turned the boat into the setting sun.

*****

Najid looked at each army officer one by one. They were loyal. Loyal to him personally.

"I will be directly in charge of this operation. When Vatican city is surrounded we will begin. Any questions?" asked Najid.

The room was silent.

"Good. Colonel Goneri, Hamdar, you're with me. It is time to move out," said Najid.

The officers saluted and filed out. Najid looked at his hands. Surprisingly steady. He was born for this moment. This destiny.

*****

The car rental was closed. Just as well. No parking hassles. Jane would have a car.

"We'll get a taxi. But first some cash," said Tom.

Wisdom nodded and followed Tom toward a bank.

*****

Jane crossed Saint Peter's Square and knocked on the door of the portable broadcast station brought in by NWN for the occasion.

"So nice to see you, Jane," said William Hamadi, holding the door and reaching for Jane's hand.

"Have you heard from Tom?" asked Jane. "I was expecting a phone call before now. We have had such a problem getting together on this trip. He sailed across the Atlantic you know."

"How could I not know. You have told me this ten times already. Is your phone on? Sometimes it is the simple things that cause the most trouble," said William reassuringly.

Jane checked her mobile phone.

"It's on," said Jane.

"So where is Nick? You are inseparable," said William.

"Vienna for the holidays. With his girlfriend. I have my assistant, Emily, with me," said Jane.

William nodded to Emily.

"Good to see you again, Emily. I have chairs for you set up in this corner here," said William, leading the way. "It is a great honor to cover the pope's speech so I am producing it myself. I know this will be hard for you, Jane, but I'd like you both to stay out of they way of my technicians. It is an important night for me."

"And you don't want me to screw it up. Got it," said Jane grinning.

William smiled back at her, touching her arm.

*****

Tom and Wisdom were making good time in the taxi until they were stopped by military police to let a convoy of trucks pass.

"This is a strange thing. The army is going to Vatican City as well," said the taxi driver.

"Strange in what way?" asked Tom.

"Strange as in I've never seen such a thing before. Especially on Christmas eve. Soldiers should be on holiday or on their bases, not jamming up the roads of the city," replied the driver. "Wait. They must be arresting the beggars. I haven't seen any on the road tonight."

"What beggars?" asked Tom.

"The immigrants. They hold signs and beg everywhere. It has become a big problem. I'm glad that someone is finally doing something about it," said the driver.

Tom looked at Wisdom. Wisdom shrugged his shoulders. Traffic came to a halt.

"I don't know why the cars have stopped. Oh, now I see. Soldiers ahead are turning cars down a side road. They have blocked the way ahead," said the driver.

"We're getting out here," said Tom. "Buon Natale."

"Buon Natale," replied the driver.

Tom led the way parallel to the roadblock ahead.

"When we knew one of our villages was to be attacked. We warned the people and they hid in the forest. Then we set up an ambush," said Wisdom.

"Why would beggars be warned of anything? Why is the army on the move? And why the Vatican?" asked Tom.

Three blocks further Tom held up his hand, then waved Wisdom forward. Six trucks sat idling.

"We'll keep circling," said Tom.

Wisdom motioned toward the trucks as the back flaps opened. Men in brightly colored uniforms climbed out.

"Swiss guards. The guys that protect the Vatican. Why here? Why now?" asked Tom.

"They look very dark. Aren't the Swiss a blond and white people?" asked Wisdom.

"Fake Swiss guards? What is this, a protestant coup?" Tom muttered to himself.

The guards formed up into two groups and marched in opposite directions.

*****

"All units have reported in place and ready," said Captain Baletto.

Najid turned to Colonel Goneri. "You may begin."

"God be with us," replied Colonel Goneri turning to his aids.

Najid stood quietly. The snipers would soon be doing their work. And his replacement Swiss Guards would conceal what would be going on inside.

*****

Jane stood up.

"Did you hear that? I thought I heard a boom in the distance," said Jane.

William Hamadi looked up.

"It's nothing. Probably some Christmas fireworks," said William.

"Do they do that here?" asked Jane.

"I don't know for sure. What I do know is that everybody likes fireworks," replied William.

"There's another one. I'm going to go out and look around," said Jane.

"No you don't. If it's trouble of any kind it is best for you to stay right here. I'll call around to my technicians to find out," said William.

He picked up his radio. "Hamadi here. Report."

*****

Major Aljahad watched the real Swiss guards forming up outside their barracks. They were arming themselves quickly. Officers were calling on radios trying to find out what was happening. They moved out double quick toward the Basilica. Toward his kill zone. He waited a few seconds more.

"Fire," he said calmly.

*****

"Gun fire," said Wisdom.
"No doubt," said Tom starting to jog.

*****

"The entrance is secure," said Captain Baletto.
"Good. We're going in. Hamdar, bring the actor. Captain,

104

position our Swiss guards," said Najid.

He would capture the pope. Then the actor would give the speech and go on to mass.

*****

"We need some high ground," said Tom looking up at an apartment building.

A third story apartment was dark.

"We're going up," said Tom beginning to climb up to the balcony.

He stood on the balcony and pulled out his binoculars. He scanned the entrance to Saint Peter's square. A mass of soldiers blocked the entrance.

"That's interesting. They are letting people in but no one is coming out. Except for a few men with head scarves. What do you make of it," asked Tom handing over the binoculars.

Wisdom scanned the view.

"I have not seen these exact colors before but I know jihadists when I see them. They are all armed but conceal their weapons," said Wisdom.

The lights of the apartment behind them turned on and a man and wife entered. Wisdom started to climb down as the balcony door slid open.

"Follow me," said Tom.

Tom raised his finger to his mouth and held out his wallet.

"Shhhhh. CIA," said Tom holding eye contact with the new arrival.

"CIA?" asked Aldo Moretti in surprise.

"Shhhhhh. Yes. CIA. What's going on over there?" asked Tom motioning toward the square.

"I don't know. The kids went ahead. Then they phoned to say no one was being allowed to leave. We headed home," said the man. "Why are you here? Why does the CIA spy on the Vatican?"

The crackle of gunfire echoed across the street.

"Here that? Guns. Someone is shooting up the place," said Tom.

"That's not possible. It is the Vatican," said the man.

"It's a brave new world. Agent Smith, we're going now," said Tom motioning toward the door.

Tom walked out. Wisdom followed. Aldo stared in disbelief.

*****

Najid grabbed the bowl from the table and smashed it on the floor.

"What do you mean he is not here! Where is he! Find him!" shouted Najid.

Colonel Goneri stood silently, waiting for orders. Mansour Hamdar touched Najid's elbow gently.

"We are not the only ones to have spies. He is gone. So what? The actor will make the speech live instead of using the recording. We control the media. I'll call Hamadi and let him know. This makes things easier in many ways."

Najid stopped fuming and paused to think.

"OK. Do it. And you," said Najid turning back to Colonel Goneri. "Search this place until you are sure the Pope has escaped. Leave no stone unturned. Hamdar, you will take charge of the investigation. Find out everything you can about his escape. God willing, you may still be able to catch him."

Colonel Goneri saluted and left the room.

"What do we do with the actor after the speech?" asked Hamdar.

"We do nothing afterward. The Pope will die tonight one way or another. Use real bullets," said Najid.

*****

Jane opened the window beside their chairs and stuck her head out. She could see the Swiss guards running toward the Basilica. There. More gunfire. The crowd at the back of the square was nervous. Heading away from the square. Something was keeping them in. She heard shots from that direction.

"Hamadi here," he said into his radio.

Jane watched. That wasn't a type of radio she had seen him use before. Hamadi turned to watch Jane as he spoke.

"It's no problem. Live feed for all. Then roll tape when we cut the feed," said William. "Yes. We can make it come out any way we want. That will be easy. Yes. And fast. We just need the footage."

Jane watched him put down the radio and talk to his technicians in Arabic. He never did that in front of her. For the first time she felt uneasy. Then she heard the crowd cheering. The pope was on the balcony. She watched the satellite feed, listened to the speech. OK. Everything was going smoothly. She had been wrong to worry.

*****

Tom brought his forty five down on the head of the jihadist. Wisdom did the same, dragging his target down the ally behind Tom. They were soon stripped and tied and hidden under some stairs.

"Fast in. Find Jane. Fast out. We'll be gone before these two are missed," said Tom hanging the strap of the R5 assault rifle over his shoulder. "Why don't you lead."

Wisdom nodded and they headed for the square dressed as jihadists. The soldiers parted as they advanced. Soon they were into the crowd of faithful straining to hear the Pope. The broadcast trucks were on his left. There was cheering and the Pope was waving.

"It's over. Let's get Jane," said Tom.

Gunfire from the balcony. The crowd gasped then went silent as a masked assailant shot the pope in the face three times then threw a rope over the side and rappelled down. Swiss guards appeared at the balcony and fired at the assassin, who fell, disappearing from view. The crowd was frozen in place, stunned. Then they began to move toward the exit. Toward the soldiers. Officers shouted at the crowd to stop. Soldiers fired once into the air. No affect. Their officers shouted orders and the carnage began. Automatic weapon fire into the crowd at close range.

Wisdom grabbed Tom's arm.

"Don't move," he shouted.

Tom froze as the leading wave of soldiers moved past, firing into the crowd.

"Now," said Wisdom, following the soldiers and pulling the R5 from under his coat. Other jihadists were moving forward as well. No one paid attention to them.

*****

Jane watched from the window in silent horror as the Pope was killed before her eyes. She looked back at William. He stood watching the camera footage as calmly as if nothing had happened. One of the technicians had left a radio like his nearby. She slid it off the desk and returned to the window to hear a barrage of gunfire coming from the entrance of the the square. The crowd near the basilica was running toward the exit. The crowd at the exit was running toward the Basilica. Two colliding stampedes. Young and old being trampled as the sound of gunfire grew louder.

Bullets tore through the walls and everyone dived for the floor.

William shouted at a his security man who went outside. Jane was drawn irresistibly to the window again. A line of armed men had formed up around the broadcast trailer. They fired warning shots at anyone who came close. William's radio beeped. Jane held the radio to her ear. It was William and a man she didn't recognize.

"Yes, we have the footage. It was as good or better than we scripted. That assassination was right on cue. The effects were brilliant."

"They weren't effects. We had to tie up a loose end."

"What ever. The speech went out to the world live without a problem. When should I release the last part?"

"Send it when you're ready. I have reports of gunfire in the square. What can you see?"

William turned to look around.

"It's chaos here. The crowd turned in panic for the exit and the soldiers opened fire. Were they ordered to keep the crowd inside?"

"Yes. To make sure we had a full count of witnesses."

"You had that. It would have been better to let them run away. The story would have spread like wildfire. The story we wanted to get out. Now we have hundreds of people shot."

"What should we do now?"

"Stop shooting. Move the witnesses into the Basilica. We have time to edit the feed to include eye witnesses who saw a large group of assassins trying to leave the square. This will explain who the soldiers were shooting at. Justify it. Then interrogate each person and repeat the story to each one. In the absence of other information, our story will be believed by each and every survivor. They will spread our story for us. We control the information coming from here. In a few more days, when the list is eliminated, we will have control of all media in Europe. We can control this incident and any others that crop up."

"I agree. I'll inform Najid. Hamdar, out."

William calmly set his technicians about their tasks and turned to see Jane holding the radio.

"You knew," said Jane slowly.

William took the radio from her hand. Gunfire was heard outside.

"Knew? More like conceived, scripted, rehearsed, produced, directed, and filmed the result," he replied.

"But all these people being shot," said Jane.

"Pure incompetence. I am not in charge of the army. If I was, no one would have been hurt. Everything would have run as smoothly as on a closed Hollywood set. No animals would have been hurt, etc.," said William grinning.

"But why? What's going on?" asked Jane.

"I marvel at your naivete, Jane. It makes you loved by the TV audience but here it makes you look just plain stupid. Europe is coming under new management. Like a bankrupt business. The old owners are being swept away and new ones are taking over. Life goes on. And I have to thank you for your hard work in our cause. All those stories supporting immigration and multicultural values. Where did you think it would lead? Did you think about it at all? Oh never mind, you are just a woman. I forgot that for a moment. Pretty. Sexy. Desirable. That is all that really matters," said William.

"Emily, we're leaving. Now!" said Jane.

"Out there. To be shot? Now you are being stupid. You don't have a chance. Don't you hear the gunfire. The army is out of control. I don't know what will happen. You leave and it could be your death," said William.

Jane dragged Emily to the door and threw it open. Another burst of bullets ripped through the top of the trailer. Emily collapsed. Crying.

"I don't want to die," she sobbed.

Jane pulled Emily inside and closed the door.

"You are one of them, aren't you. A jihadist," said Jane.

Hamadi laughed heartily.

"No, not exactly but the label will work for the moment. You didn't figure this out before now? I am shocked, Jane. Really shocked. When all the countries of the world are begging for oil, you could fly a jet around the world at the drop of a hat. Just who made that possible? Didn't you wonder why you got priority fuel rations over almost everyone? You've been working for us all along. Promoting our causes, supporting our initiatives. You and the rest of the media. Obsessed with doing good for the world as you destroy your own cultures. Yes, I'm a jihadist as you say it. And judging by what you have been doing for me over the last few years, you are too!" said William. "But enough of this. You have served our cause well and I will protect you. Become my mistress and you will be completely safe. Sign your name to that effect and be safe or go outside and die. You have the same offer, Emily."

"I'll sign anything. Just don't put me outside," wailed Emily.

"Don't do it, Emily. You don't know what you're doing. Your dignity will only be the start of what you will lose!" said Jane.

"I don't care. All I want is to stay alive," sobbed Emily.

Hamadi turned to his technicians. "Who wants her?"

One man raised his hand. Hamadi motioned him forward.

"You will be Alfredo's mut'a," said William, scribbling quickly on a sheet of paper. "Just sign here."

Emily took the paper.

"Emily, stop! I know enough about this to know that there is no going back. You are signing your rights away. Permanently. The courts are upholding these contracts," said Jane emphatically.

Emily signed her name.

"I'm not as brave as you are, Jane," she replied sadly.

"Now you, Jane," said William. "Be my mut'a. Nikah even. You know me well enough to know I will treat you well."

"I've always liked you, William, but I already have a husband. I've picked the man I want already," said Jane.

"Your marriage is not a problem for our laws. When you sign this what went before is null," said William.

"Tom will never be null to me," said Jane.

"This is your last chance. Think about your safety if nothing else," said William.

Jane shook her head. Hamadi barked orders to his security chief who moved up beside Jane and held her elbow firmly.

"We'll talk further in a few days," said William.

"I won't be around in a few days. And by the way, I quit," said Jane.

"Take her to my apartment," said William.

The security men took her and headed for the door. Emily rose to go with her. Alfredo slapped her down.

"You cannot leave! You are my mut'a. Sit on the floor next to me or I will beat you!" shouted Alfredo raising his fist.

"Jane, don't leave me here!" cried Emily fearfully.

"Goodbye, Emily," said Jane as she passed out of the door.

Hamadi watched the door close. He would win her over. He had to. She knew too much and could be the kind of rallying point that simply couldn't be allowed to spring up during the delicate phase that had begun. He returned to his mixing console, ignoring the beating Emily was receiving.

*****

Tom watched the soldiers open fire again. They were herding the terrified crowd toward the Basilica. Small groups tried to break out of their net and were shot or clubbed down. Nearing the broadcast trailer Tom froze. Jane was being escorted out by three men dressed in the same outfits that they had stolen. Tom signaled Wisdom to move across Jane's path then follow. He stood behind the soldiers and waited.

They escorted Jane toward the entrance of the square without challenge from the soldiers. Jane didn't struggle. Tom began his slow pursuit, Wisdom to his right. They both held their R5s openly.

Jane made a sudden break to her left to no avail. She was held fast. The men continued walking, past a second line of soldiers now keeping everyone out of the square. Beyond that line there were no soldiers, making Tom and Wisdom more obvious. They would have to act soon.

Jane and her escort were turning toward a side street. Tom signaled Wisdom to the left of the row of trucks and broke into a jog to the right. He turned the corner and ran full speed into the man behind Jane, throwing him sideways. The leader turned into the butt of Tom's R5 and fell silently. Wisdom was astride the inert figure of the third man. A kick silenced the first man.

"Jane," said Tom turning.

She was gone. He began to sprint toward the sound of running footsteps.

"Jane stop," he hissed.

He was gaining. Far ahead she was bending over a car door, keys out. Tom could make out the NWN logo as the engine roared to life. She smashed into the car parked behind and jammed it into first never letting off the gas.

"Jane stop," he hissed again.

He could see the terror of the hunted animal in her face as he crashed his assault rifle into the passenger window and dived into the car.

"Stop, Jane!" shouted Tom.

She was too panicked to hear him and careened down the street. He grabbed her hair and pulled her head back. The slam of brakes threw Tom into the dashboard as she broke free and jumped from the slowly moving car. When Tom looked up, Wisdom held her pinned against the car. She was sobbing. Tom threw off his keffiyeh and took her in his arms firmly so she couldn't escape again.

"It's me, Tarzan," said Tom.

Jane stopped struggling and paused to look at his face. Then she began to sob into his chest.

"Jane, get in beside me and stay low. Wisdom, take the back. I'll drive. We're leaving, now!" he said.

Hamadi looked at his three guards being treated by the army medic. Professionals not easily overwhelmed like this. Only by other professionals. Like a marine sniper named Tom Hansen and maybe others. It could be the perfect setup. A real marine sniper in Vatican City during the assassination of the pope. Open and shut case. It would be the end of Jane. He could turn the fury of the EU against them with only a few words. He turned to the detective of police.

"I have reason to believe that Jane Hansen, one of my producers, has been kidnapped. My men were attacked while escorting her back to my apartment. I have written down the license plate of her car which is also missing. Maybe you can alert your men to look for it," said William.

"Of course, we will will do that right away," said the police detective nodding to one of his assistants. "Do you have knowledge of who might have done this or why?"

"No, I don't have any idea. She was well liked by everyone," said William.

"OK. Let me know if you think of anything we should know," said the Detective.

"Could you call me if you find her? We are very close," said William.

"Of course, leave your number with my assistant," said the Detective turning back to the injured men.

It would have been so easy to destroy her. But he would be merciful. At least, for now. After all, what were two infidels when millions of them were coming under his control. And he could still implicate them later if he needed to. Hamadi headed back to the square with his new security chief.

"Her husband was arriving in a yacht. A sailboat. Forty five or fifty feet. Get your men together and search every slip and marina along the river until you find them. Don't kill them. Their capture can still serve us. If they turn out to be the Pope's murderers, bringing them to justice will distract the nation while we do our real work."

"I saw the pope being assassinated. Wisdom, what did you see?" asked Tom fighting the urge to drive faster.

"Yes, I saw the pope being shot," replied Wisdom.

"Jane?" asked Tom.

"I saw it too," replied Jane. "Then the army started killing innocent people."

"Who was your escort?" asked Tom.

"William's security men. He's one of them. He knew about the plot. He boasted that he had planned and organized it. At least the filming. I listened in on a radio that implied someone named Najid was the real boss," said Jane.

Tom fit this information into the puzzle.

"Does he know I'm here?" asked Tom.

"Yes, I told him we planned to meet tonight," replied Jane.

"Shit," said Tom. "He knows you, your car, and about my boat. What did he want with you? Will he care if you slip away?"

"He wanted me to be his mut'a. His mistress. He said he would keep me around for a couple of days. Probably under guard at his hotel," replied Jane.

"His mistress? I never did trust that snake. I want you to quit your job immediately," said Tom.

"I beat you to it," said Jane with a little smile.

"Police," said Wisdom.

Four police cars streaked past going the other direction. Lights and sirens blaring.

"These people control at least part of the army and maybe the police. With the Pope murdered everyone will be trigger happy. If William is one of them, he may set the police on us. Head us off before we can get to the boat. We should switch cars before the cops find us. Uh oh, too late," said Tom watching the flashing lights of a police car coming up from behind.

*****

Stan flipped through the TV channels again.

"Will you stop that?" said Bane turning off the TV. "You're driving me crazy."

"I'm trying to find a news program. Maybe there will be more about Malta," said Stan. "Something in English or with subtitles."

"Not in Italy, mate. We're just lucky to have good reception out here in the ocean," said Bane.

"Tom was worried about something. I know it. I'm expecting something big to come across the networks any time now."

"Like what? We watched the Pope's speech. He blessed us all with peace and happiness. It's Christmas eve. There hasn't been a hint of bad news on any channel. All is well in the world," said Bane.

"Why did Tom send us out here then?" asked Stan.

Bane headed for the cockpit.

"I never thought I would actually look forward to my watch," muttered Bane.

Stan turned the hand held radio up to full volume. Nothing. He turned the TV back on to see the words 'Notizie Buletin'.

"Uh oh," said Stan.

*****

Tom slowed and turned onto a side road. He went down the road a half block before stopping. He faced the others.

"Stay calm and cooperate. But we are not going to allow ourselves to be arrested," said Tom.

The policeman approached the car and spoke to Tom.

"Americano," replied Tom.

"OK. I need your license and papers," he said.

Tom turned to Jane. "Do you have the registration?"

"I don't know, I'll look," she replied opening the glove box.

"It's my wife's company car," said Tom.

"What happened to the window?" asked the policeman.

"We don't know. We were in the city and found the window smashed when we came back to it," said Tom.

"Anything stolen?" asked the policeman.

"I don't know. Dear, was anything stolen?" asked Tom.

"Not that I know of," said Jane. "Here. I think this is the registration."

Tom handed it over.

"Now your license," said the policeman.

"I have one from the States. Will that do?" asked Tom.

"Yes, with your passport," said the policeman.

"My wife has an international drivers licenses but she had a little too much wine with dinner so I'm driving. I hope that is OK?" asked Tom.

"Wait here," said the policeman heading back to his car.

"If there's trouble, Jane, you will scream and fall down to distract him, then Wisdom or I will step in," said Tom.

"Then what?" asked Jane.

"Then we'll see," replied Tom.

They waited. The policeman returned with the papers.

"It is very strange. My police radio doesn't work. I can't call this in. So you are free to go. Drive carefully. Buon Natale," said the policeman.

Tom handed the papers back to Jane.

"Merry Christmas," said Jane.

"Yes, Merry Christmas from all of us," said Tom smiling.

Tom headed back to the main road. Then took the next side street and turned off the lights. He headed north for the river. He hit a dead end and parked.

"We walk from here. This car is a liability," said Tom.

It was quiet in the ruins as they walked.

"This used to be the port for Rome two thousand years ago. The coast has moved a few miles downstream over the centuries. I would have loved to examine this place," said Tom.

"Maybe we'll return," said Jane.

"Not anytime soon," said Tom.

They headed for a small marina. All was quiet. Sirens sounded behind them and he turned. Lots of lights were flashing in the area where they had left the car.

"Police radio must be working again," said Tom.

"We can cross with this boat," said Wisdom, pointing to a rowboat tied to a larger yacht.

"My thoughts exactly," said Tom.

As they rowed into the darkness, two cars stopped at the marina entrance. Men got out and searched each boat. When they finished, the searchers got back into their cars and headed downstream.

"Looks like more than the police are searching for us," said Tom quietly. "There's another tributary of the Tiber to the north. We'll take a boat from there and head offshore to our rendezvous with the Constitution."

Tom helped Wisdom drag the boat ashore. They headed into the neighborhood with Tom and Jane side by side. Wisdom followed, watching behind. They kept to the side roads to avoid traffic but soon approached a large mosque. There was a lot of traffic in the area.

"Do you know why there would be so much traffic at a mosque on Christmas eve?" asked Tom.

"No," said Wisdom. Jane looked blank.

"We'll go around to the left and avoid this place. Could you go a little closer and see what is happening, Wisdom?" asked Tom.

Wisdom nodded and melted into the darkness. Tom and Jane kept walking.

"What a trip. Every plan I make has been changed. Sometimes suddenly. Like our meeting in the Canaries. Did you make it to the resort?" asked Tom.

"I don't want to talk about the Canaries," she replied quietly.

Tom could see she was holding something back. It didn't matter right now.

"And tonight. The Pope. Snatching you from armed escorts. Running from the police. It all reminds me of one thing," said Tom.

"What?" asked Jane.

Tom took her in his arms and kissed her fiercely.

"How much I love you," he replied.

Jane held him and buried her head in his chest. She felt safe. Tom turned with a start as Wisdom reappeared.

"I have seen men going in the front entrance of the mosque. Then I have seen policemen and soldiers leaving from the rear entrance. It is not what I would expect to see," said Wisdom.

"Nor I. I'll be glad when we are out at sea and heading west. Let's find a boat," said Tom taking Jane's hand.

They found the north tributary of the Tiber and soon found a sailboat to Tom's liking. Sails were all in place ready to unfurl. Plenty of fuel. The Veloce was a well kept boat. Too bad for the owner that they would have to take it.

"Cast off," whispered Tom.

Wisdom went forward. Then a truck appeared on shore four boats upstream. The engine and lights of a large powerboat came to life illuminating the shore.

"Hold it," hissed Tom.

He could start the engine and head out, but if these men were looking for them, they could shoot down on the sailboat from their high deck. They waited and watched. There were two lines of women, four in each, tied together by the neck. Their hands tied behind their backs.

"Slaves," said Wisdom.

Good. They aren't looking for us, thought Tom.

"This is terrible! You must do something," whispered Jane pulling on Tom's arm.

"Do what? Those men are armed and they outnumber us. We can't intervene unless we are prepared to kill them all. And we might get killed instead of them. We can't save everyone when we can barely save ourselves. We have to get away now. Do you know how lucky we have been to find each other and get this far? You're the only woman I would kill for. I thank god I haven't had to," said Tom.

Jane stared at the women and started to cry.

"I was in their shoes tonight. Being marched off to what ever fate William had in mind for me," said Jane.

"If we try something and fail, what do you think will happen? There will be nine lost women instead of eight," said Tom.

"If they thought they could capture me, wouldn't they try?

Would it distract them enough for you to do some kind of rescue?" asked Jane.

Tom's tactical mind sprang into high gear.

"Are you crazy? I'll not risk you. Ever," said Tom.

"I'll never forgive myself if I don't try," she replied.

"You mean you will never forgive me. We will be exchanging the lives of those men for those women. Can you live with that," said Tom.

Tom saw the look in her eyes. She was determined. Why did he fall for such a crazy woman?

"Wisdom. Count the men. Jane, come here and help me lower the dingy," said Tom.

"Five on the boat. Six on the shore. They have loaded the girls and are talking on shore about something," said Wisdom.

"When they pass by us, we will have one chance. Jane, I want you to use the motor and steer into them. Distract them. If they don't stop, there is nothing we can do. Do you accept that?" asked Tom.

"Yes," replied Jane.

Tom handed her his forty five.

"Just in case," said Tom.

Tom got into the dingy and examined the motor.

"They are moving," said Wisdom joining him.

Tom started the outboard and headed out about midstream. There would be no time to wait or think.

The big cruiser approached picking up speed slowly. Jane dropped the aft line and steered into the river. She pushed the throttle to full speed and turned on the running lights, and the stereo. Collision course. One man on the cruiser shouted and turned on a light. She hit them with a glancing blow and throttled back to match their speed. More men appeared on the railing above her as their boat slowed.

"Sorry about that. It's all my fault. I have insurance," she shouted.

"You stupid woman," shouted Hamjid.

There were four on the rail as the boat stopped. They talked among themselves.

Tom steered for the cruiser's far side. The outboard seemed to roar but no one had reacted to the noise. They bumped gently against the hull. Wisdom jumped for the railing and scrambled over. Tom left the dingy quickly and headed up the aft steps.

"What are you doing out here? Are you alone?" asked Hamjid.

"Oh yes, I'm all alone. I was just moving the boat to Fiumicino to pick up three of my girlfriends," said Jane.

117

Hamjid translated. The others nodded then talked some more.

"Wait. I will come down to you. We should talk about more insurance. Can you tie up to this rope?" asked Hamjid.

Wisdom climbed up to the bridge silently. One man at the controls. Four at the railing. He made hand signals to Tom who nodded in understanding. Tom heard nothing as the man at the controls disappeared. Hamjid was about to go down the side ladder.

"Freeze," shouted Tom jumping up.

Hamjid dropped over the side. The other three were not cowards. They turned and raised weapons without hesitation. Tom had no choice and a good firing position. Three bursts from his R5 and they dropped. There was a shot from the sailboat. Then a thump and a splash. Tom leaned over to see Jane staring at a body in the water drifting away slowly.

"You OK?" asked Tom.

Jane nodded.

"Make that line fast," said Tom.

Wisdom followed him below decks. They moved room by room ready to shoot instantly. He was relieved when they didn't find anymore men. In the lower salon were seven women tied together. The eighth was in a side room, tied to a bed. Tom tugged on the line holding four of them.

"Come on ladies. Time to go," said Tom.

The girls stared at the deck. Not speaking or moving. Tom tugged again without result.

"Do you know what's wrong with them?" asked Tom.

"Sometimes drugs, usually harsh treatment," replied Wisdom. "Do we take this boat?"

"Too risky. The owners know this boat and will be looking for it. We'll still need a second boat. Best a sailboat," said Tom.

Tom looked at the girls, puzzled. Wisdom clapped his hands loudly and spoke in Arabic. The women stood up.

"Good. I'll let you load the women while I ransack the kitchen. I'll meet you on deck," said Tom.

Wisdom nodded as he cut the ropes.

Acting captain of the Marseilles, Claude Bery, watched six trucks approach along the pier from the darkness. Asim stepped out of the lead truck and shook hands with Bery. He turned and waved to his men.

"Rochambeau is in the truck. I've already killed his family. He doesn't know it yet," said Asim. "I don't know how he will be of use to you except to blame for this mutiny if it fails."

Bery handed over a uniform and Asim put it on. Crew men jumped down from the trucks and headed for the submarine.

"Good luck," said Bery.

"Luck? I have no need for luck. It is god's will," replied Asim.

Bery saluted and headed for the sub.

The guards at the headquarters building saluted to Asim, in a captain's uniform, as he approached. He entered the control center and saluted the commander.

"Who are you?" asked Captain Lavandou frowning.

"The man who is holding your family hostage. You will remain quiet and do what I tell you or they will die," said Asim, holding out his mobile phone.

Captain Lavandou listened to his wife and children in horror.

"What do you want from me?" he asked.

"Not much. You will just stay here and tell anyone who calls that the Marseilles is still tied up at its dock," said Asim. "And that I am from special operations and not to be questioned."

"The Marseilles? Gone?" asked Lavandou in confusion.

"No. Of course not. It's tied up at it's dock," said Asim firmly.

*****

\Adrien28\   Of course I'm hot. Too hot for you!
\Barker40 has joined the room\
\Richard38\   Cool girl, when are we going to hook up?
\Adrien28\   As if! Only in your dreams, sucker.
\Celia19 has left the room\

119

\Richard38\	So you're another tease. I'll forgive you after you're mine.
\Adrien28\	Shit shit shit
\Richard38\	I like it when you talk dirty. Maybe not those exact words.
\Adrien28\	OMG. Something is wrong here.
\Richard38\	The only thing wrong is that you aren't here getting me off.
\Barker40\	What's wrong?
\Adrien28\	My parents are being arrested. They have been handcuffed. My dad's being beaten up.
\Barker40\	Where are you?
\Adrien28\	I'm next door at my friends house. My parents won't let me use this site so I snuck out.
\Richard38\	Parents? What's this about parents?
\Barker40\	What do you see now?
\Adrien28\	They are being dragged downstairs to a waiting van. It's a mix of soldiers and bobbies.
\Barker40\	Do they see you? Turn off your lights.
\Adrien28\	I don't think so. They are searching the house. What should I do? Call the police?
\Barker40\	No. Stay where you are. They may take you prisoner also. When they leave, stay where you are or go to someone not related to you that you can trust with your life. Tell your friend what happened if you can trust her or him. They may hunt for you.
\Adrein28\	I'm so afraid. I'm only thirteen. What will happen to me?
\Barker40\	Focus on not being caught for now. Live one day at a time.

\Adrien28 has left the room\

| \Richard38\ | What an imaginative little shit. She told me she was a stewardess. Twenty eight and hot for me. Not! |
| \Barker40\ | It didn't sound like her imagination I lived in South America for many years. I've seen exactly what she described with my own eyes. You never forget it. |

*****

General Bariatinsky spread the map over the large table in the center of his rail car. Armor had been loading since morning and they were ready to leave. Ivan watched the biting wind making snow drifts beside the rail yard.

"Intelligence reports confirm what you had predicted, Colonel Borovich. There has been a Muslim coup across the breadth of Europe. The situation varies from a smooth transition like in France to a paralyzed confusion like in Germany and Ireland. Most military forces are demobilized while the old officers are replaced by new ones loyal to the Muslim Directorate. Europe is changing hands before our eyes. I find it strange that America is showing no reaction to these events but there it is," said Bariatinsky.

"The American secretary of state visited the Saudis only one week ago. I suspect they secretly traded Europe for oil. They must have known about this," said Ivan Borovich.

"Now we have reports that the Turks are on the move in force. They are moving to secure their old colony, Greece. They have advanced in strength to Thessaloniki. Amphibious landings are reported on Cyprus and Crete. Overnight it appears that Greece is leaderless, doomed. The Turks won't have much problem there. That is not really our concern for now. What is our concern are the two armored columns that have crossed the frontier into Bulgaria. Bulgaria is also now leaderless and confused. The larger group is in Dimitrovgrad following the rail line to Sophia," said Bariatinsky.

Borovich traced his finger along the map.

"The old Orient Express route. Sophia, Belgrade, Budapest, Vienna. A bridgehead to their countrymen in Germany," said Borovich.

"It is too early to know how far they plan to go. The Turks are most likely taking advantage of the chaos started by the Muslim Directorate to grab what they can. This other column is of immediate concern," said Bariatinsky, pointing to the coast.

"Armored units have passed Tsarevo with advance scouts in the outskirts of Burgas. The Muslim Directorate does not have clear control of Romania and Bulgaria yet. These countries are currently not capable of resisting an invasion by a well organized and supplied foreign army. If they only meet light resistance, they could push considerable forces north to the Ukrainian border in a week. When Greece is subdued they will most likely turn their main force north to back up the advance units. That is where we come in. We are ordered to cross the frontier into Romania and grab as much territory as we can as fast as we can. Colonel Borovich, your column will head to Bucharest. Hold the Danube, cross it if you can. My column will take a western turn for Belgrade. If I can get there first, the Turk advance will be stopped. Our northern counterparts are moving through Belarus to secure Poland. Bypass small pockets of resistance and leave them for the rest of the Army that will be following as fast as they can mobilize. Understood?" asked Bariatinsky.

"Yes, sir. It is a glorious day to be an officer in the Russian army," said Borovich saluting.

"We'll see if you still believe that in a week or a month," replied Bariatinsky, returning the salute.

The train began to move as soon as Colonel Borovich stepped aboard his own command car. The General and his staff slid past his window while he turned his full attention to what lay ahead.

This is the BBC, Yasmin Abouti reporting from London. Fire broke out in the home of Dutch parliamentarian Beert Gilders overnight. Fire investigators report that he and his entire family were trapped in the fire and none survived. The festive celebration of the birth of Jesus has taken a somber tone as the ultra conservative anti-Muslim was remembered in Christmas services across the country.

An eye witness claims she saw locks and chains on the door of the house when the fire started. Officials deny this and say it is too early to know what caused the fire, but stress that there is no sign of arson.

*****

"You betrayed me!" shouted Najid, slamming his fist down on the desk.

The Turkish Ambassador shrugged his shoulders without concern.

"Your recklessness has brought the Russians into this. Their armies are on the move. We do not have full control in the east. We are still weak and unable to create a solid front to stop them. They will cross the frontier and take what is ours because you provoked them!" snarled Najid.

"You were never going to take over the entire EU in one try," replied the Ambassador.

"A self fulfilling prophecy because of your greed,"said Najid. "Why didn't you honor your word not to move?"

"We lost our Mediterranean empire as a result of the Great War in 1918. There has been little chance over all these years to regain it. We could not simply sit and watch while this opportunity slipped past," said the Ambassador.

"I promised you territorial concessions once we were secure in our victory," said Najid.

"A promise you could only keep if you succeeded. Our

intelligence was that you were strongest in the west and weakest in the east. So we have taken matters into our own hands. You have nothing to worry about from us. When you establish the Caliphate, we will be a close ally, maybe the closest one that you have," replied the Ambassador.

"It was never you that I was worried about," replied Najid coldly.

*****

"What is it?" demanded Captain Thomas entering the bridge.

"New orders from CINCLANT. Captains eyes only," said Hampton.

Thomas nodded and went to the communications booth. He was irritated. It was bad enough the he and the crew had missed Christmas, but he had just fallen asleep. He scanned the orders, then reread them word for word to be sure he didn't miss anything.

Orders:	Return to Europe and begin searching for French submarine, Marseilles, using all available resources.
Intelligence:	Marseilles has left port without NATO clearance or notification. Believed to have left Christmas eve. Not discovered until satellite sweep. Captain Rochambeau and family missing. France denying it has left Brest.
Objective:	Report position when found. Take no other action.

Thomas sent an acknowledgment signal and returned to the bridge.

"Turn the ship around, Mr. Hampton. We're heading back to Europe," said Thomas.

"Yes sir," replied Hampton. "Helmsman, set course due east, all ahead standard."

"Due east, all ahead standard," repeated the helmsman.

The ship leaned slightly as they began to turn.

"And Mr. Hampton," said Thomas.

"Sir," replied Hampton.

In the morning, inform Mr. Mueller and his team that they have been drafted," said Thomas.

"Yes, sir," replied Hampton, surprised.

Brent nursed his ale slowly. The small pub in the middle of nowhere was quiet. Clarke was busy on the phone in the back. A light snow had fallen overnight making a postcard picture of the tiny English village. Clarke put the phone down and paused, running his hand through his hair. He headed for the exit and motioned Brent to do the same. Brent finished his ale and followed.

"Someone onto you?" asked Brent.

"Not likely. But it's safest to move after using any telephone," replied Clarke scraping snow off the windshield of the car.

"Are you calling people who are wire tapped?" asked Brent.

"No. I'm calling people who will pass messages back and forth from people who are being wire tapped. It's safer but not fool proof," said Clarke. "Don't use your cell phone. That's too easy. I carry one only to give them something to do."

"News?" asked Brent.

"No. But the lack of news is the news. Half of my information network is off the air. Either I'm not getting any replies or the code words are wrong," said Clarke firing up the car.

"On holidays?" asked Brent.

"My network is never on holidays. No. My contacts are being shut down. That's the only explanation. It's started then," said Clarke.

"What's started?" asked Brent.

"The coup. The takeover," said Clarke putting the car in gear and slithering down the road.

"A coup? Here in England?" asked Brent.

"Yes, here in England, lad. Think about this. Who runs the country? The prime minister and cabinet, top civil servants, Mayors, the generals, admirals, and police chiefs. Remove these top people and put others in who are loyal to a different way of life and you have a successful coup," said Clarke.

"Put in traitors, you mean," said Brent.

"In the long run, to take over you have to have a large group of traitors. Although they probably don't see themselves as traitors. Greed has a big part in it," said Clarke.

"You mean bribes?" asked Brent.

"Yes, and promotions. The backbencher who will sell his soul for a cabinet post. The colonel who would do anything to be a general. Every one of these top spots have people lower down competing in the hopes of moving up. Take some ambitious lad aside, tell him he can have his hearts desire if he plays ball. Some will take the opportunity. Some will be deceived. Others will know exactly what they are doing," said Clarke.

"How could they be deceived? How could anyone involved not know they are traitors?" asked Brent.

"Misinformation. And a national emergency. Since Christmas eve, only three cabinet members have been seen. The others are all missing. Same with some of the generals. Two newspaper editors were found murdered in their homes this morning. Others are simply missing," said Clarke stopping the car at a small market. "Most of the leadership of the nation is being disappeared. A few are being found dead to generate a controlled level of fear. Enough to get people to obey any requests from authority figures. Not enough to create outright panic."

Clarke pulled a newspaper from his coat pocket.

"Look," said Clarke handing over the newspaper.

Brent stared at the headline.

> PRIME MINISTER OUT!
> No confidence vote called over inept handling of terror crisis. Stanley loses leadership. The honorable Alexander Smith voted in. Declares state of emergency to combat internal terror threat. He will meet with the king this afternoon.

Brent looked around.

"It's so peaceful here. Where's the crisis? The noise? The shouting?" asked Brent.

"You're thinking of revolution. A coup is a quiet affair by its very nature. The coup must replace the old leaders with their own before anyone notices. At first, life goes on as before. Changes start after power is secured," said Clarke. "I know Smith is a Quisling for the Muslim Directorate. They were wise to put an English face before the nation to maintain the sense of continuity. It will be interesting to see how long they keep him around."

Two police cars with lights flashing passed by, heading down the road they had come.

"For us?" asked Brent.

"Quite possibly. The new PM will clearly go after anyone who has stood up to the Muslims in the past. They will be labeled racists, blamed for the assassinations, and rounded up with the support of a frightened nation. Not a good time to be in the BNP," said Clarke.

"What about the press?" asked Brent.

"Two murdered editors will silence anyone even thinking of speaking up. Our newspapers are the courageous defenders of the truth until their lives are in danger. Then they are just a bunch of cowards like the rest of us. Damn, Damn, Damn!" said Clarke.

"What now?" asked Brent.

Clarke took the paper and showed the back page.

"The honorable Lord Haynesford has publicly converted to Islam. The bastard is hedging his bets. Going over to Islam while his brother is a top general in the army. I've lost my faith in the peers of the realm. Instead of leading the fight to defend out heritage, they scramble to maintain their place at the top of our society however the wind blows. Haynesford's defection will encourage other opportunists and cowards to blow with the winds of change and convert as well."

*****

"You'd better get up here," shouted Stan nervously.

Tom climbed to the cockpit and followed Stan's arm pointing at a collection of boats approaching from the southwest. He reached for the telescope, then stopped, and raised the binoculars instead. Three boats, sails with motors. Lots of men on each. Trouble. He looked up to the tell tale. Inconvenient wind.

"All hands on deck. We're taking down the sails. Stan, start the motor. We're changing course to north west," said Tom.

Wisdom and Bane took in the situation and got busy. Tom picked up the radio.

"Jane. Respond immediately. Please!" said Tom. The radio crackled to life.

"Good thing you said please, dear. What's up?" replied Jane.

"This is serious. Three boats are on a course to intercept us. I want you to take down your sails and turn on the motor. Then you need to close up on us and turn north north west. If there's a problem we'll screen you," said Tom.

"I don't like the sound of this," said Jane.

"Me neither. Just do what I say, OK?" asked Tom.

"Yes dear," said Jane.

Tom watched the sails drop as Jane changed course. Her boat, the Veloce, gained on them then began to move to their starboard as their courses diverged. He turned to watch the approaching boats. Nothing. Maybe they weren't dangerous. Then gunshots were heard. They looked at each other.

"I don't like the sound of that," said Bane.

The three boats changed course.

"Damn," said Tom. He picked up the radio.

Jane, come in," said Tom.

"Yes, dear," said Jane.

"The boats ahead have changed course to intercept us. They're armed, too. I want you to make a run for it. Stay on your current course and make all speed. Clear?" asked Tom.

"Yes. Be careful, Tarzan," said Jane.

"I always am, out," replied Tom replacing the mic.

He went below and opened the drawer under his berth. He broke out the stolen clothing from Rome.

"Wisdom, Bane get down here," he shouted.

The two men came below to see an arsenal spread out before them.

"Take two forty fives each plus the rifles we captured. Wisdom and I will take the flare guns. If things go bad we'll start fires on their boats. That will distract them enough for us to get away, I hope," said Tom.

Tom began to wrap a keffiyeh around his head. Wisdom followed suit.

"You too, Bane," said Tom.

Bane looked at the blood stained cloth with disdain and did nothing.

"We three will be on deck trying to look like Arabs. Maybe Wisdom can talk us out of this. If not I expect every man to do his duty. What ever happens I want the girls out of this," said Tom.

"Ok, Admiral Nelson, I get it," said Bane, picking up the cloth.

"Bane, you take the wheel so Wisdom can do the talking," said Tom.

"What will you be doing?" asked Bane.

"The killing," said Tom. "Stan get down here."

Stan gave the wheel to Bane and went below.

"We're in the shit aren't we?" said Stan nervously.

"Maybe. All good boy scouts must be prepared," replied Tom.

Tom moved to each side window he had modified to open.

"Stay down here out of sight. If shooting starts I want you to pick the window with the best view and spray the other boats with bullets. Try to hit the men if you can but make sure you make a lot of noise. Every bit of noise and confusion will help us," said Tom handing over the AR-15 and six clips. "You already know how to use this."

"Yes . . . um. Yes sir," replied Stan putting on a brave face and staring at the weapon.

"Good man," said Tom putting on his ammunition pouches and grabbing the forty fives, the flare gun, and an AR-15.

He placed his M-40A1 sniper rifle on a hook by the gangway. Lastly he brought up the flag box. Moroccan, Spanish, French, Maltese, Italian flags he had gathered on the voyage. Plus the Stars and Stripes, Canadian, Australian, and British flags. Which would be best?

"No change in course. They are coming for us," said Wisdom crossing his arms.

"Good," said Tom. "Make them think you are the boss. Tell them that they can have all the rich yachts anywhere they choose along the coast of Europe. It's all for the taking. Maybe they will leave us for richer spoils."

Wisdom nodded.

"Who the hell are they?" asked Bane.

"Haven't you heard of the Barbary Coast pirates?" asked Tom.

"Pirates? Get off!" replied Bane laughing. "Maybe off Somalia, but never in the Med."

"From the halls of Montezuma to the shores of Tripoli. Why would US marines be in Tripoli? To fight the pirates that captured merchantmen and sold their European crewmen into slavery. They've been held at bay by the warships of the Royal Navy and the other European powers. And the Americans. Without that restraining force they will return to seizing ships and raiding the coast of Europe. They raped, burned, pillaged, and took slaves from Europe for centuries. Only one thing has ever stopped them," said Tom patting his rifle.

Tom watched the three boats approach. The men aboard curious about the forty seven foot sail boat. They made no effort to hide their weapons.

"Stop. Let's have a talk," shouted a man on the leading boat in Arabic.

"He wants us to stop," said Wisdom.

"If we don't?" asked Tom.

"No chance to fool them. They will attack," said Wisdom.

Tom looked at Jane receding into the distance.

"OK," said Tom. "Get ready."

Twelve men on the first boat. Seven or eight on each of the other two. All of them eager.

"Where are you headed?" asked the leader from the bridge.

"Home," replied Wisdom.

He pointed at the flag on the flagstaff. The Moroccan flag waved lazily as the wind dropped.

"Morocco," said Wisdom.

"Who was on that boat that was close to you," asked their leader.

"French sailors. Heading for Marseilles. Harmless," replied Wisdom.

"French, aye? French sailors are always wealthy," said the leader.

"Not these. We went aboard to rob them already and they had nothing of value. They were just sailors enjoying the sea," said Wisdom.

"Surely you found something of value. I would have," said the leader.

"No, nothing," said Wisdom.

The second boat crossed his bow and turned to his starboard side. The third boat was making to cross his stern. The situation was deteriorating fast.

"I don't believe you. You must have taken something. Their yacht if nothing else. We'll come aboard and see for ourselves what you took. These are our waters and everything here belongs to us," said the leader.

"That would be a mistake," shouted Wisdom.

Tom watched, ready, as the pirates brought their rifles to bear.

"A mistake. Why?" asked the leader.

"Have you not heard? Italy is in turmoil. There are no police. No law. There is looting and robbery everywhere. You could go there and grab anything you wanted. A yacht. A super yacht. Don't waste a moment. Get there as fast as you can and you will all be rich men!" shouted Wisdom.

The pirates looked at each other. Interested.

"Any yacht? Why not this one. You are so much closer. From what you say, you probably stole this boat for yourselves," said the leader.

"You are right, we have. But this is worth nothing compared to the yachts we saw at Capri. Much better than this unworthy craft.

And each one filled with beautiful women," shouted Wisdom.

"We'll search your boat and decide if it is unworthy. Stand away from the wheel and go forward," said the leader.

"They are coming aboard," said Wisdom softly.

"Like hell they are," said Tom as the second boat bumped into his Starboard fender.

The roar hit them with a shock to their senses. Was the air sucked out of his lungs or was it his imagination? Tom looked forward to see the twin engine fighter climbing and turning to make another pass. Everyone had stopped to stare at the jet in awe. Tom pulled down the Moroccan flag and reached for the Stars and Stripes. Up it went, unfurling in a sudden gust. One of the pirates turned to see what Tom was doing and began to shout. He raised his rifle but Tom was faster. The Arab fell back, blood spurting from his neck, a surprised look on his face.

Tom got off three quick shots with the flare gun. The first bounced off the hull of the lead boat, the other shots found openings. Bane and Wisdom crouched to fire at the first boat. Stan opened up to the starboard while Tom turned to the third boat at his stern. One man down. Two down. Shit! Only winged the third man.

The jet passed again with an overwhelming roar. Subsonic but on the deck. The pilot gave a wave as he passed. Tom reached down and pushed the idling motor to maximum. Stan had kept the second boats crew under cover with automatic fire. Its deck was clear for now. Tom jumped aboard firing as he went. Flames were now visible and the three men fighting the fire looked up to see Tom shoot the three other men holding rifles.

Tom threw his AR-15 onto the Constitution and turned back with his forty fives. The three fire fighters raised their arms and so did Tom. He fired two shots through the hull and ran to the stern, leaping onto his accelerating sail boat.

Tom added his firepower to the others as they pulled clear.

"We're leaking," shouted Stan from below.

"Put your fingers in the hole! Do something," shouted Tom reaching down for the M1. He lay prone on the deck and took aim. Damn. One miss, two hits. He was out of practice.

A plume of water rose high into the air far to port. Then the whistling noise caught up to them. A destroyer in the distance was raising a bow wave visible from the Constitution. Armed and dangerous. And very fast. The remaining pirates saw the destroyer and began shouting. The shooting stopped as they turned their boats south as fast as they could. Tom picked up the radio microphone.

"American Yacht Constitution. Attacked by pirates. They've broken off the fight and are heading south, over," said Tom.

No response.

"You OK?," asked Tom looking at Wisdom and Bane.

"Fine and dandy," said Bane.

"What's that?" said Tom pointing to the red stain on Wisdom's side.

Wisdom looked down and opened his shirt.

"I have been shot four times. This is nothing. Bullet must have bounced once before it hit," replied Wisdom.

"We should get you aboard that destroyer. They could patch you up real good," said Bane.

"No. I am not leaving Captain Tom or this boat," said Wisdom firmly.

"You will see a real doctor. The Americans love to help the needy," said Bane.

Wisdom shook his head firmly.

"OK. It's your life," said Bane looking away.

"This is American warship, Medford. We understand your situation and will take care of it for you. Continue to steer north west over."

"Understood. Out. And thanks," said Tom thumbing the mic.

The fleeing pirates were dead meat. Tom went below to see Stan patching three holes in the stern.

"If we move our weight forward, I can patch these holes permanently," said Stan displaying the foam pads jammed into the holes. The leakage was slow and non threatening.

"Let's do it," said Tom returning to the deck.

He picked up the mic again.

"Jane, come in, over," said Tom.

"Are you OK? I heard the shooting. What happened?" asked Jane.

"We're all OK, honey. Change course to steer West south west. I'll fill you in when we meet up," said Tom.

"You better, sweetie, out," said Jane.

Tom put down the mic and looked east. No doubt about it. Carrier group. The destroyer screen was passing. There were more jets in the air. Lucky for them the sixth fleet was passing by. He picked up the binoculars. What the hell. A line of ships. White. Bigger than the carrier itself.

"Well, I'll be damned," said Tom.

"Why, what now? " asked Bane.

Tom handed over the binoculars to Wisdom who passed them to Bane.

"Looks like cruise ships. A lot of cruise ships. So?" asked Bane.

"Those boats go south for the winter. What are they doing here?" asked Tom.

They raised sails and got back on course. Tom collected the weapons. The sails of the Veloce were visible and closing.

Tom continued to examine the cruise ships. Something was nagging him about those ships. Bane picked up the binoculars.

"They are flying the American flag. That's odd. They're usually registered in Panama or Norway or some other odd country," said Bane.

The gears clicked.

"They knew. They knew this shit was coming. They've gotten these cruise ships here to take Americans home from the mess happening in Europe," said Tom.

"American tourists?" said Bane. "More likely the American NATO contingent attached to the navy and air force. The fleet's leaving and they are taking the shore personnel at the same time."

"Oh yeah? I'm still suspicious. It looks like there are way more ships in that line than they could need for the military. They're flagged American to make sure there is no mix up. Damnation," said Tom.

"In my land, power and treachery go hand in hand," said Wisdom, putting down the binoculars.

*****

Colonel Ivan Borovich stared at the map again.

"Give your report, Baransky," said Ivan.

"The Turks arrived in Varna without trouble and split their forces. About a third is continuing up the coast. They are fast units. The others found trains to move their armor to the Danube at Buse and unloaded their forces there. They secured the main bridge and have stopped for the night" said Baransky.

"Why didn't they keep going to Bucharest. By rail?" asked Captain Litvinov.

"They would be vulnerable while loaded on trains. No, they have to be able to maneuver should they meet Romanian resistance. They will have to move by road," replied Baransky.

The radio man handed Ivan a message. The room went silent.

"We have good news. The advance train has found an open route around Bucharest onto the south line toward Giurgui," said Ivan. "We will move at midnight to reduce the chances of detection. We will proceed south of the city and cross the Arges river. There we will unload and move west toward the highway. At dawn we will be in position east of the road they must take to Bucharest. They will be completely surprised and if they move early, we will have the sun at our backs."

"Do they know we are coming?" asked Litvinov.

"Of course they know we are coming. But do they know where we are right now? I think not. Otherwise they wouldn't have stopped in Guirgui. They would have raced on to beat us to the city," replied Ivan pouring vodka all around.

"Victory!" shouted Ivan.

"Victory!" shouted the others in return.

DECEMBER 28

This is the BBC, Gaston Dhaoui reporting from London. A spokesman for the Berlin government has announced arrest warrants for two German generals. Calling them rebels, a search for generals Schmidt and Ramstein has begun. These warrants came about as evidence emerged that these men were plotting the over throw of the government. When some of the plotters decided to pull out, they were murdered, along with a large number of other military officers. The army has returned to lawful control as new commanders, loyal to the Berlin government, are sworn in around the country.

*****

Ivan stood on his tank facing his men.

"Very soon now, a column of tanks will be moving up the road in front of us to capture the city of Bucharest. Most of you are wondering why we have been sent to this foreign land to fight in this place this morning. I will tell you. Europe has collapsed. The fine wines, beautiful women, perfumed villas, and riches of western Europe are up for grabs. Anyone who is strong enough can take this wealth for his own. History, culture, and geography make it clear that this prize belongs to us! Europe belongs to us! But now the Turks and the other Muslim peoples want to take what is ours. This enemy that approaches is the tip of the sword that tries to sever our claim on the wealth of Europe. I will lead you into battle to keep what rightfully belongs to us. Will you fight with me?" shouted Ivan.

"Da" shouted the men in a growing chorus.

"Return to your tanks. Good hunting!" shouted Ivan.

He stood with his hands on his hips as the men disbursed.

"That went well," said Ivan.

"Yes. After the men we planted cheered, the rest joined in of their own accord," said Baransky. "They are soldiers, they would have done what you ordered anyway."

"They will start a battle with only an order. But will they stand and fight or run when things get tough? That's when morale is important. Soldiers fight best when they have more of a reason to fight than orders," said Ivan.

*****

Ivan watched the moving column in his binoculars. He saw no sign that they were seen or expected. He felt calm but was perspiring anyway. The attack would begin when he opened fire.

"Surprise is complete," said Ivan to himself.

He looked down the line of brush covered tanks and support vehicles. The enemy was in range.

"Fire," said Ivan into the microphone.

His tank lurched in recoil. Then the entire line opened up on the enemy. He watched a cloud of dust rise in a line stretching from left to right. The targets were now hidden by dust. Ivan had ordered two shots would be made before his tanks would advance. The position of his line was now marked by the gun smoke they had created. His tank recoiled again.

"Litvinov, advance to the south and hold any who retreat," shouted Ivan into his microphone.

Ivan was outnumbered. Everything depended on the accuracy of the first two volleys. He needed to disable half the enemy to make things even. After that the day would be won by courage and determination. The T105 could shoot when moving like the American Abrahms tanks, which is what the Turks were using.

"Shoot smoke grenades," said Ivan.

The Turks began to return fire. Sporadic at first, then with more determination.

"Squadron Sahkalin ready to drop on target," came over the radio.

"Sakhalin this is Yalta. Drop on red smoke. They are on the road. We are to the east," replied Ivan.

"Understood. Sahkalin out," said the pilot.

Ivan switched radio channels.

"Hold positions for bomb drop," said Ivan.

A line of SU-34 fighter bombers swept in from the north moving just below the speed of sound. Precision guided missiles preceded their arrival. Two hundred kilo bombs followed. The jets rose and turned for home before the roar of their engines washed over the battlefield. Explosions rocked the ground. Hits were marked by red fire and dark ordinance clouds. Misses were marked by the brown dust that filled his vision.

"All advance. Repeat. All advance," said Ivan.

His line moved toward the dust and smoke ahead. The Turks that were left returned fire steadily adding to the deafening noise of guns and explosions. A few enemy tanks could be seen turning toward him and attacking his line. Other Turkish tanks fired on him as they retreated. There was no strategy on their part. No command control. It was everyman for himself. He was leading the charge across open ground. The machine gunner opened up on the enemy infantry. The tank to his left exploded, the turret flying ten meters into the air. They picked targets and fired as fast as they could. Now they were among the burning enemy wreckage. Some of the enemy were jumping out of their vehicles trying to surrender. His men fired into them. Their blood lust was up and he wasn't going to stop it. The Turks dropped like puppets with their strings suddenly cut.

The Russian line swept through the enemy position leaving death and destruction in its wake.

"The Turks are running to the west. All units pursue at full speed. Destroy them all," shouted Ivan, caught up in the overwhelming urge to kill. They passed through the enemy line into the clear air beyond.

"Stop here," he said to his driver. "Group one, form up on the road with me. Group two, three, four, and five continue the pursuit to the west."

He listened to the continuing roar of battle moving in pursuit. Then explosions built to a steady roar to the south.

"Litvinov, report," shouted Ivan.

"Engaging strong enemy force retreating south," replied Litvinov.

"Everything depends of you, Litinov. Can you hold them?" asked Ivan.

"Yes, colonel, ..."

The radio went dead.

"Litvinov! What happened? Are you there?" shouted Ivan.

The noise to the south continued at full volume. Ivan couldn't advance to support him as long as Litvinov's forces continued fighting. He couldn't risk friendly fire.

"Yalta, this is Ivonovich. All enemies to the west have been destroyed. No prisoners," said Ivonovich.

"Return to the road and form up behind me. All groups return to the main road for resupply. Yalta out," said Ivan. "Supply units, advance to the road.

His tanks were rearmed and refueled as he waited for news from the south. The explosions to the south were fewer and fewer. It was almost over. But who had won?

"This is Litvinov. It's over. They are stopped," he said.

"Move off the road. Resupply and fall in with the supply train when it gets to you," said Ivan.

Yes, colonel," replied Litvinov.

"All group commanders, meet me in group three right now," said Ivan jumping out of his tank.

He jogged over to the waiting officers.

"We're going to capture the bridge at Giurgui. Fall in behind me. If I meet resistance, groups two and four will move to my right, groups three and five to my left. Understood?" said Ivan. "We have a chance to capture the bridge before the remaining forces can set up a defense. Move out!"

This is the BBC, Mansour Jahfel reporting from London. Pre-dawn London was rocked by a bomb blast at Buckingham Palace. Authorities are reporting that a massive truck bomb was exploded on Constitution Hill shattering windows and leaving a crater sixty feet across. The nearest corner of the palace was severely damaged and looks close to collapse. The death toll is at twelve. The early hour prevented a much greater loss of life. Minutes later, similar blasts occurred at Windsor Palace and at Balmoral. Security services report that the King has been moved to an undisclosed location for his safety.

*****

The mayor of Gabrovo kissed Colonel Ivan Borovich on both cheeks.

"Save us from the Turks, please!" begged Grigor Nedelcho.

"Of Course, that is why we are here, Mayor Nedelcho," said Borovich.

Captain Baransky motioned from the doorway of the mayor's office.

"Excuse me for a moment, Mayor," said Borovich heading outside.

"I have a report from General Bariatinsky. He crossed the frontier near Arad and made for Szeged to seize the rails and highways and stop the Turk's advance. A lucky Turk air strike took out his fuel supplies forcing him to abandon his advance and take defensive positions in Szeged. The Turks had already passed Szeged and turned back to counter this threat. Another division approached from the south to surround the city. Bariatinsky is trapped in Szeged. Reinforcements are a couple of days away at the earliest," said Baransky.

Borovich spread out his map.

"He is too far away for us to do anything before the relief column arrives. But maybe we can help him from here. Where can we do the most damage?" asked Borovich.

*****

Nick crossed the Augarten and stopped in front of Heidi's house. It was her father's house but she still lived with him. He dialed his mobile. The sound of sporadic gunfire came from the north.

"Hello, Nick," replied William Hamadi.

"William, I'm in Vienna. There's a story breaking here. I tried to contact Jane but she doesn't answer my calls. Do you know where she is?"

"I'm afraid not, Nick. She has been off the grid since she met up with her husband Christmas eve. I honestly don't know where they are. I can find you another reporter if you have your camera gear," said William. "What is the story there?"

"The skin heads have risen up and taken control of the city. They have barricaded the inner ring and all the bridges leading to Leopoldstadt," said Nick.

"How did this happen? Where are the Police in all this?" asked William.

"I've been gathering information all day. As I understand it, the police started rounding up all the skinheads and taking them to the sports stadium. Then they started executing their prisoners. Somehow word got out and the others rebelled against the police. They stormed police headquarters and took revenge. There are no police left. Vienna has no lawful authority to guide it," said Nick.

"I'm surprised that a few skin heads could organize such an attack," replied William.

"You are right. Now all the rumors say that a high ranking officer in the army is behind it. He brought all the men loyal to him and all the heavy weapons he could get into the city. There are soldiers and officers mixed in with the skin heads. I'm in the middle of a revolution and it's happening fast," said Nick.

"I'm glad you called. Keep me posted. Call me with the news as you get it anytime day or night. I'm especially interested in who is behind this and where they are . So we can get an interview," said William.

"I'll do what I can. I'm not going anywhere. No one is being passed through the barricades. I'm trapped here," said Nick.

William paused in thought.

"Hello, are you there?" asked Nick.

"Yes, I was just thinking. I've changed my mind. I'll use other

141

sources and personnel. Don't get involved in this. Stay out of sight and keep your Australian passport with you at all times. Are we clear, Nick?" asked William.

"Quite clear. But why. I'm right here on the inside," said Nick.

"It's too dangerous. I hear things in my job that I don't spread around. Trust me, OK?" asked William.

"OK, it's your call," said Nick.

"Goodbye," said William.

The line went dead. Strange. William loved getting the story. And here they could cover a street fight in Vienna from the inside. But William knew what he was doing. He was out of it. End of story. Nick climbed the stairs to Heidi's apartment to find her in the living room wringing her hands.

"What's up?" asked Nick.

"It's father. He's lost his senses," said Heidi Kraus.

"What do you mean? Is he ill? Has he had a stroke or something?" asked Nick taking her hands.

"No my boy, nothing of the kind," said Gunther Kraus striding into the living room.

He carried a blanket and packed it into a knapsack. Beside it stood a Mauser k98 and a box of ammunition. Gunther followed Nick's eyes to the rifle.

"This was my father's. It kept him alive on the retreat from Russia. It's accurate out a thousand yards," said Gunther patting it affectionately.

"Father's going to join with those NAZI criminals in the street. I am so ashamed," said Heidi, tears beginning to well up.

"My darling," started Gunther reaching for her.

She backed away.

"Nick, you have always had my blessing to marry Heidi. I wanted you to take her to your home in Australia so she could avoid something like this. Too late now. Just stay with her. You've been to war zones in your work. You know what happens to women without men to protect them," said Gunther.

"You have my promise on that," said Nick taking Heidi into his arms.

"My friends and I are all old but we're not fools. We saw this coming. Now we go to fight for our country like our fathers before us," said Gunther. He shouldered his rifle, nodded to Nick, and closed the door behind him.

Heidi burst into tears.

The cold northeast wind drove them on to Gibraltar. Stan scanned the horizon with the telescope. The rock of Gibraltar was prominent in the distance.

"Lieutenant Bane, there may be trouble ahead."

Bane came up the ladder and took the telescope.

"A bit of smoke. Yes, I'd better use the radio and call ahead. We're in range of the guns." said Bane.

"Just what I was thinking," said Stan. "We could run up the Union Jack also. It might help if anybody with a gun gets jumpy."

Bane nodded nodded and went below.

*****

The whole crew was on deck watching as they rounded the point and headed toward the naval dockyard. Bane pointed ahead.

"Make for that dock there. I'll go ashore and make my report. Best if you wait on board," said Bane.

The radio masts of two patrol boats jutted out of the water in the dockyard. Sunk. No other ships were visible in the harbor. The smoke was coming from the direction of the airfield. Groups of fully armed and armored marines looked down from sandbagged enclosures as they passed. The dock towered above them as they made fast to a float with a stairway leading up. Jim rafted the Veloce to their starboard side.

"Right, off I go. I'll get back as soon as I can and let you know what's going on," said Bane, straightening his uniform and climbing the steps. The marines saluted as he passed them.

"It sure is quiet. I don't see a ship or anything else moving," said Stan.

"There has been a battle. The fighters are regrouping. It is always quiet after a battle. Everyone is tired. The people are hiding," said Wisdom.

"Well, I'm going to take a look around," said Tom stepping off the boat.

The others showed no interest in leaving the boat. Wisdom reluctantly followed. Tom climbed the stairs and headed for the sandbag emplacement. He sat on the bags and looked around.

"Here mate, best get down from there. You might fall off," said the sergeant.

"Or get shot off," said one of the privates. The others chuckled.

"I'm okay here. I've done this before. Kuwait, Somalia, Bosnia, Fallujah," said Tom.

"So you're a yank. I heard about Fallujah. Marine?" said the sergeant.

Tom nodded.

"Well, it's good to have you with us. Any more of you aboard?" asked the sergeant nodding at the boat.

"No. Just me, one African jungle fighter, three tourists, and eight eligible bachelorettes," replied Tom.

The privates all leaned out for a better look at the sailboats.

"Too bad. I saw your fleet pass two days ago. They didn't even slow down. Quite rude actually, I thought," said the sergeant. "It's nice to see reinforcements when the shooting starts. Felt abandoned. It's just us now."

"Against who?" asked Tom.

"We don't really know. We were attacked across the airfield Christmas morning. We were caught napping. Who'd expect this happening? The Spaniards have been good chaps and we're in Europe after all. We tried to regroup but everything was chaos. Pure luck brought two destroyers into the harbor just as it started. They put men ashore and used ships guns in support. They advanced to the air field and threatened to cut off the attackers. So the bastards pulled back giving us time to regroup."

"What happened to your ships?" said Tom nodding toward the wrecks.

"The ships were refueling as fast as they could when artillery started landing on the airfield. It was coming from the city and other civilian areas. We couldn't just blast at Spain. They are our allies in the Euro force. They hit some of the ships before they could pull out," said the sergeant.

"After that?"

"Quiet since the Americans passed. We're ready now. A sneak attack was their only hope," said the sergeant.

"A siege then. This attack doesn't make sense. Whoever thinks they're in charge isn't. This faction was out of control. What did the enemy look like?" asked Tom.

"They had Spanish uniforms but somebody said they were

Arabs. Can't see much difference between them. They're both dark," said the sergeant. "What have you seen?"

"The same thing in Rome. Italian soldiers shooting up the place. Chaos. Confusion," replied Tom.

"London too. That's the rumor. But not Arabs. White racists. The National Front or somebody. Attacking parliament and killing a lot of people. Supposed to have ruined Christmas for everybody. Bastards," said the sergeant.

*****

Brent watched Clarke's face as he listened to the voice on the phone. Clarke listened steadfastly, only closing his eyes in pain momentarily.

"I'm safely hidden for now. I'll be moving again soon. How about you?" asked Clarke. "I'll confirm that when I know for sure. Thanks for letting me know. Goodbye."

Clarke put down the phone and leaned back in his chair, rubbing his eyes. He stared at the ceiling.

"Well?" asked Brent.

"The evil of our time astounds me. Things are moving faster than I ever imagined possible. France has fallen completely into the hands of the Muslim Directorate. With thousands of assassinations and constant media propaganda, the fifth republic of France is a thing of the past. Liberty, equality, fraternity has been replaced by Allah Akbar already," said Clarke.

"You said they would fall first and hardest. That they were the most infiltrated country in all Europe," said Brent.

"Yes, I did say that. It doesn't make me happy to be correct. Things are happening that I never imagined could happen in Europe again. Even the Nazis conducted their holocaust in secret," said Clarke.

Brent waited.

"This morning the Catholics of Lyon went to church as usual. When they filed out of one of the churches, they found an angry mob of Muslims waiting for them. They stopped and stared in confusion, not recognizing their deadly peril. Those nearest the mob were dragged down the steps and forced to kneel. Each victim was told that if they denied Christ and embraced Islam, they would be spared. They were told this in the only true language, Arabic. Few victims understood what was said, what was happening. In fear, they crossed themselves as they had done their whole lives. This was taken as a sign of resistance. Of defiance. They were beheaded. Almost all of them. A few

145

understood and submitted," said Clarke evenly. "Did you know that Islam means submission? Islam is a code conceived by a conqueror intended to motivate and maintain discipline in his army and provide guidance on what to do with conquered peoples. They call themselves compassionate because they offer the conquered the option to join Islam instead of being killed."

"My god, where were the police, the army, somebody?" asked Brent.

"All under the control of the Muslim Directorate. The mobs must have been carrying out the will of the Directorate. The de-Christianization or the Islamization of Europe, however you want to call it, is underway. It was already happening slowly, quietly. This violence will accelerate the process. A recent poll found that less than twenty percent of Europeans go to church regularly. France is the lowest. Eleven percent. Will the other nominally Christian people fight for something they don't believe in? Not when they face extermination if they do. Everyone in France will know what happened by nightfall. Most will cry one small tear then do what they can to survive. The media brainwashing will continue full force. Those who don't want to believe this story will accept the media's denial as truth. So much easier than doing anything about it," said Clarke. "The Muslim Directorate's firm control of France gives them a base to keep the ball rolling in the other countries. A domino effect. I can only hope that this story will strengthen the will to resist in other places."

"What can we do?" asked Brent.

Clarke smiled briefly and shook his head.

"You Americans are really something. Always sticking your noses where they don't belong without being asked," said Clarke wistfully.

"I was raised to get up off my behind and make things happen. To take action for my own benefit and the benefit of my community. You say this isn't my business. But they took my girl. It's personal. I should have woken up when they took out the World Trade Center. I didn't. Our leaders kept saying that the attack was the work of a small extremist group called Al-Qaeda. That Islam was the religion of peace and we should embrace it. Well fuck that idea," said Brent evenly. "So I say again, what can I do?" asked Brent.

Clarke paused in thought.

"I will think of something. But it may be dangerous," Clarke replied.

*****

146

The sergeant entered the military headquarters of the Muslim Directorate of England. He walked to Farouk Aziz and touched his shoulder. Farouk looked up.

"Many Pardons, sir. But there is a girl outside asking for you. She is hysterical. What should we do with her?" asked the sergeant.

Aziz turned to see that his boss, Anwar Saidi, had overheard.

"Take care of it, Farouk, and be quick about it," said Saidi turning back to his staff.

Farouk stood.

"Bring her up the stairs," said Farouk to the sergeant.

The sergeant nodded and escorted Celia Banks up the stairs. She was emotional, breathing hard, her hijab in place.

"Why haven't you returned my calls? I have been trying to talk to you," said Celia.

"I am an important man and I am busy. Your problems will have to wait until this crisis is over. Now go back home and wait," said Farouk quietly.

"My business can't wait. I must talk to you now. Let's go outside," said Celia.

"No. Tell me here. I will give you ten seconds to tell me this problem then you must leave," replied Farouk, crossing his arms.

"I am having your baby, Farouk. No one knows yet. We can avoid scandal if we marry right away," said Celia.

"Go home now. I am done talking to you," said Farouk turning away.

Celia grabbed his shoulder and spun him around.

"Aren't you listening to me? We have to marry. Right now!" cried Celia.

Farouk raised his arm and slapped her hard.

"Shut up!" he hissed. "Now go!"

The slap only fired Celia's determination.

"Is this how you treat your wife and child?" shouted Celia.

"What you are is an unmarried woman with child. How do I know who the father is? Unmarried women with children are whores. You are a whore. I will deal with you later," said Farouk.

Celia wrapped her arms around him. Tears falling onto his chest.

"How can you say that! You know I have been faithful! There are no others, only you. You said you loved me! You said I was your wife in your heart already. How can you treat me like this?" cried Celia.

Farouk pushed her away.

"I would never marry a whore like you. Now go!" said Farouk.

Farouk turned to see the whole room staring at him. Saidi frowned and motioned with his head to the exit. Farouk was being humiliated by a mere woman in front of the entire leadership committee.

"I still love you with all my heart and you said you loved me!" repeated Celia crying.

"I never loved you. I used you like many others to achieve objectives of my own. Look around," said Farouk gesturing to the room. "We are changing the course of history. We no longer need the wombs of women to get what we want. We are taking what we want like men! With our strength!"

Celia removed the hijab and stared at Farouk, puzzled. Then everything became clear to her.

"You lied to me! You bastard! You fucking bastard," she screamed, clawing him with all her strength.

Her nails gouged his face and it hurt. His anger turned to rage. She would not humiliate him here of all places. Farouk grabbed her arms and pushed her away from him with all his strength. She flew back into the air and disappeared down the stairs. After a few thumps there was silence. Farouk turned to the sergeant.

"Take her out and get rid of her!"

Night was passing. There was a glow in the east. Colonel Borovich looked over his position. All his men had dug in as best they could during the night. Rocks and dirt for protection, branches for cover. It was the best they could do. He looked down on the city of Chirpan. A few lights still visible in the approaching dawn. In his binoculars, he could just make out the Marica River valley.

"We open fire at dawn," said Borovich.

"We haven't been discovered yet. We could make it to the Marica and capture the highway and railway. At least blow them up. The Turks at Szeged would lose their supply lines," said Captain Ivanovich.

"We would be caught in the open and destroyed. No, we will stay in the hills. Just knowing we are almost to the Marica will be enough to scare them," said Borovich.

"Yes, Colonel," replied Ivanovich.

The morning sun hit the command tank.

"Fire," said Borovich.

Noise and smoke enveloped him. Borovich watched the debris clouds rising across the valley through his binoculars.

*****

"Captain, I'm picking up a lot of radio chatter all of a sudden," said Smith the radioman.

Captain Thomas stared out the window without concern. "What's it about?

"A tanker is being ordered to stop to take on borders. Spanish ships, I think. A Dutch escort ship is warning them off."

"Shall we intercept?" asked the exec.

"No. Stay on our current sweep. This isn't our beat anymore," he replied.

"Missile track! Thirty miles south ..... heading west," Radar man Stepney called out.

Captain Thomas looked at the chart. One hundred miles southwest of La Coruna, Spain. A very busy shipping lane. Almost everything heading to or from northern Europe passed this way. The exec was looking at him, waiting.

"Plot a course to intercept the tanker. Smith, call them and ask what's happening."

"Aye Captain," replied Smith.

"All ahead full," said the Captain.

"All ahead full, aye sir," replied helmsman Blanchard.

"Mister Carpenter, make regular reports to headquarters as we go."

"Regular reports, aye aye," replied Carpenter.

"Second missile track!" shouted Stepney.

"Details?" asked the Captain.

"It's heading east along the track of the first missile!" shouted Stepney.

"Mr. Stepney," said the captain

"Yes sir,"

"Keep your voice down. The missiles aren't coming our way. At least not yet," said the captain turning to his exec. "Mr. Hampton."

"Sir," replied Hampton.

"Sound battle stations," said the captain.

"Battle stations it is sir," replied the exec grinning.

The ship's bells sounded battle stations as the ship turned and brought its 50,000 horse power to bear.

*****

Hansen studied the orange line streak across the northern sky, then the bright flash on the horizon.

"Jim, take down the radar reflector. Be quick about it," said Tom urgently.

Jim watched the horizon.

"Now," said Hansen.

Jim went forward to the main mast. The metal disc fell down as he let the rope slip through his hands.

*****

"The tanker has increased speed to thirty knots, course north north east. Bogey One is catching up at forty knots."

Thomas picked up the radio mike. He thumbed the transmit button.

"This is the captain of the American warship Trenton, who am I talking to? "

"Captain Aromedes of the tanker, Pride of Sawakin. Full oil tanker on our way to Amsterdam," he replied.

"Who's firing the missiles?" asked Thomas.

"We left Algiers with a Dutch escort. Two ships claiming to be Spanish came toward us. We are off the Spanish coast so what is to worry about? They attacked our escort and ordered us to slow down and accept borders," replied Aromedes.

"What happened to your escort?"

"He took a hit and I saw a fire. I haven't heard anything from them since. They did hit one of the Spanish ships and it has turned east," said Aromedes.

"What are you going to do now? Our radar shows the Spanish ship overtaking you," said Thomas.

Aromedes began swearing.

"Captain," interrupted Smith. "The Spanish captain is calling."

"Hold on a minute, Captain Aromedes, I have to take another call," said Thomas. "Hampton, have we heard back from CINCLANT?"

"Nothing yet," replied Hampton.

"Try to verify his story," said Thomas turning back to the microphone.

"This is Captain Thomas of the American war ship Trenton. Who am I talking to?"

"This is Capitan Abasson of the Spanish cruiser, Mendez Nunez."

"What's going on, Captain. Why have missiles been fired?" asked Thomas.

"We are rendering assistance to the Pride of Sawakin. They reported a pirate attack. We had to defend ourselves when we were threatened," he answered. "The tanker is now safe but we need to do an inspection to confirm this."

"We're closer. We'll save you the trip and do the inspection for you. You can look for survivors off the ship you attacked." said Thomas.

"Not possible. This is our coast and our responsibility," said Abasson.

"I've relieved you of that responsibility," said Thomas coolly. "Thomas out."

The bridge crew listened in a tense silence.

"We have no right to intervene. Spain claims these waters and they are our NATO allies," said Hampton.

"The NATO treaty ends at midnight. It didn't stop them from

firing on a fellow EU member," replied Thomas. "There's a bad smell to all this. It's obvious and in our faces. Smith, is Aromedes still there?"

"Yes sir," replied Smith.

Thomas turned to marine lieutenant Kenney.

"Mr. Kenney, prepare a boarding party. Take the launch and and as many men as you need to inspect and secure that tanker," said Thomas.

"Aye aye, captain." said Kenney saluting, then leaving the bridge.

"Hampton, send Midshipman Penaloza across with the marines," said Thomas.

"What are you thinking, sir?" asked Hampton.

"That derelict is going to need an American officer to assume command and get it to a friendly port," answered Thomas.

"Derelict?" asked Hampton.

*****

Captain Abassom of the Spanish destroyer put down the binoculars and looked at the radar again.

"Damn Americans," he said.

"They will get there before us easily. Nothing we can do about it," said executive officer Obeidi.

"We must. Our orders to divert this tanker to England come from the highest authority," said Abasson pacing the bridge.

"We can only stall them until we get closer. Keep them on the radio. Maybe we can talk them into leaving," said Obeidi.

"No. We sank a Dutch ship. There's blood in the water that no one can ignore. The American sounds relaxed but he is clearly no fool. We can't go back, there is only forward. The closer we are the shorter their reaction time. I'll talk to them again," said Abasson nodding to his radio officer.

"Sir, they are ignoring my signal," replied the radio officer.

Captain Abasson pounded his fist on his chair.

*****

"We have no reason to intervene, Captain Aromedes. What's to fear from a ship of the Spanish navy off the coast of Spain? They are members of the European Union after all," said Thomas.

"You idiot! They are pirates. They attacked our escort. That can't be ignored. If you don't stop them, they will capture my ship and I don't want to think about what they may do to us," shouted Aromedes.

"Not my problem. Unless . . ."

"It's like I always said. You Americans have the fancy weapons but you are all cowards deep down," shouted Aromedes.

He paused.

"Unless what?" asked Aromedes.

Thomas turned to Smith.

"No change in course or speed," replied Smith to the look from his captain.

"Hampton, order Penaloza and the marines across, then give us some maneuvering room," said Thomas.

"Aye aye, captain," replied Hampton turning to give orders.

Thomas looked at the radar screen.

"That bastard's not changing course and it means only one thing," said Thomas to himself.

Helmsman Blanshard looked sideways at the captain but remained silent.

"Aromedes. If you declare your ship unfit for sea we can come across and take possession. Then I will defend your ship like I would defend my own," said Thomas.

Thomas waited during the deafening silence.

"This is an outrage! This is piracy! You force me to choose between American pirates or Spanish ones. You god damned bastard!" shouted Aromedes.

"I didn't seek this confrontation. They did. You can give me your ship and get protection and most likely get your ship back. Or you can take your chances with the other guys who have already shown themselves to be killers. You have one minute to decide. Thomas out."

Thomas looked across at the tanker with his arms crossed. The radio crackled to life.

"I have no choice. OK, I accept your terms," said Aromedes angrily.

"One of my officers is on his way with a company of marines. Welcome them aboard then resume course," said Thomas. "Full stop, send the launch."

"Aye, full stop," repeated Blanchard.

"I won't forget this. Not ever," replied Captain Aromedes.

"None of us will. Thomas out," said the captain. "Alright everyone listen up. The only reason that Spanish ship is still coming is to attack us and soon."

"All weapon systems armed and standing by, captain. Launch is away," said Hampton.

"Send the chopper up. It will be safer in the air," said Thomas. "Any word from CINCLANT?"

"Nothing," replied Hampton.

"That's odd. They must be having a busy day. All ahead full. Let's get some maneuvering room," said Thomas.

"Aye, all ahead full," repeated Blanchard.

"Missile away, heading for us. Make that two missiles," said Stepney.

"Return fire, Mr. Thurston. Two missiles. Present our stern, Mr. Blanshard.

"Aye, aye. Firing one. Firing two."

"Incoming. Twenty seconds to impact," said Stepney.

Thomas looked at his watch. Why bother. Time was irrelevant now.

"Ten seconds" said Stepney.

Radar jamming was at maximum. Automatic Phalanx defense cannons roared, loud even on the bridge. Thomas gripped his chair and waited.

There was a flash of fire one kilometers behind the ship. The cannons kept firing. A second flash bang shook the ship. The cannons stopped. It was silent by comparison.

"Zero," said Stepney. "Nothing incoming on radar. Outgoing three, two, one, zero."

There was a flash on the horizon. They waited.

"Bogey One is slowing and changing course," said Stepney.

Thomas waited.

"I'm receiving a Mayday signal from the Spanish ship," said Smith.

"They've turned south east and are slowing steadily," said Stepney.

"A wise decision. Let's catch up with the tanker, then we'll resume our sonar sweep," said Thomas.

"Aye aye, captain," replied Hampton.

*****

Midshipman Penaloza looked nervously around the bridge of the tanker. From Annapolis to his first command in only five months. Who'd have believed it. He put the radio down and turned to Captain Aromedes.

"Sir, my captain has decided there are no safe ports to make for in Europe right now. He has ordered us to turn west and head for the United States," said Penaloza.

Aromedes stared in disbelief.

"Cross the ocean when I am heading for Amsterdam? Are you crazy? I already know your Captain is crazy but I had hoped for better from you!" said Aromedes advancing toward the green midshipman.

"Lieutenant," said Penaloza quietly.

"Marines, stand by," said Kenney.

The Marines brought their weapons up. Aromedes stopped in his tracks. He threw down his cigar in disgust.

"The whole world has gone crazy!" he cursed as he stomped out of the bridge.

"Steer due west, helmsman," said Penaloza.

The helmsman just stared at him. Penaloza pointed.

"That way," said Penaloza.

The helmsman nodded and turned the wheel.

Tom lifted his binoculars toward the yacht in the distance as Stan and Jim took down the sails. First light had found them only one mile away from the stationary vessel. Two men stared back with binoculars from the mystery ship.

"Continue with your story, specialist," said Tom.

"Radio specialist Jose Maria Martin shivered in the blanket.

"Before the Dutch missile sank our ship, our Captain began shouting at the Captain of the Mendez Nunez. He cursed the Muslim Directorate in the conversation. Then the first officer shot him and took command. Minutes later we were hit by the missile and abandoned ship. I had to jump into the water with the others because our ship was going down so fast. I still don't know why our sister ship didn't come to our rescue. I did see missile launches to the north. Then the blessed virgin smiled on me and brought you to save my worthless life," said Martin.

"Are you a member of the Muslim Directorate?" asked Tom as he watched the yacht lower a launch.

"No. I am a loyal Spaniard," said Martin.

"A Muslim?" asked Tom.

"No. Catholic, of course," replied Martin.

Tom watched as the launch was manned and cast loose.

"What do you make of that yacht?" asked Tom, handing over the binoculars. "Jim, wake Wisdom and Bane. I want everyone armed. Let Jane sleep."

"There is nothing distinctive about the boat. The men in the launch are carrying automatic rifles," said Martin.

Tom switched on the diesel and turned the Liberty away from the yacht. He had a full tank of fuel and four fuel drums lashed to the forward deck.

"Wisdom, Bane, take station in the stern. Be ready," said Tom.

Wisdom nodded. Bane yawned.

As the launch approached, the man in the bow picked up a megaphone. He wore a uniform. Military.

"Please stop. We would like to talk to you. Only talk," said the

156

man.

"Wisdom, fire a burst into the air," said Tom.

Shell casing bounced off the deck as he fired. The launch stopped and waited. Tom turned to Martin.

"Well?" asked Tom.

"A Spanish accent," replied Martin.

Tom waved the launch closer and shut off the motor.

"The uniform is Spanish army," said Martin.

"Don't shoot. We want to buy your fuel if you have any to sell. You can continue with your sails but we are in the embarrassing position of running out of fuel during the night," he replied.

"And you are?" asked Tom.

"Capitan Christopher Manual Cortez Oliva of the Spanish Army," replied Oliva.

"Of the Muslim Directorate, you mean," said Tom.

"Of course not, how dare you make such a statement!" asked Oliva arrogantly.

Tom turned to look at Martin. He shook his head. Oliva collected himself.

"And who are you?" he demanded.

"Sergeant Tom Hansen, United States Marines, retired," said Tom. "Who's on the yacht?"

"It's is best that you don't know that. Best that you don't ask that," replied Oliva sternly.

Oliva reminded Tom of all the staff officers he had met. Full of themselves.

"Fuel is hard to come by. Especially out here on the ocean. I'm willing to sell some of it," said Tom.

"How much?" asked Oliva.

"How much you got?" asked Tom, in his best Brooklyn accent. "Tell General Salazar I'll give him a special price."

Oliva reached for his pistol. He stopped when Wisdom fired another warning burst.

"You just gave him away, Captain Oliva. Were you told to kill us if we didn't cooperate? Or was it your own idea?" said Tom.

Oliva and his men waited silently.

"Martin, go aboard the launch and take his radio," said Tom.

Oliva swore at Martin and he replied in kind. Wisdom fired again and they fell silent. Tom looked at the yacht. Armed men were now visible on the previously empty decks. Martin handed over the radio.

"Put the general on. Hello, General Salazar, we met at Tenerife Sur. . . . In the control tower. . . . I'd be happy help you out . . . "

*****

General Salazar poured the scotch and handed a glass to Tom. The tequila sunrise went to Jane.

"We barely had enough fuel to make the coast when the battle broke out ahead of us last night. A slow fuel leak made it worse as we waited. So here we are, stranded. Dead ducks waiting for the EU to find us and do their business," said Salazar. "What do I owe you for the fuel?"

"I'll trade for information," said Tom.

"Specifically?" he asked .

"What is going on?" asked Tom.

"You saw what happened on Tenerife. I was blamed for everything. Even things that happened before I arrived. I was tipped about the EU arrest warrant and ran. I was in the Azores, hiding. Waiting to make a dash for the new world. On Christmas day my contacts in Spain were severed almost overnight. My brother officers who I would trust with my life, were being replaced then murdered. Along with their families. My family is now safe so I can return to fight for my country. For the future of my Europe," said Salazar staring out to sea.

Jim signaled that they were ready to cast off. Tom waved back.

"Specialist Martin wants to go with you. Will you take him?" asked Tom.

"Of course," replied Salazar.

"Martin mentioned something called the Muslim Directorate. He said the first officer shot the captain while arguing about this group," said Tom.

"The Muslim Directorate is the political organization pushing the Muslim agenda across the EU. They blamed me for the murder of Mansoor Wadi, head of the Muslim Directorate in France. A lot of highly placed people know I couldn't have done it. Why I was chosen to be blamed for the murder still mystifies me," said Salazar.

Tom sipped his scotch.

"It's easier to blame somebody already in trouble than to frame a new man," said Tom.

"Truly. The Muslim Directorate has to get me out of the way somehow. I represent old Europe. Old Europe must be removed before new Europe can be established," said Salazar.

"Is the new Europe the EU or the Muslim Directorate?" asked Tom.

"One is leading to the other. Or maybe they are now one. I can't see the whole picture yet. Does this satisfy you?" asked

Salazar.

"No, but it will have to do for now. I have one more request," said Tom.

"Yes?" asked Salazar.

"I'd like a picture of us together," said Tom.

"Certainly. But you understand that such a picture could put you in danger," said Salazar.

"There comes a time when men are forced to pick sides. I'm picking your side," said Tom.

General Salazar raised his glass.

*****

The ground shook six times in successions. The benefit of a near miss was that it raised a dust cloud that obscured their positions. What was left of them. Borovich surveyed the area. The Turks had responded yesterday afternoon. Now the area was a series of craters without vegetation. Captain Baransky crawled into the trench next to the command tank.

"Ivanovich?" asked Borovich.

Baransky shook his head. "The reinforcements led by General Koronski crossed the frontier near Deta and are heading for Beograd. The Turks have abandoned Szeged and are racing south to avoid being cut off. General Bariatinsky is saved."

Borovich looked down into the valley. An armored column was moving north on his right. Another was moving north on his left. He would soon be trapped.

"Time to save ourselves. Were pulling out in twenty minutes. Pass the word," said Borovich.

"Shouldn't we wait until dark?" asked Baranski.

"It will be too late by then! Go!" shouted Borovich.

*****

"I have news that the Pope is in Warsaw," said Hamdar.

"Logical. Warsaw is the last catholic stronghold in Europe," said Najid.

"There is more. Our attack on Vatican City has made him more dangerous to us than before. Our best source is saying he will give a speech tomorrow calling on Christians everywhere to end their conciliatory relations with Islam and begin a crusade to remove Islam from Europe. He has called on the catholic cardinals around the world to join him there for this announcement," said Hamdar.

"Do we know if he ...." asked Najid.

"He has changed his name from Constantine the second to Urban the ninth," said Hamdar.

"Hmm, Interesting choice. He had the name of a Roman emperor who pushed Christianity on our ancestors by force. Now he takes the name of a pope who launched the first crusade. Will the struggle be an armed one or an ecclesiastic one?" asked Najid.

"That I don't know," replied Hamdar.

Najid paced to the window and looked out at Saint Peters Square.

"He has no real power. And we have convinced the world that he is dead. But still. We cannot allow a rallying point to develop while we are still vulnerable," said Najid. "We must arrest him tonight. Silence him. Do we control the police there?"

"Loyal men are in positions of leadership but control is uncertain. The legacy of the Soviet period left a lack of faith in leaders. I don't know if we will succeed. Our numbers are not great in Poland," said Hamdar.

"Then it's time to see where we stand. Order his arrest immediately. First the police. Then the army. He must be assassinated along with as many cardinals as possible. It will leave the church in complete disarray for some time. No longer a threat to us. This must be done before midnight. Report to me then. We must silence him now or we may not be able to. If we can't stop him tonight it means that we are losing control of Poland. Did you know the Russian army is on the Polish border asking for permission to enter?" asked Najid.

"No, I did not," replied Hamdar.

"The Russians have already grabbed Romania. They are about to grab Poland. I think it is time that they know we control the Marseilles and that we have the will to use it. Two birds with one stone if we can't stop the Pope by conventional means," said Najid.

"Warsaw?" asked Hamdar.

Najid nodded "Send Asim in."

"Yes, sir," replied Hamdar leaving.

Asim moved into the room looking left and right. Assessing possible danger from years of habit. He waited silently.

"The business in Lyon is unacceptable. Murdering Christians can only work against us. Christians are not our enemies. They are our dhimmis, our servants, our slaves. Of course, if they cause trouble, we must crush them absolutely. But I'm not aware of any trouble from them in Lyon, are you?" asked Najid.

Asim shook his head.

"Go to Lyon. I mean, Kubri al Bukra. Find out who was behind this. Do whatever you need to do to reestablish our control there. No one can disobey us, Muslim or infidel. I will pass the same orders to all of the Muslim Directorates immediately," said Najid.

Asim nodded.

"When that's done, do the same thing in Gibraltar," said Najid.

*****

Captain Claude Bery stared out at endless ocean. Nothing on radar. Nothing on Sonar. Darkness was a comfort and he knew that the sky was clear of American satellites. He took the chance to come up and enjoy the fresh air. He would probably never be called on. Everything would fall into their laps as planned and he could return to port soon.

"Coded transmission coming in Captain" said the radio officer over the speaker.

"Bring it up," said Berry.

This was the first message he had received. It was agreed he would only receive two messages. A recall order or a launch order. It was too soon to be recalled.

"Here it is," said the radio officer from the top of the hatch.

Bery took the paper and held it under his light. He studied it. The rest of the watch stood silently. Launch. He hoped this would never happen. But he was a naval officer of a nuclear submarine. He had been prepared for this type of order for years. He turned to his exec.

"This is not a drill. Change course and go to missile launch depth. We have been called to do our duty. Allah Akbar," ordered Bery.

*****

Captain Thomas heard the knock on his door and woke up quickly. He swung his feet to the floor.

"Come in," said Thomas.

Exec Charles Hampton, stepped in, out of breath.

"Missile launch fifteen minutes ago," said Hampton,

"Type?" asked Thomas.

"Ballistic," replied Hampton.

"This is confirmed?" asked Thomas.

"Yes, verified by SAC," said Hampton.

"Target?" asked Thomas.

"It should be hitting Poland about now," said Hampton.

"Set our course for the origin of that launch. All ahead full," ordered Thomas.

"Yes, sir. Already done," replied Hampton.

"How far?" asked Thomas.

"Two hundred and fifty miles," said Hampton.

"Start our search pattern there. It must be the Marseilles. Maintain standard watches. I'll see you in the morning," said Thomas.

"Yes, sir," said Hampton closing the door behind him.

A night launch would make the missile visible for miles. So they were hiding from satellite coverage. That made it very plain. They were a renegade boat with thirty nuclear, no, twenty nine nuclear missiles. Why Poland? He'd learn that tomorrow. It would be a busy day.

Thomas swung his feet back onto the bunk, fighting the desire to be in control of the action on his bridge. He needed his sleep to be sharp in the morning.

This is the BBC, Namir Wahidi reporting from London. In a tragic accident, an American warplane carrying nuclear warheads crashed on the outskirts of Warsaw last night. The impact set off one of the warheads destroying the city and leaving a radioactive holocaust in its wake. The fatalities are beyond count as the survivors head out of what is left. EU commissioners have called for a full investigation and point out that if NATO had been disbanded sooner, then maybe this accident would never have happened.

The American military deny having any planes over Warsaw last night. An unofficial source claims a French ballistic missile submarine, the Marseilles, fired the missile from the Atlantic Ocean. Commissioner of EU Security, Ahmoud Antillier, calls this preposterous, claiming that the Marseilles was at it's dock in Brest at the time of the accident. He demanded that any remaining American nuclear warheads in Europe be removed by EU forces.

*****

The Santa Ana had entered the harbor at Marin just before dawn. General Salazar paced the deck, waiting.

Three men approached the yacht, walking in the light drizzle. Salazar turned to his men. They nodded back. He walked across the gangway to the pier. His men followed.

The first of the three strangers walked forward and embraced Salazar. The others shook his hand.

"Thank god you have returned. You are our last hope. The men are with you. We have to get to the base and take charge before word can spread to our enemies," said Capitan Diaz.

"General Gomez, Capitan Torrez?" asked Salazar.

"Missing. Presumed dead. Comandante Alvarez is in hiding but I can contact him. I have only two cars but we can borrow a city bus for your men," replied Diaz looking over Salazar's growing entourage.

"Aren't those your trucks?" asked Salazar pointing to the three army trucks that appeared at the end of the pier and began unloading soldiers.

"Mierda! We are betrayed!" replied Diaz looking in horror as the soldiers formed up across the entrance to the pier.

General Salazar walked calmly toward the soldiers. His men followed.

"Present arms. Prepare to fire!" shouted Coronel Jaffa to his men.

Two rows of soldiers raised their automatic rifles. Salazar stopped ten meters from the line.

"General Salazar, you are under arrest by order of the EU for insubordination, murder, and crimes against immigrants. Place your hands in the air while we take you and your men into custody!" shouted Jaffa.

Salazar stood quietly looking at the soldiers. They looked back in awe of this famous general.

"Subteniente Garza, Sargento Lopez, Sargento Pena, Cabo Ortega, Soldados Ruiz and Cruz. It is good to see you all again," said Salazar warmly.

"It's good to see you also, General," replied Sargento Lopez lowering his rifle.

Salazar's men called out to the soldiers they knew as well. The soldiers began lowering their weapons. A few remained firm.

"I have returned to Spain not as a criminal but as a patriot. I am falsely accused. You know me. Have I ever let you down? Have I ever let Spain down? I am here to save our country! Who is with me? Who is loyal to Spain? Who loves this country the way I do!" said Salazar with emotion.

The men cheered their support.

"Fire! I said fire!" shouted Colonel Jaffa.

The soldiers turned on Jaffa and the men still loyal to him. They were disarmed and herded together.

"I will see you all hang for this!" shouted Jaffa angrily.

Four soldiers took Jaffa and picked him up off the ground.

"What are you doing! Put me down!" shouted Jaffa struggling to get free.

The others gathered around and followed Jaffa to the edge of the pier. The cheers grew louder each time the four men swung the screaming officer toward the water. On the third swing they let go and Jaffa flew out into the water making a big splash. The men laughed and shouted happily. Salazar raised his hands to quiet them.

"Thank you all! Our work is just beginning. On to the base!" shouted Salazar as he marched toward the trucks.

Salazar's men and the soldiers meshed together as they marched. A band of brothers reunited.

*****

Farouk Aziz paused in the doorway and cleared his throat.

"Yes?" asked Anwar Saidi from his desk.

"The tanker. It's not coming," said Aziz.

"What happened?" asked Saidi, concerned.

"The ships sent to intercept it were attacked by the Americans. They hijacked the tanker. It's heading to America right now," replied Aziz.

"Who told you this!" demanded Saidi.

"Najid's lieutenant, Mansour Hamdar. He's looking around for another tanker for us, but everyone is clamoring for fuel. He didn't make any promises," replied Aziz.

"I need a rapid strike force in the center of England to put down any potential threats. That force needs a lot of fuel to be effective and will leave us dangerously short everywhere else. Where am I supposed to find it!" asked Saidi rubbing his eyes.

Aziz stood silently.

"Summon the staff. Our fuel shortage has reached a crisis. I want all ideas on where to get more fuel. We'll siphon the gas tanks of every car, truck, and train in England if we have to. Something doesn't feel right about our takeover. I can't say what it is but we need that force fueled and ready and we need it now!" shouted Saidi.

Aziz nodded and turned to go.

"And Aziz," said Saidi.

"Yes, sir?" asked Aziz.

"Have those sons of the devil who sold our fuel supplies on the black market, shot before sun down today! They hurt us more than anyone knows," said Saidi.

*****

Clarke carried his things into the small room at the back of the barn while Brent closed the doors behind the car. Clarke soon had a warm fire going in the stove. Brent looked around. A stove, a kitchen table, four bunk beds, no windows. They hovered around the stove.

"Tomorrow we part company," said Clarke. "Today, one of my

contacts gave me the final word about Lorrie. It was confirmed that she was loaded onto a boat in Italy. By now she has been transported to North Africa. There is nothing you nor I can do to save her. Someday she may escape on her own. That's it. You have no reason to stay in England. You should go home," said Clarke.

Brent stood silently.

"Bastards," he said quietly.

"I am going to try to explain what is happening to the military while there is still a chance. I have a friend in military intelligence near here. If no one will listen, I will have to use the escape route I set up for myself. Unfortunately, there's only room for one in my plan. You will have to go back to America on your own. Before you are caught with me," said Clarke.

"I understand what you are telling me. But I don't want to leave until I get even. Even a little bit," said Brent.

"There is one small thing you can do for me before you fly out. The only way I can fight back," said Clarke.

"Shoot," said Brent.

"I need you to take this briefcase to my apartment in London. And make six phone calls. Then get out of there fast and disappear. Can you do that?" asked Clarke patting his briefcase.

"What's in the case?" asked Brent. "A bomb?"

"No. It contains details about my entire information network," said Clarke.

"What? Are you giving up or are you one of them all of a sudden? I'm not going to do it," said Brent crossing his arms.

"Five members of my network have been murdered. Ten more are missing, presumed dead. This is the only way I have of striking back," said Clarke.

"By giving the rest of them away?" asked Brent.

"No. By creating confusion. By implicating known traitors as my allies. I've created documents naming men they thought were loyal. It's the only way I have of getting back at them," said Clarke.

"So you aren't giving away your network?" asked Brent.

"No. Of course not," replied Clarke.

"I get it. Misinformation. Count me in. Fifteen minutes at your apartment and I'm out of there," said Brent. "No problem."

"Good man," said Clarke. "Remember. Don't hang around. Make the calls and get out."

"OK. I got it," replied Brent. "You think your apartment will be watched?"

"Without question," said Clarke.

166

Brent awoke to the sound of diesel motors. He went into the barn and peeked through a window. There was an inch of new snow blanketing the landscape. In the adjacent pasture he could see a military truck and a car. Soldiers were getting out of the vehicles.

"What do you see?" whispered Clarke, sneaking up behind him.

"It's the army," said Brent. "Should we run for it?"

"The police are looking for me. The army probably isn't," replied Clarke. "We'll drive away like two normal residents when we're ready."

Two high ranking officers got out of the staff car. One of them began berating the driver who had also gotten out. Brent could hear the anger in the officer's voice but not what he was saying. The snow seemed to deaden all sounds.

The soldiers had climbed down from the truck with their weapons. A third officer got out of the lead car and joined the argument. The senior man shouted at him and pointed back toward the road and the barn. The officers walked to the stone wall between the pasture and the barn and stopped.

"Uh oh," murmured Brent.

While the three officers were arguing, a sergeant walked up behind the first two officers with a pistol in his hand. He shot each one in the back of the head. They dropped onto the snow. The third officer directed the men to stack their rifles and take up picks and shovels. The ground was hard and they worked slowly.

"Shouldn't we run away?" asked Brent.

"It's too late. We're witnesses. They'd have to kill us," replied Clarke.

Holes were dug. The bodies dropped into them. Then covered over. The men returned to their vehicles and drove back onto the road and away.

"Thank god they didn't come any closer. Let's get out of here before they return," said Brent.

167

Clarke began searching the barn.

"Do you know how lucky we are?" shouted Clarke from a side room.

"I sure do. I've never been in a position to be murdered before. I'm happy to be alive," replied Brent.

Clarke reappeared with two shovels.

"What are the shovels for?" asked Brent uneasily.

"Come on," said Clarke heading outside. "This is evidence that can't be ignored!"

"What do you mean? Let's get in the car and make a run for it before anyone comes back," pleaded Brent.

"This could be my only chance to prove a campaign of assassination is being waged!" said Clarke.

Clarke went out and began digging up the grave with enthusiasm. Brent looked at the main road cautiously.

"Get to work, Brent. We can leave when we get the bodies up," said Clarke between breaths. "If only I could prove who ordered these murders, I could put the blame squarely where it belongs. That would be a turning point. Dead bodies can't be ignored. It means prison for some one!"

"It will be us if we're caught out here," said Brent. "Evidence like this will be hard to explain."

Clarke paused in thought.

"You're right. Stop digging. Do you have a camera with you?" asked Clarke.

"No. What about my mobile phone?" asked Brent eying the road again.

"It will have to do," said Clarke.

They returned to digging and soon had the bodies up. Brent handed over his mobile phone and Clarke took some photos. Clarke went through their pockets. Brent hung back. The bodies had become disfigured, not like the living men they had been only an hour earlier. He took some close ups of their faces.

"Right then. We'll move them into the barn for now. It's cold enough in there," said Clarke. "It's vital I get this information to a friend who can do something about it."

They placed the bodies in a cellar under the barn and returned to the car. Clarke pointed to the briefcase.

"Now you know what we're up against. Still willing to do what I asked?" said Clarke.

Brent stared out the barn door and shrugged his shoulders.

"I said I would and I will," he replied.

"Good man. It's off to the train for you. While I use the last of the petrol to get where I'm going," said Clarke starting the car.

*****

Clarke walked silently beside Corporal Wilson.

"Captain Sykes' office is just ahead. We don't normally escort civilians across the base but we have new security rules what with the crisis and all," said the corporal.

"I understand. We can't be too careful right now," said Clarke.

"Here it is," said the corporal, knocking on the open door. "Your visitor, sir."

"Oliver, it's good to see you," said Sykes coming around his desk to shake hands. "Carry on corporal."

The escort saluted and marched away.

"Take a seat. Haven't seen you since our tenth reunion. What kind of trouble are you in now?" asked Sykes smiling.

Clarke paused and looked into the hallway. Then he closed the door.

"I have news that you will find hard to believe. Something I can only divulge to someone I trust with my life," said Clarke.

"You know you can trust me. What happened?" asked Sykes.

"I witnessed a murder this morning. Actually two murders," said Clarke.

"My god. How terrible. What are the police doing about it?" said Sykes.

"Nothing yet. I wanted to talk to you first," said Clarke.

"Me? Why? If you are involved in some way I can't protect you," said Sykes.

"I'm not involved. I only witnessed the crimes. I came to you because the victims were high ranking army officers. Executed by other army personnel. An officer, a sergeant, and a squad of infantry," said Clarke. "Two vehicles stopped in a pasture next to where I was staying. After an argument the two victims were shot then buried."

Sykes paused. "You still need to call the police."

"I can't. I was told they are looking for me already for things unrelated to these murders," said Clarke.

"Then I will call for you," said Sykes reaching for the phone. Clarke covered the phone with his hand.

"I need you to come with me to the scene. Look at the bodies. Help me identify them then try to identify the killers. This isn't an isolated incident. The newspapers are full of accounts of murders and disappearances. You must have even more knowledge of events than the papers," said Clarke.

"Yes, internal terrorists. A bad lot we should have put away

169

long ago," replied Sykes.

"Wearing army uniforms, driving army vehicles, and shooting their own members?" asked Clarke. "No. These were soldiers killing other soldiers and you are in a position to find out what's going on."

"What you are describing isn't possible. Not in England. In third world countries with active death squads maybe, but not here. I can't believe it. That would suggest that these murders are being carried out by the army. Like a coup plot in Africa or somewhere," said Sykes.

"It is unthinkable. It is unbelievable. That's why you must see it with your own eyes. I took some mobile phone photos but they aren't clear enough," said Clarke holding out the phone.

Sykes looked through the photos.

"I certainly can't identify them from this. So you want me to go with you, take a quick look. Is that it?" asked Sykes handing back the phone.

"Yes and we don't have time to wait," said Clarke.

There was a knock on the door and it opened. Captain Jalal scanned the room. He looked at his clip board. A senior officer walked in. Sykes rose to attention.

"This is Captain Sykes, intelligence officer," said Jalal.

"At ease," said Colonel Rahman extending his hand. Sykes shook it. Rahman turned to Clarke.

"Who are you?" he asked.

"Burton, Richard Burton. An old friend of Sykes here," said Clarke extending his hand. Rahman shook it absently. Clarke examined Rahman's uniform. Jalal looked familiar.

"I'm here to tell Sykes about his girl Martha. She's in a terrible state. Maybe kill herself she will. I figure Sykes is the only one who can handle the matter. We've all been friends since school days. Old school ties and all that. I'm sure you know how it is, general," said Clarke.

Rahman frowned and turned to Sykes.

"I like to have a sit down and get to know my officers right from the start," said Rahman.

"Yes, sir," said Sykes.

"Sorry to interrupt but we have to leave right now to save Martha. That's why I'm here," said Clarke.

"I see. Jalal, who is next on the list?" asked Rahman.

"Lieutenant McGovern in the maintenance building," replied Jalal.

"All right Captain. I'll move you to the bottom of the list. You may take care of this private matter but be here tomorrow morning early. We're in a crisis if you hadn't noticed. We need everyman on his toes including you. Carry on," said Rahman walking out.

Sykes saluted and sat down frowning.

"Great. It's settled then. You'll need to get a car. Mine is out of petrol," said Clarke.

"This better be good. I've just buggered my relationship with the new commander," said Sykes.

"So? What's one black mark, aye?" said Clarke.

"Because it's my career. There's only one British army. I can't move from army to army like some business man. Too late now. Let's get this over with," sighed Sykes.

*****

The daylight was fading when they arrived. Sykes parked the army car in front of the barn.

"Follow me," said Clarke heading for the pasture. He pointed to the blood near the stone wall.

"This is where they got it. Here's the grave. The truck was over there. You can see the tire tracks."

"And you disturbed the crime scene by digging them up," said Sykes shaking his head.

"Yes, well, too late now. We filled the holes back in in case anyone came back," said Clarke.

"Ok, show me the bodies," said Sykes turning back to the barn.

Clarke opened the basement storage room and turned on the light. The two corpses lay staring at the ceiling. Sykes froze, his mouth open. He knelt beside the bodies.

"It's Colonel Haig," whispered Sykes in shock. "And his adjutant, lieutenant Allenby. Until this morning he was my commanding officer."

"Then Rahman arrived to take over?" asked Clarke.

"Yes, Rahman brought orders that Haig had been promoted and was to leave immediately for his new post. The newly created Crisis Control Center outside Cheltenham. We all gathered to toast his good fortune this morning. Then Colonel Rahman officially took command," said Sykes.

"How was he to get to Cheltenham?" asked Clarke.

"By car with an armed escort because of the terrorist attacks. Oh god, a car and a truck. Captain Jalal was in charge," said Sykes, his shoulders sagging.

"That's what I saw this morning," said Clarke. "The other officer looked like Jalal but I can't swear to it."

"It had to be. Even I can see that," said Sykes. "What do we do now?"

"Get your camera from the car. We have to document this. Then we get the word out to everyone we can trust," said Clarke.

Sykes looked at Clarke. "But who can we trust? This murder was led by Captain Jalal. And that suggests that Colonel Rahman knew about it. Maybe even ordered it. This can't be happening."

"I knew you'd have to see this with your own eyes. Everything you believe about England is out the window. Sorry old man. That's the new reality and we have to face it squarely," said Clarke.

Sykes stood looking more determined. "Who is Rahman working for? And what are they planning?"

Clarke clapped him on the back. "Now that is something that I do know something about."

*****

Brent turned the key in the lock and stepped into Clarke's flat. It was good to be in familiar surroundings after being on the run. He put some frozen food in the microwave then went to the phone.

He opened the briefcase and began dialing the phone numbers as instructed. He hung up after getting any response whether it was recording or human. No answers got eight rings.

Brent gathered his food and drink and put his feet up in front of the television and flipped through the channels as he ate. The comfortable flat was warm and quiet.

*****

The surveillance specialist at Scotland Yard heard a chirp from his computer and clicked on the phone icon. This brought up another file and he called his supervisor.

Harold Smythe walked over. "What's up"

"Someone entered one of my flats. The door trigger has been tripped and the phone has been used," said the specialist.

"Any conversations?" asked Smythe.

"No. Lot's of dialing but no talking," said the specialist.

"Whose place is it?" asked Smythe.

"An Oliver Clarke. I don't know why he's being watched," said the specialist.

"What do the flag notes say?" asked Smythe.

"I am to notify Special Operations when anyone shows up

there," replied the specialist.

"Good. Call them. Refer them to me if there is anything you can't handle," said Smythe.

"Yes, sir," said the specialist.

*****

Brent woke to a test pattern and white noise.

"Oh crap," said Brent rubbing his eyes. He was supposed to leave right after the phone calls. Hours had passed. He went around wiping his fingerprints just in case. He locked the door and headed down to the entrance with his knapsack.

*****

The surveillance van was parked to see both the windows of the flat and the front door of the building.

"Wake up, Farshad. The lights went out. Someone must be coming out," said Abdul Shabaz.

"I'm not sleeping," said Farshad becoming awake instantly.

"Of course not. OK. There's someone leaving the apartment," said Abdul looking at a hand held TV screen.

"Let's intercept him," said Farshad opening his door.

"He's coming out the front door. Hold on," said Abdul.

He pulled slowly from his parking space. When Brent headed for the street, Abdul gunned the motor and shot forward.

Brent looked up in surprise as the passing van gave him a glancing blow and sent him to the pavement.

"Now!" shouted Abdul jumping from the driver's seat.

He kicked the stunned Brent and turned him on his stomach. The plastic cuffs were on when Farshad threw Brent over his shoulder and dropped him roughly in the back of the van.

"Clear," said Farshad jumping in and closing the rear doors.

Abdul nodded and hit the gas pedal.

This is the BBC, Hassan Wady reporting from London. As a result of the Norwegian government continuing to defy the EU with plans for a succession referendum, the entire Norwegian delegation to the EU has been taken into custody by security forces. Prime minister Norstad called this a gross violation of diplomatic courtesy and a criminal act by the EU. He said these actions add fuel to the conflict instead of defusing it. Commissioner Ahmoud Antillier spoke for the EU saying that succession was a crime and all those who were connected to it in any way were criminals.

*****

Farouk Aziz parked his Jaguar just inside the wide doors of the deserted warehouse. He entered the side room to see Farhad and Abdul drinking coffee. He looked through the window into the small room where the subject sat, unconscious.

"What did you find out?" asked Aziz.

"He's been with Oliver Clarke for the last three weeks. Out in the west country mostly. He went to the apartment to carry out some sort of disinformation campaign. Making phone calls to loyal men to make them look disloyal," said Abdul.

"Yes, I heard about the phone calls before I left," said Aziz. "What else?"

"He says he knows nothing about Clarke's resistance network. He met the man only after he says we stole his girl. Apparently she was kidnapped and sold south," said Abdul.

"I don't care about his personal problems. The only reason I'm here is to capture Clarke or at least infiltrate his network. You haven't achieved either one is that right?" asked Aziz.

Abdul looked at Farhad. "No, we haven't."

Aziz removed his gloves and jacket. He rolled up his sleeves.

"Let's get to work then," said Aziz.

They entered the room and Farhad switched on the electricity.

Brent recoiled and woke up. He stared at the men without further reaction. Aziz looked at the card Abdul handed him.

"You are completely under my power. If you do not cooperate fully you will be subject to so much pain you will beg me to kill you. Do you understand?" asked Aziz.

"Who are you?" asked Brent, his voice hoarse from screaming.

"It is unimportant to know who I am except that I am a powerful man who holds your life in his hands. So. Let's begin. Where is Oliver Clarke?" asked Aziz.

"He said he was going to an army base to see a friend about the conspiracy," whispered Brent.

"What base?" asked Aziz.

"I don't know," replied Brent.

Aziz nodded to Farhad who turned up the voltage. Brent shook uncontrollably and moaned through clenched teeth.

"We went over that for hours. We got nothing," said Abdul.

Aziz pulled out his cell phone and dialed.

"Put the word out that Clarke has recently been on one of the army posts in the west country. I don't know which. Investigate every one west of Reading. Just do it and do it right now," said Aziz angrily.

He snapped his phone shut and turned back to the prisoner.

"So you were working for Clarke when you came back to his flat," said Aziz.

Farhad gave him a shot of electricity.

"Yes," replied Brent clenching his muscles.

"Then what? What more damage did he instruct you to do?" asked Aziz.

"Nothing else. He told me to leave England when I finished," said Brent.

"And go where? For what purpose?" asked Aziz.

Farhad gave him a larger jolt.

"To America," said Brent.

"To recruit fighters?" asked Aziz.

"No," replied Brent.

"To raise money?" asked Aziz.

"No," replied Brent.

"Then why, why, why?" demanded Aziz slapping Brent's face with each question.

"Clarke told me to go home and stay out of Europe and its problems," said Brent.

Aziz paused.

"Home? What do you mean, home?" asked Aziz.

"I'm American," replied Brent spitting out the blood pouring from his nose.

Aziz turned to his men. "Is this true? Is there proof?"

Abdul looked at his boss nervously then stared at the floor. Farhad pointed to a table where a small pile of items rested. Aziz picked up the passport and examined it. He dropped it on the table shaking his head.

"You bloody idiots. He's American. Didn't you see the order? The order directly from Asim himself. Americans and Russians are to be left alone under penalty of death. Well?" shouted Aziz.

"You told us to interrogate him so we did," replied Abdul firmly. "He is working for a known enemy. Besides, what is one American more or less."

Aziz grabbed his men by their collars and dragged them from the room and slammed the door.

"Do you know who Khalil Asim is?" shouted Aziz.

"I saw him at a conference once. He didn't look like much," replied Farhad.

"Asim is Najid's right hand man. His enforcer. Asim can have any of us killed for any reason. Didn't you hear about the mess in Lyon? Seven loyal men like you were executed for disobeying Najid's orders. Beheaded in the central square. By Asim himself! Curse you!" shouted Aziz.

Abdul and Farhad stood silently.

"There are records of you two going out to intercept him. What am I going to do now!" said Aziz pacing.

Aziz stopped in front of the table.

"Burn his identification then dump him near a hospital. Pour alcohol on him for good measure. He doesn't know who we are so we should be safe. As for you two, forget everything that happened here. No reports, nothing. If Asim ever finds out about this, you're dead. But he'll only get to execute you if I don't do it first!" shouted Aziz.

*****

"Mr. Smith, tell Steele and Beecher that we have lost the Marseilles. Ask them to spread out another twenty miles from their current positions," said Thomas.

"We haven't lost them!" interrupted Moeller.

Thomas stared at Moeller cooly.

"Sir," added Moeller.

"Do it," said Thomas.

"Yes sir," replied Smith.

"Hampton, come with me into my cabin," said Thomas.

"What's up?" asked Hampton when they were alone.

"I'm sending Steele and Beecher away so I have a free hand in this matter," said Thomas.

"Oh?" said Hampton.

"I can't stand by and let another city be vaporized. Something is wrong at headquarters. I've been trained to act in this situation. To stop any and all nuclear threats. Now our orders go against everything that I know. It makes no sense to me. I'm going to be acting alone if I act at all. I'm damned if I do and damned if I don't," said Thomas in frustration."If I take a fall over this you will likely fall with me."

"If you do nothing and a nuke hits America, you will be damned by everyone in this crew as well as everyone at home. We're with you. All the way," said Hampton pointedly.

"Thanks for that," said Thomas.

******

The internet cafe was empty except for two men.

"I'm done. I've contacted everyone I trust," said Captain Sykes.

"So have I," said Clarke. "I hope it's enough because it's our only chance to turn things around."

"No one has taken me seriously. They tell me I must be mistaken, even crazy," said Sykes.

"No one in England has experience with this. That's why they don't believe us. It's like when a mad gunman starts shooting people at a shopping center. Afterward the witnesses all say they thought it sounded like fire crackers. They have experience with firecrackers but not with automatic weapon fire," said Clarke. "So it's back to the farm house."

"Not me. I'm going back to the base," said Sykes.

"You're not serious? Your commander ordered the murder of two officers. Any of you could be next. You can't go back there," said Clarke surprised.

"I've done everything you asked of me and nothing has come of it. I missed my appointment with Rahman this morning and I don't know what excuse I'll use but I'll think of something. I have to get back to my job, my life," said Sykes.

"Your life is precisely what you could lose if you go back now. Besides I need your help. I have no credibility with the people who count. This information has to come from a brother officer and that's you. You are all that stands between the country you love and a brutal take over. I need you, your country needs you, you can't quit now!" said Clarke.

"I've decided. I'm going back. I'm not important enough to be a threat to anyone. It may be a reprimand for me but life will go on. Maybe I can help from the inside. I can watch Colonel Rahman and Jalal. I'm not doing any good out here," replied Sykes standing.

"I hope you're right. It's too late to report to Rahman today. At least stay with me tonight and we'll go back together in the morning. Something may break by then," said Clarke.

"OK, but tomorrow morning for sure. Let's get some food. And you're buying," said Sykes walking out.

Brent tottered on the crutches. The nurse steadied him.

"I want you to walk about for a least fifteen minutes, right?" said the nurse. "You better get control of your drinking problem. I don't want to see you back here."

"Yeah sure," mumbled Brent.

He paused before the mirror by the door and gasped in pain. His face was swollen and he was black and blue all over. Some ribs felt broken but that was inconclusive according to the doctor. He wandered the hospital, feeling a little better as he went.

He didn't pay much attention to where he was going. The events since being kidnapped went round and round in his thoughts. Helping Clarke had got him into this. But why did they let him go? And were they still watching, waiting? Hoping he would lead them to Clarke? He wasn't proud about what happened. He'd told them everything he knew. Except one thing. Witnessing the murders. Spilling that would have been suicide.

Hold on. Did he see a familiar face? He backed up and looked into the room. Six clipboards hung on pegs outside the door. He was right. Brent walked into the room and looked down at the the young blond woman.

"Hi, remember me?" asked Brent. He tried to smile but it only made his face crooked.

"Sorry, mate. I've never known anyone as hideous as you," she replied staring at a magazine.

Brent was devastated.

"Oh this," he said pointing to his face.

He started to laugh but his rib pain cut him short.

"I threw beer on you outside a pub. Then you came to my place and cleaned up, remember?" asked Brent.

"I remember vaguely. And you are?" asked Celia raising her eyebrows.

"Brent. Brent Swain," he replied.

"Right. Yes. Of course you are. The American. So what are you doing here, Brent Swain?" she asked.

"Some Arab guys kidnapped me, beat the crap out of me, then dumped me in a ditch nearby. They made me look like a drunk by pouring Gin all over me," said Brent.

Celia stared at the ceiling thinking about her fiance, Farouk. She blamed the miscarriage on the fall. How she came to fall down the stairs she hadn't revealed to the doctor.

"Surprising how often that happens," she said. "Did you tell anyone? The cops?"

"No," he replied.

Who would believe him? Those guys may have been the cops that were after Clarke. All he wanted was to get back to the States as soon as possible. Until now.

"Hey, this is great! We can recover together. I'll come up as often as I can," beamed Brent.

"Super. I can't wait," she replied sarcastically returning to her magazine.

*****

The sonar officer removed his headphones.

"Sir, There is a ship approaching," said Shekar Danzai, the sonar chief.

"Why should that concern me?" asked Captain Bery.

"It is moving fast. A naval vessel for sure. And I've heard it's sound signature three times before," replied the sonar man.

"Probably the Americans. By now they know we are not in port. They are wondering just what is going on. And they have sent their sub chasers out to find us. But they will fail just as they failed during the maneuvers," said Bery.

"How could they get close to us four times. Such luck has to be suspect," said Shekar.

"We could head for deep water just to be sure," said Ali Mouti, Bery's exec.

"Make it so. It won't change the situation. But it won't hurt us either," said Bery.

*****

"They have changed course again, sir," said sonar chief Yablonski.

"New course?" asked Hampton.

"Three oh five degrees," answered Ralph Moeller from the jury rigged console next to Yablonski.

Thomas had the new system monitors moved to the bridge. Hampton looked at the chart.

"Deeper water, sir," said Hampton.

"Have they changed depth or speed?" asked Thomas.

"No sir," replied Yablonski.

"They aren't sure if we are on to them. But they aren't taking chances," said Thomas. "Smith, send a message to Steele and Beecher asking them to close up and take position ahead of us but off to the sides, say ten miles."

"Yes sir," replied Smith.

"Do you think they will pick up the Marseilles?" asked Hampton.

"No. But they will be closer if the Marseilles gets away from us and tries to surface," replied Thomas.

"If they surface we'll have them," said Hampton.

"Our orders said to find them, not stop them. If we are close enough, I'll tip my hat and their Captain will tip his back. Then we'll watch them dive again," said Thomas.

"Or launch another nuke!" said Hampton.

"I'll be in my cabin on a secure line to find out just what our options are. Keep after them," said Thomas.

"Yes, sir," replied Hampton.

*****

"It's almost time," said Mouti.

Bery looked at Danzai.

"I haven't heard anything for two hours," said Danzai from the sonar station.

"Very good. Surface for radio reception," said Bery. "No. Don't surface. Make radio depth and extend the antenna."

Ali Mouti looked closely at his Captain. The mask of unshakable confidence had a crack in it.

*****

"They are heading for the surface," said Moeller calmly.

"Stay close but not too close," said Thomas.

"What are we doing just watching?" asked Hampton.

"You heard the orders. No interference for now. We will obey our orders," replied Thomas.

"They could launch against the United States as easily as any other target," said Hampton.

"They, like us, respond to orders. It's dark and no birds are

181

overhead. They are coming up for orders," said Thomas. "Smith, I want a sweep of all frequencies. Shout out if the Marseilles broadcasts anything."

"Yes, sir," replied Smith.

"Now we wait," said Thomas.

Hampton clenched his teeth and turned away.

*****

"Well?" asked Bery.

"Nothing yet," replied radioman Zehani.

Bery looked at his watch. Time was up. Nothing tonight.

"Take us down," said Bery.

"Yes, sir," replied Mouti. "Ahead half, planes down twenty. Level at two hundred."

The helmsman repeated the order and pushed the wheel forward.

"Planes down twenty, level at two hundred."

*****

Colonel Borovich watched his small column cross the bridge at Giurgiu. After a running battle through the night, the Turks had given up the chase. The distance and Russian jet cover had discouraged them. Russian reinforcements could have moved in strength to secure the lower Danube Valley, but higher ups had ordered the retreat back across the Danube.

They had lost an opportunity but maybe it was enough to have gained control of Estonia, Latvia, Lithuania, Poland, Slovakia, parts of Hungary and Serbia, plus Romania. It doesn't pay to over extend your forces. The last of his column entered the bridge.

"Go," said Borovich into his microphone.

He followed with his gun turret pointed into Bulgaria. Half his men dead or wounded as a result of his bold advance. He could have stayed here at Giurgiu the whole time. Did he cause the Turks to retreat or was it General Boronski's advance to Beograd? Someday he'd ask one of his Turkish counter parts about that. Now he faced the small but real possibility of reprimand. He'd never faced that before. But he had never led an armored column into battle before either. No Russian had since Chechnya.

There was a new political order in Europe. Russia was a power to be reckoned with once again. Colonel Borovich felt very much a patriot.

*****

Edmund Bane stepped off the bus in front of the main gate. Hansen followed him, automatically scanning the surroundings. The sign at the gate said Rapid Reaction Corps.

"I shouldn't be long. I'll just check in and let the navy know I'm back. With my ship sunk, I doubt they'll know what to do with me. Probably a weeks leave at least before I'm sorted out. I'll requisition a car then we can all head to my home for a few days. I'll return the hospitality you've shown me," smiled Bane.

"Will there be room for all of us?" asked Tom.

"Room? Ha, ha. The ancestral home has sixty rooms. Twelve guest suites. My father is the Duke of Warford. There's room for a regiment. I know because one was posted there during the war. Anyway, this business shouldn't take long. I'll be back with transportation and we'll be off," said Bane.

There was a bench at the bus stop. Hansen waited. It was a frosty morning with only a weak sun shining through high clouds. An hour passed. Then two. The guards at the gate had been watching him with suspicion for some time. Then Bane walked out cursing.

"Damn. Just when I thought I was away, that bloody Colonel made me wait while he sent to headquarters for orders. Seems that I've been posted to something called the Crisis Control Center. All the best men are being sent there to head off this damn terrorist crisis. No visit home for me. But I'll ring up my father and he'll put you up until you're rested and ready to continue your voyage," said Bane.

"Thanks for the invitation. We'll definitely take you up on it," said Tom.

"Here's the address. Just get close. Everyone for miles around will know how to direct you," said Bain. "Goodbye old chap."

Hanson shook Bain's hand. "Until the next time."

Bain nodded and went back to the base. Hansen turned at the sound of a car approaching the gate. It was a military vehicle but the man who got out was a civilian. The man waved to the officer driving then stared after the car as it entered the base. The man walked to the bus stop and Hansen made room on the bench. The new arrival didn't sit. He began to pace instead.

"American?" asked Clarke.

"Yup," replied Tom.

Clarke watched a military car and truck move toward the gate

183

and stop. A wave of fear swept through him. He began rubbing his hands nervously.

"Problems?" asked Tom.

"You wouldn't believe me if I told you," said Clarke.

Hansen looked at his watch. It would be a long wait for the next bus and he was bored.

"Try me."

*****

Sykes walked past the newly arrived vehicles to see Colonel Rahman and Captain Jalal talking to a lieutenant he didn't recognized. They shook hands and the lieutenant got into the waiting car.

Shit. I'm in for it already. Food poisoning. That's my story thought Sykes.

Rahman looked at Jalal and nodded when he saw Sykes approaching. Jalal nodded and walked to the truck where Sergeant Alhoun stood with his squad. Jalal pulled a photo out of his jacket and handed it to Alhoun.

"Take one of your men and see if you can find this man. He is a friend of Captain Sykes. Word came down he is a high priority target. Bring him here and hold him until I return," said Jalal.

Alhoun picked his man and moved out. Jalal returned to his commander.

"I don't like being stood up by a junior officer, Sykes," said Rahman coldly. "I'd be sending you to the stockade on the double but you're not my problem anymore. You've been transferred so I don't care what happens to you so long as I never see you again. Do you understand me!"

"Yes sir. Thank you sir," stammered Sykes.

"Another officer is leaving the base right now and you can ride with him," said Rahman gesturing to the convoy.

"Where am I going, sir," asked Sykes.

"You're going to the Crisis Control Center. Colonel Haig asked for you personally," said Rahman. "If he wants to put up with your incompetence that's his business."

Sykes turned white. He stared at the open gate. Got to make a break for it.

"I'll dash into my office and get my things, sir," said Sykes moving toward the headquarters building.

Rahman stopped Sykes with his clipboard then turned him back toward the waiting car.

"No time now. I'll have a man pack your things and send them

184

on. Now get in the car and be on your way," said Rahman herding Sykes toward the car. Rahman saluted and Sykes returned it out of habit. The driver held the door and Sykes got into the back beside Bane. Captain Jalal got into the front seat.

"Lieutenant Edmund Bane, late of his majesty's destroyer Valient. Pleased to meet you. That was quite a dressing down you got. Nothing serious I hope," asked Bane holding out his hand.

Sykes shook it absently as the car headed for the gate. He felt helpless as disbelief changed to despair.

*****

Clarke watched the army car pass. He saw Sykes make a slashing motion across his neck as the car went by.

"Oh god," said Clarke standing.

"So a convoy just like this one headed out to a remote pasture where you witnessed the execution of the previous commander of the base. And he was told that he had been posted to the Crisis Control Center? Bane told me he was posted there and was leaving immediately. Your friend was with him. Going to the same place most likely," said Tom.

"To their deaths," said Clarke angrily. "But you don't believe me do you!"

Clarke saw two soldiers leave the gate heading his way.

"Shit," said Clarke turning up his collar and walking rapidly across the street.

Hansen remained sitting as the two soldiers loped toward him like hunting wolves.

"Hey, how's it going?" said Tom smiling broadly.

Sergeant Alhoun didn't reply. Just another stupid American. He watched the other man head into the village. He looked at the photo again. It might be Clarke but he didn't get a good look. He motioned to the private to follow him.

Hansen stood and felt the butt of the forty five in its holster. He flipped into combat mode. The hunters would become the hunted.

Ahead he could see that Clarke was running out of time. So was he if he was going to save Bane. The soldiers were gaining. Just ahead a young man got into his car and started the motor. The next thing he knew he was lying on the street with Hansen's forty five in his face.

"I'm taking your car," said Hansen jumping in and closing the door.

He sped down the street and threw open the passenger door.

185

He pulled close to Clarke.

"Get in!" yelled Tom.

Clarke looked up in surprise but reacted well. Hansen watched the soldiers finally pulling out their pistols. There was a thump followed by a bang as they raced around a corner.

"The bastards shot the car. Good thing it's not mine. You OK?" asked Tom.

"Yes," replied Clarke looking at his clothes. "I thought I was done for."

"Those two looked like killers. Your story sounds true to me. We have to act fast to save our friends," said Tom.

"You believe me?" asked Clarke, surprised.

"A General I know told me a similar story," said Hansen. "Where are we going?"

"Right here then the next right again. If they are going to the same place we'll catch them before they get to the farm," said Clarke. "By the way, my name is Oliver Clarke."

"Tom Hansen, U.S. Marines, retired."

Clarke laughed nervously. "Marines to the rescue, ay?"

"Are you prepared for what we will have to do to save our friends?" asked Tom.

"What do you mean?" asked Clarke.

"I just arrived from the Med where I killed six criminals who were selling women into slavery. No loss. Then I killed a couple of pirates who were going to kill me and my friends. Self defense there. But this is different. We'll be killing members of the British army. It will be called murder if we are caught. Life in prison at least," said Hansen.

"Do we have to kill them?" asked Clarke surprised.

"Get real. How will a squad of heavily armed assassins react when we show up," said Tom.

"I hadn't really thought about it," said Clarke.

"I have to know where you stand before I make plans. I only have one gun. Once we start, there will be no stopping. You know that don't you?" said Tom.

"I do now. Sykes has been a good friend since school days. If a man won't stand with his friends, what good is he?" said Clarke.

"Good point. Do what I say when we catch them," said Tom looking ahead. "I smell diesel."

"There they are," said Clarke. "What now?"

"I'll just have to stop them on the road. The farm will be too late," said Tom.

Clarke was gripped with fear. "Ready." He was committed. What ever would happen would happen. Too late to stop. That

186

thought reduced the fear a little.

Hansen gained on the vehicles then stomped the gas pedal to pass. He pulled abruptly in front of the lead car and slammed the brakes. He was rear ended.

"Take out the driver!" shouted Tom jumping from the driver's seat.

"Sorry about that," said Hansen, smiling as he ran past the army car.

Jalal and his driver looked in surprise at the strange man running past the car. Then Jalal saw Clarke and pulled his pistol. Sykes saw his chance and jumped forward slapping the pistol down and grabbing Jalal by the neck. The driver stared in surprise then reached for his pistol as Clarke pulled the door open to attack him.

"What the hell are you doing, Sykes?" shouted Bane in confusion.

"Hi! How are you doing?" said Tom to the truck driver as he leaped up beside the cab. He threw the door open and fired twice. Pushing the driver inside, he put the truck in reverse and started it going slowly backward down the road. He jumped from the cab to see two confused faces peering around the rear canvas.

"Just a little fender bender," shouted Tom waving happily at the two confused men.

He ran back to the car as three shots rang out and glass from the windshield shot into the air. Hansen pushed the forty five past Clarke and shot the driver in the chest. He leaned farther inside and shot Jalal's brains into the ditch.

"Take his weapon and drive!" he shouted racing around to the passenger seat. He hurled Jalal into the ditch and jumped in. "Go, go, go!"

Clarke pulled the driver out and jumped in. He was breathing hard and shaking as he got the car moving.

"I'm not good at this," said Clarke.

"If this was a regular war, you'd get a medal. You did good," said Tom starting to chuckle.

Clarke and Sykes joined in.

"Good god, Hansen! What have you done?" exclaimed Bane in shock. "You'll hang for sure."

"He saved your life Bane," said Sykes. "I won't forget this."

"What are you talking about?" asked Bane.

Sykes gave him the whole story then turned to Hansen. "What now?"

"We have to ditch this car. Is there anywhere safe in this whole country?" asked Tom.

"My home isn't too far. We can take the Rolls. Jaguar if you feel like slumming it," offered Bane. "You look like hell, Clarke. Maybe I should drive."

*****

An hour later Bane spoke up. "Almost home. The entrance is just ahead."

Hansen woke up and studied the driveway. Three military trucks rolled down the driveway and were almost to the main road.

"Keep going. Don't pull in," said Tom. "Do you usually have military vehicles on your property?"

Bane looked ahead. "No."

"We have to scout the house then. Can you park where we can approach unseen?" asked Tom.

"Sure. I know just the place," said Bane.

They turned down a side lane. Parked. And headed toward the mansion on foot. They crouched in the bushes with a view of the side of the house. Three cars and one army truck were parked in front. Fresh mounds of dirt filled the extensive garden area in back.

"Mother is going to be angry when she catches these bastards. Look what they've done to the garden!" hissed Bane.

They heard an engine rev up as the last truck disappeared down the driveway. In the silence of the garden they could hear voices crying out in the basement.

"What's in there?" asked Tom pointing to the double doors in the basement that faced directly towards them.

"Gardening supplies. Tools. That kind of thing," said Bane.

Automatic weapons fire sounded on the other side of the double doors. Then the flash of a strobe light. Eight times. Two single shots followed. They waited.

The doors opened and three soldiers appeared pushing wheel barrows. On each barrow, two corpses dripped a trail of blood on the fine gravel walkway. Hansen pointed at two of the soldiers then at Bane and Sykes. He made a slash across his neck. They nodded. When the soldiers passed, Hansen lead them out, knife in hand. They attacked from behind. Hansen finished them and pointed at the double doors. They entered to see a sergeant filling out some paper work. Two more bodies lay in a pool of blood. The smell of urine and excrement was strong.

"Dump these two and we're done for today," said the sergeant absently, not bothering to look up until Bane was right in front of

188

him.

"What in bloody hell is going on here!" shouted Bane into his face.

The sergeant flinched and stood seeing the two officers. His momentary confusion turned to a decision as he reached for his pistol. Sykes was quicker and shot his brains out against the wall.

"So trucks come in and wheel barrows go out," said Hansen motioning to the the bodies on the floor.

"Someone is running a death camp," said Clarke.

"They don't take prisoners. We won't either," said Bane.

Hansen passed out the three SA80s leaning against the wall. He handed his forty five to Clarke. "Watch our backs. Remember, shoot first and don't ask any questions."

"Follow me," said Bane heading up the stairs.

They listened to the sounds of men talking on the main floor. Hansen peeked into the room and then ducked down. "Five visible. Maybe three in the next room."

The four men burst up the stairs into the house running from room to room firing as they went. Surprise was total. It ended quickly. Bane heard a car door slam and led the way to the front of the house. Two cars were starting to move. A spray of bullets shattered their windshields. The cars rolled to a stop. Silence filled the grounds. They returned to the house to see Clarke firing up the ceremonial staircase. A body rolled down the stairs stopping in front of Bane. Hansen nodded his approval.

"I'm getting the hang of this," said Clarke weakly.

"We have to do a room to room search. Then we can rest," said Tom. "Bane, you lead."

*****

After dinner, Bane stood staring out at the garden. Sykes cleaned up. Hansen checked out the weapons. Clarke sat in front of a computer.

"Check this out," shouted Clarke.

He turned the screen as the others gathered around.

"They photographed each victim. Before and after. It's a who's who of the blue bloods. It's a very long list. If I was to guess, I'd say that Bane here is the last member of the aristocracy left alive," said Clarke.

"What of my mother, father, sisters?" asked Bane.

"I'm sorry, Bane. They are all in here," said Clarke nodding at the screen.

"Damn! Damn them all to hell," said Bane turning to look into the gardens.

"Mass graves. We can give them all a decent burial later," said Tom.

"Prepare yourselves for a shock. See those lights and the TV camera in the library? I recognized the room from the King's speech ordering us all to obey lawful authority. It was either recorded or broadcast live from your house, Bane," said Clarke.

"So the King is ..."

"Dead. The entire dynasty is buried in your garden," answered Clarke. "I wanted our feudal system to disappear, but not like this."

"Kings and dictators must be killed for any coup to succeed," said Tom. "It was a long and successful run. From the Norman invasion until now. Almost a thousand years."

"My god. The King is dead, long live the .... who?" asked Sykes. "It feels strange to have no royal family. Like a boat without a rudder."

"You'll get used to it," said Tom. "We've done very well for ourselves without a monarchy."

"This isn't America," said Sykes.

"Don't I know it," replied Tom.

Clarke slammed his hand on the table.

"We now have proof about the murders all across England. We can expose them," said Clarke happily. "But there is more! There is a complete lists of targets. One file tells who has been killed. The master list tells us who is still a target. I'm on this list. So are you, Bane. Sykes, you were added two days ago. There are lots of others. I know from personal experience what it's like to be on somebody's death list. When they know they are targeted, it will damn well motivate them to fight back!"

"Finally, a break," said Tom.

"I'll send the evidence to everyone in the country," said Clarke. "This will turn the tide in our favor. It must! Or all is lost!"

"We could probably escape on my boat if we left right now. If we stay, there is no turning back. It's a fight to the death," said Tom.

"It already is. I'm in," said Sykes.

"Me, too," said Clarke.

"I'm not about to walk away from this," said Bane nodding toward the garden.

"Then here's a toast," said Tom pouring. "To the bitter end!"

They drained their glasses.

The telephone rang. Hansen hoisted the SA80 and came fully alert. He scanned the front yard. Nothing moved. The frost on the grass was undisturbed. Clarke was face down on the computer desk, exhausted. Bane turned over on the couch ignoring the interruption of his sleep. Sykes picked up the phone.

"Yes?" said Sykes. "I'm Captain Sykes. There's only four of us. Yes, he is. Bane, it's for you."

"Can't you see I'm sleeping you dolt! Take a message," said Bane turning again.

"It's important. It's Admiral Sommerville's aide. The Admiral wants to talk to you," said Sykes. "He's coming, sir."

Hansen tipped the couch.

"Bastard," said Bane collecting himself from the cold floor and shooting Hansen a deadly look.

Bane took the phone. "Yes, this is Lieutenant Bane .... Yes, it's true. All of it. I've seen it for myself ... Dead ..... He's dead ..... she's dead ..... they're all dead. The back garden is a ruin of mass graves. Plus one of my mates witnessed a colonel being executed. I was next. Me and Captain Sykes. They had orders for us to report to the Crisis Control Center. We'd have got the chop a few miles down the road ....   Very good sir ..... Yes of course .... Goodbye."

Bane put down the phone and walked to the window. "He called me milord."

"You are now the Duke of Warford," said Sykes.

"By murder! Look at the bloody garden! My parents are out there. Most of the people I've known are out there. All the girls I was going to shag at Ascot are out there. In that freezing muck!" shouted Bane.

Clarke stirred at the desk. "What did the Admiral say? Did he believe you?"

"Yes, he and dad were friends. He's known me since I was a lad. He's on his way with a forensic team and at least a company of marines. He got the message and has ordered everyone else to sit tight until he gets here and verifies our story," said Bane.

"When?" asked Sykes.

"He's sailing for Bristol bay from Scotland and will get here as soon as he can. He said an advance party of marines will arrive tomorrow sometime," replied Bane.

"The sooner the better," said Clarke.

"This is good news. If the navy is on our side we have an even chance. The more fellow traitors the better," said Tom.

"What do mean traitors? No one is more loyal than I am," said Sykes indignantly.

"Loyal to what? To who? Parliament? We have exposed the coup. Exposed the puppet prime minister and the Muslim Directorate. You will be taking on the elected government of England. Necessarily by force. We are headed for civil war," said Tom.

"So be it! I swear on my family's graves that heads will roll!" said Bane.

*****

Anwar Saidi sat down and convened the meeting. "What have you come up with?"

Abu Alhasan spoke. "The navy is refusing to supply us and we haven't got control of them yet. That leaves only one large fuel depot left in England that we can tap."

"Why is the navy not cooperating?" asked Saidi.

"Because they know the truth," said Farouk Aziz striding in from the doorway. "One trouble maker who eluded us stumbled upon the operation at Middlebourne Manor last night. He found the mass graves and the death list. He's been sounding the alarm all night. Admiral Sommerville and every surviving officer are conspiring against us as we speak. Sommerville has ordered everyone he can to wait for further orders from him pending an investigation."

"Sommerville? Why isn't he dead? He was high up on the list," asked Saidi frowning.

"He was aboard his flagship with his officers Christmas eve. A party. He must have heard something that worried him. We haven't been able to get past his security," replied Aziz.

"His family?" asked Saidi.

"With him on vacation," replied Aziz.

"We must take advantage of his order to wait. We'll retake the initiative. Recapture the estate and move the evidence. We can still shift the blame where we want it," stated Saidi.

"If we got there before him, it would still take too much time. And if caught by his marines it would mean open warfare," said Aziz.

"Which we are not ready for because you still haven't secured the fuel we need," said Saidi turning to Alhasan angrily.

"There is enough fuel for our needs at RAF Fairford," said Alhasan.

"Then what are you waiting for!" demanded Saidi.

"The Americans are still there. They control it. They have been moving their NATO personal through there as a refueling and transport point. You know the order about Americans," said Alhasan.

"We are into the new year. NATO is dissolved. Why haven't they packed up and left?" demanded Saidi.

"I don't know for sure. Their president was supposed to be there for the big NATO closing ceremony. It was canceled because of the crisis," said Alhasan. "The strike force could easily take the base if you ordered it."

"Of course, it could. If it had the fuel to maneuver," said Saidi.

Alhasan shrugged.

"Farouk, you contact the Americans and ask them for the fuel. Offer to buy it. Americans will do anything for money. If that doesn't work, come up with a strategy to take it by force. Meanwhile, I'll speak to Najid personally about this."

*****

The Bristol marina was quiet and peaceful. Jane Hansen was finishing her breakfast aboard the Constitution when her mobile rang.

"Hello?"

"It's Tom."

"Where are you? Why didn't you call? I've been worried sick since yesterday. You said you would be right back!" said Jane angrily.

"Bane got into some trouble. I couldn't involve you in a potential murder rap until I knew where things were going," said Tom. He told her what had happened.

"You made this discovery and you aren't doing anything with it yet?" asked Jane.

"Sommerville is taking over and he'll be here soon," replied Tom.

"Soon isn't good enough. You've been out scooped. The press

is already announcing the find of bodies at Middlebourne Manor. And again it is the work of you racist traitors," said Jane. "By the time Sommerville finishes his investigation all this will be old news. Minds will be set against you. You have to tell your story now! And I mean right now or it will be too late! In the absence of other information, people believe the first thing they hear. And there is an unfortunate but true corollary. He who lies first wins!"

"I can't do anything about it. I have a bigger problem to solve. Stay with the boat and sail for America if you have to. I'll call when I can. I love you."

The line went dead. Jane gathered some things. Tom couldn't do anything about the situation, but she could. He had committed himself. So could she. The crew were on deck. She explained what Tom had told her.

"I have to go to Middlebourne Manor and meet with Admiral Sommerville. I can make a difference there. But I want you to stay with the boat and sail for America if you have to. I'll call when I can. I love you guys," said Jane giving them each a hug.

Wisdom went below and put a forty five and an extra clip in his knapsack. "I am going to Middlebourne also. Will you travel with me?"

*****

Najid entered the meeting room briskly. His full staff was present. The air was strained.

"Well?" asked Najid.

"Saidi called. He is worried. The navy is turning against him. He needs fuel right away to stop them," said Hamdar.

"We all need fuel and we already lost a tanker trying to help him. He must succeed with what he has on hand," said Najid.

"He's desperate. He wants your permission to take it from an American air base by force if necessary," said Hamdar.

"No! Out of the question!" said Najid slamming his fist on the table. "No force against the Americans. Period. Make that very clear, Hamdar."

Hamdar nodded.

"Was there something you wanted to add, Asim?" asked Najid settling himself down.

"Yes. General Salazar landed by boat near La Caruna four days ago. He was able to hide his operation until he was ready to strike. Yesterday five cities rose up against us along with Galicia, Asturias, and some adjoining territory. All the military posts in that region are now with him," said Asim.

"You know the standing order. Why is he alive?" asked Najid.

"It's very hard to kill a military man who knows he is a target," shrugged Asim.

"General Salani, what can you do right now?" asked Najid.

"I have drawn up plans to attack the Galicia region and end this threat," replied the General.

"Why not attack the cities where Salazar isn't. Surely that would be easier," asked Najid.

"Loyalty is a delicate matter right now. Ordering Spanish soldiers to attack their own cities, their own people, is risky. Many would go over to the other side making things harder. If we attack a denounced criminal, a condemned enemy of the people, I will be able to keep the army together while we are still vulnerable. Also, this uprising is the work of a single man, not a movement or organization. When he is silenced the others will likely give up," said Salani.

"I believe the General is correct. Remove one man and the rest will fall," said William Hamadi. "Let Salani move his troops to Galicia and I will stop the uprisings in the other cities."

"How?" asked Najid in surprise.

"Television is a very powerful weapon when you know how to use it," said Hamadi smugly.

*****

Clarke put down the phone.

"The army has put together a strike force to stamp out resistance but it's low on fuel. It can't move very far to fight."

"How can that be? They are the military," said Tom.

"Apparently you missed the scandal. Some bad eggs sold military fuel supplies on the black market. Got filthy rich at it. The military is hurt. Civilians have it worse. We're being rationed but there isn't enough fuel to bother. OPEC joined with the Muslim Directorate in the fight with the EU and slashed fuel shipments drastically," said Sykes.

"This is good news. Their fuel problem gives us time to rally. Patton said he could have ended the war in 1944 if he'd gotten enough fuel," said Tom.

"And did he tell you that personally, old man. Or is it just another one of your limitless silly anecdotes," said Bane sarcastically.

"Behave yourself, Bane, or I'll come over there and box your ears," said Tom.

"All right children, let me get to the bad news. The strike force has found the fuel they need here, at Fairford," said Clarke pointing to a spot on the map.

"Fairford. Sounds familiar for some reason," said Bane.

Hansen started to speak then stopped.

"It's a refueling base currently controlled by the Americans. It has huge storage tanks and the Americans have agreed to sell half of their fuel supplies immediately and give the rest away when they leave," said Clarke.

"Bloody Americans," said Bane looking at Hansen.

"We have to stop them," said Tom.

"Good luck! All the air bases in England are connected by a pipeline system. They only have to open a few valves and turn on the pumps. It may be too late already," shouted Sykes from the dining room.

"It isn't too late. My source is in a critical position to help us. The plan to bugger the pipeline is already in motion. When the fuel doesn't flow they will send a convoy of tanker trucks," said Clarke. "The Admiral will arrive here tomorrow in force and then send his marines on to Fairford. But will he arrive in time to stop them?"

"We can't leave this to chance. We'll have to go to Fairford and make sure," said Tom.

"You and what army?" asked Bane.

"I have an idea," said Clarke.

Captain Oliva burst into General Salazar's barracks room. Salazar put down his razor and grabbed his pistol.

"Come quickly! You must see this," said Oliva urgently waving the General into the hall toward the television set. "Look! You are dead!"

Salazar stared in surprise. The footage showed soldiers storming a barracks and engaging in a firefight with the occupants. He turned up the volume.

"Early this morning, EU security police surrounded the hide out of the notorious criminal, General Ernesto Salazar. After a fierce gun battle, the General and all his followers were killed."

The TV showed a man who looked like Salazar being carried out and laid beside about twenty other bloody corpses.

"Since the General's death, NWN has confirmed that the uprisings that he instigated in Salamanca, Valencia, San Sebastian, Badajoz, and Cadiz are over. Those responsible have surrendered to military authorities ending the crisis. This is William Hamadi, NWN, reporting from outside La Caruna."

"But this isn't true. He is lying," said Salazar straightening his uniform.

"It's been broadcast non stop since early this morning," said Oliva.

"No one will believe him," said Salazar.

"I tried calling our supporters to reassure them. I can't reach anyone who is with us," replied Oliva flatly.

Salazar paused. The gravity of the situation hit him. He was dead and the uprising had no leader. He was losing everything without a shot being fired.

"Call my staff together immediately," said Salazar. "And get my car. No make it a convertible. I must show myself before Galicia surrenders around me!"

Leyhill was a clean looking place set in green rolling hills. It lacked the menace he normally associated with prisons. Clarke had said it was an open prison. He could hear Sykes arguing with the director.

"Damn it, I'm from the Crisis Control Center! I still have my transfer orders in my pocket to prove it. Look!" said Sykes handing over his transfer papers.

The director scanned them briefly and handed them back.

"You aren't the officers that came before," said the director.

"What do you mean before?" asked Clarke.

"The other officers that came for the Muslim prisoners. They were all transferred to London because of race problems in the prison. They told me not to trust anyone because anyone could fake the orders. It was very irregular but I went along with it because I wanted to do my bit for the crisis and they had the correct paper work," replied the director meaningfully.

Clarke looked at Hansen. "Probably recruited into their army. And I thought we were clever."

"You know who I am," interrupted Bane. "At least you knew my father. He is dead and now I am the Duke of Warford. Why would I be in league with traitors? Think man! I'm a peer of England!"

The Director paused.

"We need men for a work detail. They will be returned soon, you have my word on that. Working for the army will be a good experience," said Bane.

"You already have a community work release program. This is the same thing," said Clarke.

"All right. But you will have to sign something. A transfer to your custody at least," said the Director.

"Yes, of course. I'll sign right now," replied Bane. "We need about one hundred and fifty men."

The director nodded.

*****

The men shivered in a large group on the green lawn next to the main road. The cold wind had dropped to a breeze. Captain Sykes stood in front of Bane, Clarke, and Hansen.

"I am Captain Sykes. I need volunteers to help me fulfill my mission to protect England during this crisis. First, I want you men to line up fifteen wide and ten deep. Then I'll tell you what this is about."

The men moved slowly into position, muttering among themselves. Hansen moved down the side inspecting them.

"You've all heard about the crisis going on," started Sykes.

"Crisis? What crisis?" shouted a man in the back. The others laughed.

"Quiet in the ranks! And stand to attention!" shouted Bane.

"What? You think we're in the bleeding army?" shouted the man in the back. More laughter.

"That is precisely who I am looking for. Men willing to join the army and fight for their country in this moment of grave peril," said Sykes.

"What do we get out of this other than the grave you just mentioned? Fight. Ha! Not bloody likely," shouted the man in the back. The others grumbled their agreement.

Hansen zeroed in on the loud mouth. He tapped him on the shoulder.

The man turned. "What in bloody hell do you want?"

Hansen gave him a right to the jaw with everything he had. The man crumpled to the ground. Hansen picked four men he wouldn't trust with a gun.

"Take him back to his cell. Then you're all excused," said Hansen.

The four men took an arm or a leg, and made for the barracks. The other men weren't enthused.

"You mean fight with rifles. With real bullets? Like shoot somebody and maybe get shot?" asked a man in front.

"Yes. That is exactly what I'm saying," replied Sykes.

"What about the bleedin army? That's what you're for. For fighting and such. Not us," said another man.

Clarke stepped forward.

"This man is completely correct. It is the army's job to do the fighting for you. What you don't know is that most of the army has been taken over by enemies of England. Your England. We have all been lied to. There is no gang of racists sneaking about assassinating people."

"Who then?" asked another man.

"The Muslim Directorate is behind the assassinations. They now control parliament and most of the army. Anyone who could rally the country against them has been killed," said Clarke.

"So what can we do? Sounds like we have already lost. Who's going to lead us? We're a bunch of nobodies," said another man.

"Yeah, if this is all true why hasn't somebody said something on the tele. Where's the King in all this," asked another.

"The King is dead. Murdered. All the royals are dead. I and my companions discovered their bodies at Middlebourne Manor yesterday," said Clarke.

The men were silent. Listening now with their full attention. Clarke continued.

"This is a dark day in our history. A war is breaking out on English soil that will determine the future of this land and this people. Who will lead us you ask? Where are the Wellingtons, the Nelsons, the Montgomerys to lead us. We have none! We are in this fight because of a total failure of leadership in England and across Europe. Are we then defeated before we begin? I say no. Take heart! We don't need famous leaders. Englishmen have risen to the needs of history without failing. When the Spanish armada threatened our shores how many Spaniards did Drake kill? None. Common men like you and me did the killing. How many Frenchmen did Nelson kill at Trafalgar? None, the killing was done by common Englishmen many of whom were pressed men and prisoners like you. How many Frenchmen did Wellington kill at Waterloo? Again, none. The battle was fought and won by common soldiers. Did Monty shoot a rifle or a tank gun at El Alamein. No! Grandfathers that you have known, grew up with, fought and carried that day. This same fighting spirit lives on in each of us still. When we are called upon to fight. We fight. And we win."

The men muttered their agreement.

"We will not be fighting alone. Admiral Sommerville and his royal marines are heading here with all speed to win the day. But he will not get here in time. It has fallen to us. The men you see around you. We must meet the enemy and stop them until the marines arrive. Who will join Captain Sykes, Lieutenant Bane, and Sergeant Hansen and myself? Who will fight for England!" shouted Clarke.

The men cheered. Around a hundred of the men moved forward. Others moved toward the back. Hansen looked them over. It would be enough.

"Men with military experience, step forward. Everyone else remain in your rows. Those at the back who will not fight are excused to return to the prison," said Tom.

Ten men came forward while those at the back drifted away. Hansen looked at Sykes who nodded back.

"You are all now temporary sergeants. I want each of you to pick a squad of nine other men and line them up. You will report to me. I'll report to Lieutenant Bane. He will report to Captain

Sykes. Mr. Clarke is our special intelligence man. You know the drill. Carry on," said Hansen handing out the spare SA8os to his sergeants.

The confusion sorted itself into ten squads of ten. Captain Sykes stepped forward.

"Thank you men. We must act swiftly and decisively. The enemy is heading to RAF Fairford to capture the fuel there. If they do, they will control the country. Our job is to stop them long enough for reinforcements to come down from the north to turn the battle. We stop them there and we can drive them back to the sea and rescue our country."

Bane tapped his shoulder from behind.

"What now? We don't have any trucks or fuel," said Bane.

Clarke faced the men. "Raise your hand if you have ridden a horse."

A quarter of the men raised their hands.

"How many are willing to learn to ride today?" asked Clarke raising his own hand. The rest of the men slowly raised theirs.

*****

Embassy employee, David Polaski, put the envelope down next to Brent's hospital bed.

"Here is your new passport and some emergency funds from your parents," said Polaski.

"That was fast," said Brent.

"Yeah, we can really move along when we need to. I already arranged a flight home for you," said Polaski.

"First class, I hope," said Brent.

Polaski chuckled.

"Dream on, kid. Because of the fuel shortage, the wait to get home is a month long. A medical case like yours gets bumped up the list," said Polaski.

"With who? United or Delta?" asked Brent.

"Neither. You'll fly out courtesy of the Air Force from Fairford in two days. A bus is leaving from the embassy tomorrow. Be there early. Good luck," said Polaski.

"Thanks," said Brent shaking his hand.

He couldn't wait to tell Celia the good news. He was down to one crutch as he hurried to her room. He pulled up the chair where he had spent most of the last two days. He told her the news.

"Good for you, Yank. Now I can catch up on my sleep without interruption," said Celia sarcastically.

She saw the hurt expression on his face and regretted her words.

"Will you be out soon?" he asked. "You never told me why you were here?"

"Simple story. I had a miscarriage. My fiance threw me down a flight of stairs," she said.

"What a bastard," said Brent.

"He was using me to increase the Muslim population. Then he changed his mind and said he didn't need me any more. If I ever see him again he'll be sorry. His picture's in my purse. Bring me some matches so I can burn it," said Celia.

Brent got the photo and paused.

"Hey, I recognize him. He did this to me," said Brent pointing to his face.

"Then we'll kill him together," said Celia.

"Deal," said Brent shaking her hand.

He didn't let go. She didn't pull away. He made up his mind.

"Ever been to America?" he asked.

"No," she replied.

"Ever wanted to?" asked Brent.

"Not really. Anything special there?" asked Celia.

"Me," said Brent.

"You," said Celia.

She thought about her feelings. He was nice enough, maybe better than most. It had been obvious he wanted her since the day they had met. Farouk had paid the rent. That was over. She would be homeless as soon as she left the hospital. She'd been poor her whole life and knew that if she didn't make hard choices, they would be made for her.

"Are you sure you want me. After what has happened?" she asked.

"Absolutely sure. These last two days have been the happiest ever for me. Come with me, please," he begged.

"Alright," she replied.

*****

They marched eight miles in two files. Low gray clouds and lightly falling snow had turned the country side into an endless panorama of gray and white. Hansen looked back at the men.

"The French retreat from Moscow would have looked like this. Rag tag bands marching through the snow trying to get home," said Tom.

"There it is," said Clarke pointing to a side road ahead. "The final resting place of the Blues and Royals."

"What are they doing out here? I thought they pranced around London with the Royal family?" asked Tom.

"They did until the 'new' British complained that they were symbols of the oppression of colonialism. Symbols which still created mental anguish and pain. A greater London referendum voted them out of the city for good. They were put to pasture out here."

"It's a nice spot for horses," said Tom looking around.

They marched down a long driveway past four large stables toward the house at the end of the row. One military Rover was parked in front.

"Now what? How do we get the horses?" asked Bane.

"I thought we'd ask nicely," replied Clarke turning the door knob and stepping inside.

A young lieutenant with a blues and Royals emblem sat watching the tele with his boots on the desk.

"Who the hell are you!" snapped lieutenant Preston.

"We're here to requisition your horses. Lieutenant ....," said Captain Sykes, stepping forward.

"Preston, sir," replied Preston, standing and giving a sloppy salute. "I haven't received any notification about a requisition. And what would the navy be doing with our horses anyway."

"We're from the Crisis Command Center, a multi service command. We have a priority need for these animals immediately," said Bane waving his transfer papers in the air.

"If headquarters gives permission that's fine. I could care less about the horses actually. Being stuck out here in the middle of nowhere is no big honor. But you'll have to wait for clearance," said Preston reaching for the phone.

Hansen yanked the phone cord from the wall and lowered his SA80.

"What's plan B?" asked Tom turning to Clarke.

Clarke shrugged his shoulders. Hansen turned back to Preston.

"We can shoot you here and now or tie you up and leave you. Which would you prefer?"

"You can't do this," said Preston weakly, confused by the sudden turn of events.

"We have a hundred armed men outside. How many do you have?" asked Tom.

"One corporal and six locals to care for the horses," replied Preston slowly.

"We win. Where is the corporal?" asked Sykes.

"In town shopping," replied Preston, wide eyes staring up the barrel of the SA80.

"Bain, round up the local people and get them to saddle up the horses. I'll guard Preston," said Tom. "Where do you keep the shiny plates and hats?"

"The cuirass and helmets? They are in the storage building behind the saddle room," said Preston.

"Locked?" asked Hansen.

"Of course," said Preston.

"Grab your keys and lead the way.

One hour later, seventy men stood next to their horses, rifles and gloves courtesy of the Blues and Royals. A horse trailer was hitched to the Rover and the remaining men filled it with shovels and all the supplies that could be gathered.

"I'd like to lead the attack on the trucks. Bane, you're the best rider. You should come with me," said Tom.

"You'll need intel about the truck's route so I'd better come also," said Clarke.

Sykes looked disappointed. "That leaves me with the spare men."

"Go to Fairford. Use the tools to dig in. We'll meet you there tonight or tomorrow," said Tom. "That's where the real fight will be."

Clarke pointed to his map.

"I have spotters on three routes. It looks like they are taking this road here," said Clarke. "We can be at this intersection in three hours with thirty minutes to spare."

"If anyone gets separated we'll meet at Fairford, OK?" asked Hansen.

"Tomorrow then," said Sykes. The others nodded.

Bane jumped onto his horse. "Mount up, we're moving out!"

*****

Hansen stood behind the overturned tractor, listening. A man ran back around the sharp corner in the road.

"They're coming," he shouted.

Hansen turned to Clarke. "Stay with our horses. I need you to calm them and cover our retreat if things go wrong."

"Right," said Clarke heading into the woods beside the road.

Hansen heard the trucks approaching. It was dark and the light snowfall limited visibility. He took two men and walked beside the road ahead of the barrier. They took up firing positions on the bank overlooking the corner.

The tanker truck convoy was led by a Rover. It came down a

long straight slope and turned left around the blind corner. The driver saw the roadblock and stopped. Hansen had a clear shot into the passenger window and took it, firing repeatedly. The Rover rolled forward into the barrier as all his men began firing. This was the signal Bane was waiting for.

"Charge," he shouted, cantering out of the forest beside the road. He went to a gallop, firing into the line of trucks as he past them. Sixty riders followed him, firing into the trucks out of the darkness. Surprise was total. The convoy had lost its commander in the first seconds. The drivers didn't know what was going on and they had no orders. Out of instinct they tried to back up or leave the road altogether but they were too close together to maneuver. Some fired weapons into the darkness. Then the darkness was lit up as one truck caught fire.

Bane led his men to the end of the column and then galloped back down the other side. Three trucks had made a break across the opposite field. The ground was hard and frozen but the snow still made it slippery. The others weren't moving.

"Burn them," shouted Bane. "Burn them all!"

The frenzy of battle died down. Once again the falling snow deadened the sounds of the night. Bain led his cavalry back to Hansen's position.

"We showed them!" laughed Bane jumping off his horse.

Bane advanced on the four men sitting beside the road with their hands on their heads. Two others lay wounded. Bane raised his SA80. Hansen pushed it down gently.

"Who are these?" asked Bane.

"Prisoners," replied Hansen. "Did you take any?"

"Hell no," said Bane. "They all went to their better place. And so should these."

Four were dark. Two were fair. One with red hair.

"They are soldiers. Like us," said Hansen.

"Have you forgotten what they did to my parents? They don't deserve any better!" shouted Bain.

"Some of the army will come over to our side when they know what's going on. We have to wait until Sommerville joins us. Then we can gather all who are still loyal to our side. Meanwhile, I insist we take these men prisoners," said Hansen firmly.

"We can't take prisoners! What will we do with prisoners?" shouted Bain.

"This Rover still runs. We could detail two men to take the wounded to a hospital. Send the others to Middlebourne with any trucks not destroyed and let Sommerville sort them out. Then meet us at Fairford," said Hansen.

The blood lust was fading. Bain shouldered his rifle.

"Oh, very well," said Bane turning to his men. "Go out and gather up all the weapons you can. We're moving out in thirty minutes!"

Hansen looked on approvingly. Bane would be a good officer someday. With his guidance, of course.

Captain Sykes looked through his binoculars to see Bane leading the cavalry across a nearby pasture. They drifted out of the light snow looking tired and cold. Sykes had commandeered a warm pub for his men to spend the night. They were fresh. Sykes walked out to his friends.

Clarke pointed down one of the roads.

"They will be coming up that road. With tanks," said Clarke.

"I'll take my men and start digging in," said Sykes.

"About a mile down the road," suggested Hansen.

"Now I know why our ancestors only waged war in the summer," said Bane miserably.

"You all look like hell. How did it go," asked Sykes.

"Complete surprise. Total victory. One man dead. He was shot but I think it was falling off his horse that killed him," replied Bane.

"I have hot food and drink waiting over there," said Sykes pointing. "Otherwise I'll get started digging."

The cavalry moved on to breakfast. Hansen saw an American jeep parked nearby. A lieutenant and sergeant watched them. The sergeant was taking photos with a telephoto lens. Hansen wolfed down his breakfast and walked toward the jeep. He tried to look cheerful. Clarke followed.

"Hi. Could you spare some weapons this morning? We could really use some anti-tank rockets. Dragons would be good. Javelins would be better. How about it?" asked Hansen, smiling.

The medium brown lieutenant stared at Hansen in disbelief.

"Who the fuck are you?" asked Lieutenant Clayton.

"Tom Hansen, Sergeant, U.S. Marines, retired," said Hansen holding out his hand.

Clayton looked at Hansen's hand like it was fresh dog crap.

"It's obvious you're not English. Probably a clansman from Alabama. Am I right or am I right? So you're the racist militia group that we've been hearing about on the TV and radio. I've seen your kind all my life back in the states. The beady unintelligent eyes. The shifty criminal stoop. Help you? Go to hell you racist bastards. We've been told not to get involved. But if you try to get onto this base, we'll open fire. I've dreamed my whole life of getting into a firefight with you mother fuckers. So go ahead. Make my day!" said Clayton.

"We aren't a racist militia. Everything you're being told on the radio is untrue. We are patriots fighting to save this country from a coup and a return to the dark ages," replied Clarke angrily. "I believe the fate of England rests on what happens here today."

"Tough shit, asshole. I hope you get what you deserve. And that's six feet under. Remember what I said. Don't go near the base," said Clayton walking back to his jeep and driving away.

"What was his problem?" asked Clarke.

"Old wounds. The media blitz from the Muslim Directorate is punching his buttons. We won't get any help here," replied Hansen.

They mounted and found Sykes digging furiously under the road. Others were putting in trenches on a rise overlooking the road.

"What are you doing?" asked Bane.

"It's a tank trap, I hope," said Sykes, out of breath.

The cavalry dismounted and joined in the digging. The snow stopped around noon. Then two horsemen galloped up the road.

"They're coming," they shouted riding past.

"How long?" asked Sykes.

"Three miles back. Moving slowly," one replied.

"Take your positions!" shouted Bane.

The few men still digging put down their shovels and looked to their weapons. Sykes went to the middle trench works. Clarke to the rear. Hansen and Bane to the front.

*****

Farouk Aziz scanned the scene with his binoculars from the Rover. His view from the hill in the forest showed him the positions of his enemies. He only saw infantry with automatic rifles. Looking to the rear of the enemy position he paused. Could it be? Oliver Clarke? Yes it was him. He smiled. It was going to be a good day. He would get the fuel and kill the man who had exposed his operation at Middlebourne.

"You may send in the tanks, colonel. And get some mortar fire on that last trench. The one by that sign post. I see an old friend who needs a wake up call," said Aziz smugly.

The officer spoke into his radio.

*****

Sykes could hear them before he could see them. The rattle of tank diesels approaching. A challenger tank appeared on the road followed by two others. Infantry gave close support. The lead tank's gun was depressed to fire when the road gave way beneath it. The front of the tank dropped, the barrel dug into the road jamming it. As the lead tank tried to reverse out of trouble, the two following tanks left the road and spread out. Mortar rounds began falling.

"Fire," shouted Sykes.

His men opened up. Bullets did nothing to the tanks. It did force the infantry to bunch up behind them.

Two tanks advanced in a wide line. They opened up with canon fire. Clarke watched the men start firing ahead of him in fascination. It seemed unreal until the mortars hit.

"Now!" shouted Sykes into his mobile.

Hansen popped out of the snow and fired almost point blank at the men behind the tanks. Others popped up throwing paint balloons at the tank sensor arrays and viewers. Still others followed with Molitov cocktails. Then they all fired at the infantry.

The soldiers that survived the initial onslaught returned fire as they ran for their lives. The tanks fired machine guns blindly, then began to retreat. They would have to be able to see to continue the fight. The lead tank got another round of molitovs. It's crew suddenly tried to abandon the vehicle. Two got away. Two didn't.

Hansen dropped a molitov into the hatch then jumped down.

"Fall back to the second trench!" shouted Hansen running.

The infantry had recovered and were increasing their fire. That and the mortars were taking their toll. Wounded men hobbled and crawled to the rear. Hansen and Bane jumped into the middle trench next to Sykes who directed the covering fire. The sound of helicopter blades was heard over the din of battle. Hansen searched the skies below the low clouds.

"Now we're really fucked. We were lucky to stop the tanks. We have nothing to stop helicopters. We can't hide from them. We have to retreat!" shouted Hansen.

"Go ahead. Run away. I'm staying to the end with any one who will fight with me!" replied Bane angrily.

"Use your head. We're beaten. We still have time to get to the horses and ride out of here. This is only one battle. We haven't lost the war. We will live to fight another day. Think about the future," yelled Hansen.

"If they win here I have no future!" shouted Bane ducking his head.

"Damn you! OK. We'll fall back to the fuel storage area and make a stand there. They can't fire missiles or they will set the fuel on fire. Now will you retreat with me?" demanded Hansen.

Bane slapped him on the shoulder and began running back to the horses. The survivors followed as best they could while Clarke and his reserve men gave covering fire.

Hansen grabed Sykes. "Take Clarke and all the wounded you can and head for Middlebourne Manor. Find Sommerville and keep fighting. Bane and I will make a stand at the fuel depot."

They all mounted up and headed for the Fairford base. Suddenly, a break in the low clouds showed two attack helicopters circling overhead.

"Oh shit!" said Hansen to himself as Bane led the men toward the base.

He looked back to see the helicopters turn and follow as they assessed the battle field and searched for targets. Hansen could see a post of marine sentries watching in surprise as the mounted men thundered toward them. The helicopters behind opened up with 30mm chain guns on the stragglers. The marines ahead raised their weapons. Hansen fired over their heads to get them to take cover. His men thundered over the marines taking fire and giving it while the Apache Longbows began their business.

The pilots couldn't tell friend from foe in the mass of moving men. Two missiles took out the marine post. Hansen led his men behind the fuel bunkers and jumped from his horse. He looked for cover and began firing at the Apaches. The men rallied to him and added their fire. Bain led a second group of men fifty meters away. The helicopters broke off the attack and began circling.

"If we can't save this fuel we have to burn it!" shouted Hansen.

Hansen ran to the nearest valve and began turning it. The others followed suit. Finally, one of the men got some fuel to gush out. Hansen ran over, closed the valve, and handed the man his lighter.

"What's your name?" asked Hansen.

"Malcom," replied the man.

"If we can't hold them I want you to turn this valve all the way and light the fuel on fire. Got it? Wait for my signal," shouted Hansen.

The rattle of tank diesels approaching spoiled his sense of

relief. Two tanks came into sight, badly scorched, but with machine guns blazing. A line of infantry followed in support.

"Uh, sergeant, take a look at that," said the man beside him pointing to the rear.

Four Bradly fighting vehicles were rolling down the runway heading their way.

"Do we shoot at the Americans also?" asked the man.

"Bane!" yelled Hansen pointing to the rear.

Bane looked and nodded. "To the death!"

Bane saluted. Hansen returned it.

"Is it as bad as that?" asked the man next to him.

"Listen up!" shouted Hansen. "The soldiers with the tanks do not take prisoners. If you are captured alive you will be executed. Do you understand me?"

His men looked up at him in shock.

"I didn't sign up for this," shouted one of the men.

"But you're here. You have no choice but to fight. Fight for England. Fight for the future. Fight for your very lives!" shouted Hansen.

Hansen was going to tell them to crawl toward the Americans if they were wounded, but that would only give them the idea that they could survive this battle. Desperate men were more dangerous. He ducked down as the bullets began to whiz over his head again.

The men fought with the desperate courage of those who were trapped and had no choice. One by one they fell, unmoving, to the withering enemy fire. The sound of helicopter blades came to him again. We are out of time thought Hansen.

"Malcom," shouted Hansen. He made a turning motion with his hand.

Malcom nodded and began turning the valve. The smell of kerosene filled the air. Hansen could see the enemy helicopters lining up behind the tanks and now he heard more helicopters coming from the fog bank behind him. More helicopters? We won't survive this day.

"Light it!" shouted Hansen.

Malcom raised the lighter and saw his hand turn into a cloud of crimson as a bullet passed through it. He fell to the ground screaming. Hansen crawled toward him. He searched the snow. Where was the damn lighter? He flattened himself to the ground as the sound of a missile passed overhead. Then two, three, four, five, six more. He felt the explosions through the earth and some of the heat from the air. He grabbed Malcom.

"Where is the lighter!" demanded Hansen searching in the

snow.

Malcom looked at him in pain and pointed toward the tanks. Hansen rolled quickly, bringing his SA80 to bear. He looked in time to see one of the Apaches falling to the ground in a ball of flame. The other was no where in sight. Both tanks were on fire. This time the turrets were blown off. Four choppers passed overhead. It was the Navy! Sommerville had arrived!

The sound of gunfire faded into the distance. Hansen stood up and turned off the fuel valve. He could see a line of British marines marching from the south through the pastures firing at stragglers and gathering prisoners while the choppers circled overhead.

*****

Farouk Aziz's smile of victory turned to a gasp of horror as he saw his tanks and helicopters destroyed before his eyes. He scanned the marines advancing onto the battle field. Only a few of his men now stood between him and the enemy. His tanker trucks were trapped.

"We've lost!" shouted Aziz in disbelief.

"They will capture us if we stay here!" shouted the colonel.

Aziz reacted quickly. "Retreat."

"Retreat! All units retreat!" shouted the colonel into his radio.

"Go, go, go!" shouted Aziz to the driver.

They sped toward the forest track where they had watched the start of the battle. Another Rover followed. Aziz looked back to see that no one else followed. It was a total disaster.

*****

Bane approached Hansen.

"You fought well today," he said slowly.

"Me?" laughed Hansen slapping him on the back. "I was ready to cut and run. It was your stubbornness that kept me here. You're going to go down in history for this. I know. I'm a history professor!"

The survivors gathered around laughing and grinning, lucky to be alive. One of the choppers set down nearby.

"It's Sommerville," said Bane advancing to meet him. "Just in time, sir. Another few minutes and it would have been over."

"Glad you made it, Bane. Quite a firefight. Took longer than I hoped to get into position. But then we had them didn't we!" said Sommerville with enthusiasm.

A second chopper landed. Clarke and Sykes hopped out.

"Good job, boys," said Hansen embracing them. "We were about to go down like the Seventh Cavalry until you showed up."

"You've all done splendidly! Right down the line," said Sommerville to the group. "Sorry about your parents, Bane. I was shocked at what we found at Middlebourne. Your evidence has convinced me that the government is involved in outright murder. No telling who is involved. Or who I can trust."

"No one who has any power or standing with parliament can be trusted. It's now completely controlled by the Muslim Directorate," said Clarke.

"I am coming to the same conclusion," replied Sommerville. "That is why I have invited all loyal officers that are left to Middlebourne Manor. To view the evidence for their own eyes and to hold a council of war. I want all of you there as well."

"Yes, sir," replied Sykes.

"Sir, I'd like to return to Middlebourne to help with the forensics. I know a lot of the people buried there. I can help identify them," asked Bane.

"Of course, Bane. It is your home after all. You're entitled to pick your post after what you did here today. Carry on lad," replied Sommerville warmly.

"One more thing," said Bane. "My men are prisoners from Leyhill. I promised them pardons if they fought for me."

"Of course. They earned it. Captain Sykes, why don't you take command of these irregulars along with ..."

"Sergeant Hansen," replied Tom.

Sommerville's eyebrow shot up at the accent but he made no comment.

"Very good. Carry on," said Sommerville turning to talk to an approaching Marine Captain.

Hansen let out a sigh of relief. He turned to look at Fairford. The US marines had taken up firing positions next to their vehicles. Hansen waved. Lieutenant Clayton gave him the finger. The sun broke through, blinding him as he surveyed the field. Red patches were in stark contrast to the dazzling white of the snow. Sykes organized his men and the wounded. Clarke and Hansen strode toward the tanks for a look.

"Aziz got the first of what I hope are many surprises. He was leading the attack," said Clarke.

"Who?" asked Tom.

"My counterpart in the Muslim Directorate. Intelligence director. Chief assassin. All around bad hat. He shot me a while back in Hyde park. In my calf," said Clarke pointing to his leg.

"Hopefully he was killed today."

"His kind always finds a way to survive. I saw two Rovers make a get away to the east. Probably him," said Tom looking absently at the charred torso laying under the tank turret.

"It's so quiet here now," said Clarke.

"Yes, always is after a battle. You don't notice how loud it is until it stops," said Tom.

"This is my fourth gun battle. Each one has been bigger and more desperate than the last. I hope this was my last one," said Clarke.

"I hope so too. You are too valuable to use as cannon fodder. It was your information that made this victory possible. Where to intercept the convoy last night. Where the enemy would attack from today. What weapons they had. It made all the difference. One more rifleman wouldn't have mattered," said Tom.

Clarke nodded appreciatively.

"To quote an old movie, with my brains and your good looks we'll go far," said Tom.

They laughed. Then stopped when eight US marines came suddenly from around the tank.

"Cuff them," said Lieutenant Clayton smugly.

"What the hell are you doing, man!" shouted Clarke as he was manhandled.

Hansen said nothing to the barrel of the M16 in his face.

"This is outrageous! I demand that you contact Admiral Sommerville immediately!" shouted Clarke.

Lieutenant Clayton nodded to the marine in front of Clarke who jammed his rifle butt in Clarke's face.

"The battle's over. We won. Why are you doing this?" asked Tom as the cuffs closed behind him.

"I took your photos and contacted Interpol. Looks like you racist pieces of shit are wanted men. They sent us an arrest order. And since America is a member of Interpol, we're arresting you in the name of the law. We're going to send you to Brussels for trial. You're toast, you fucking bastards!" said Clayton, joining in the beating.

Hansen went down and tried to protect his head.

*****

Farouk Aziz sat in the dark on the outskirts of Wantage. There had been no sign of pursuit. He got out of the Rover and dialed his mobile.

"What news?" asked Saidi.

"Bad. We overpowered a small militia but then Sommerville arrived in force. I was lucky to escape with two Rovers," said Aziz.

"And your men?" asked Saidi.

"All lost. Sommerville has the fuel at Fairford and the evidence at Middlebourne Manor. You must give me command of the whole strike force. I can still achieve our objectives!" demanded Aziz.

"You no longer inspire my confidence, Farouk. You have lost Middlebourne Manor and two tanker convoys. If you lost the strike force as well we would lose all of England in one day!" said Saidi.

"I have a man inside Sommerville's staff. All our enemies are meeting at Middlebourne Manor tonight. If we mobilize immediately I can re-capture the fuel and move on to seize all our enemies at Middlebourne. One bold stroke and this fight is won!" insisted Aziz.

"Return to headquarters. You will now assist Alhasan in securing new fuel supplies to make up for your failure. I will convince Najid that now is the time and the place to use the Marseilles. Out," said Saidi.

Aziz snapped his mobile phone shut angrily. Attacking Middlebourne was obvious. Any good leader would have seen this. Saidi wasn't up to the job. He would return to headquarters and bide his time. Saidi's days were numbered. He held up his hand then looked at the trees. Checking the wind direction.

*****

Brent stepped off the bus inside the Fairford main gate. It was late. The long detour due to road repairs hadn't helped. Why the army would be doing road repairs in the middle of winter was a mystery. Just another English quirk that reminded him he was in a foreign land. The guard at the gate took his paperwork.

"Your flight leaves at four am. You're expected at the officer's mess. Plenty of couches there to sleep on till you are roused at three for pre-flight. Here's a map," said the guard handing Brent a hand sketch of the base.

"Thanks, man. You don't know how glad I am to be going home," said Brent.

"I hear you. England used to be the safest posting you could get. But just this afternoon there was a firefight at the edge of the base. Tanks, helicopters, missiles, and a lot of casualties. It wasn't an exercise, either. Lot a shit's happening around us. Too much. Go that way," said the guard pointing.

Brent headed into the base. After a while he stopped under a light to check his map. He didn't pay attention to the banging sound until he heard the sound of breaking glass. There was a face at a small high window waving at him. Curiosity took him to the space between two buildings.

"Brent! Brent! Over here!" said a voice.

What the...?

"It's me, Tom Hansen!" whispered Tom.

"Professor Hansen. What are you doing here? Why are there bars on the window?" asked Brent.

"We were arrested. Oliver Clarke is here with me," replied Hansen.

"Oh shit. They caught you with those bodies!" said Brent.

Clarke appeared, clinging to the bars.

"That's just the beginning of the trouble we're in," said Clarke.

"What can I do?" asked Brent.

"Sykes?" asked Hansen.

"We don't know where he went and Brent wouldn't know how to find him. It has to be Bain," said Clarke.

"You have to get to Edmund Bane at Middlebourne Manor. He'll figure out what to do. He owes me big time," said Hansen.

"Where do I go and how do I get there?" asked Brent.

"Clarke can tell you how to get there. Steal a car. We're being moved in the morning. Probably to a place of execution," said Hansen.

"Like those officers!" said Brent.

"Exactly like them," said Clarke. "Our lives are in your hands."

Brent memorized the directions and then headed for the gate. The guard looked up with a question on his face.

"I'm headed into town. It's my last chance to get laid in England," he said cheerily.

"Good luck, kid. Just be back by three am," said the guard.

Brent walked into the village of Fairford looking for a car to steal. He'd miss the flight home. But there was a silver lining. He could stay with Celia until her passport was ready and they could go to America together.

*****

"It's time," said Mouti.

Bery looked at the sonar man, Danzai.

"Still nothing," said Danzai from the sonar station.

"Very good. Make radio depth and extend the antenna." said

216

Bery.

"Yes sir," replied Mouti.

*****

"They are coming up again, sir," said Moeller.

"Mr. Blanchard, all ahead full," said Thomas. "We're going to park ourselves right above them from now on. Let them try something sneaky then."

Hampton and the others smiled.

*****

"Captain, a fast ship is making straight for us. I think it's the same one I heard three days ago," said sonar chief Danzai.

"Maintain speed. Come left ninety degrees," said Bery evenly.

The helmsman nodded. They waited in silence.

"The ship is changing course to intercept," said Danzai.

"How could this be! We out maneuvered the Americans at every pass. Nobody could follow us!" said Bery angrily.

"You have forgotten that Americans are treacherous," said Mouti evenly. "They lied to you. They found you in the maneuvers but didn't admit it."

Bery began to pace, clearly unnerved by this conclusion.

"Orders?" asked Mouti.

"Increase speed. Come right forty five degrees. Climb to radio depth," commanded Bery.

Mouti smiled in agreement, releasing the pistol in his pocket.

*****

"They leveled off. No wait. They are climbing again and increasing speed, sir. Course change also," said Moeller.

"Sound battle stations, Mr. Hampton," said Thomas.

"Yes, sir. They may hear our sirens," said Hampton.

"Just one more thing to keep them off balance," said Thomas.

"Sir, I'm picking up some frequency spikes way above the background," said Smith from the radio panel.

"Direction?" asked Thomas.

"East, sir," replied Smith.

"Have decoding get on it with everything they have," said Thomas.

"Aye, aye, sir," replied Smith.

"Has the forward gun checked in yet?" asked Thomas.

"Yes, sir," replied Hampton.

"Have them fire three shots near where the Marseilles is expected to surface. We want to keep their heads down until we get there," said Thomas.

"Yes sir," smiled Hampton.

*****

"Explosions on the surface. Three of them. Ahead of us," said Danzai.

"It's clear now. They mean to stop us," said Bery.

"Not if we act first. We have torpedoes in the aft torpedo room, do we not?" said Mouti.

"That would be an act of war. It might bring the Americans into the fight for Europe," warned Bery. "You know the rules of engagement regarding Americans."

"We have already launched one nuclear weapon. We are at war already, are we not?" said Mouti. "We have detected only one ship. The Americans did nothing about the Liberty. They won't change policy over one more lost warship. I am certain of this. Besides, we don't know that this is an American."

"Out here this far it would only be British, Russian, or American. And not much chance of it being British or Russian right now," said Bery.

"We are soldiers. We must destroy everyone who stands in our way," said Mouti.

"The Marseilles was built to hide, not fight. If we can not hide we are beaten. I'm not going to throw my life away and the lives of this crew in a hopeless gesture. Not while I'm in command," said Bery angrily.

The bang was loud in the confined space. Bery fell to the deck. He looked in surprise at his lifeblood pouring out of his chest.

"You are relieved. You were never really one of us. Not fully," said Mouti.

Bery looked up at Mouti and died.

"Does anyone else feel like Mr. Bery?" asked Mouti.

The control room was silent.

"Good. Climb to one hundred meters and load fore and aft torpedo tubes. Turn to course 225 degrees. We're going to hunt the Americans," said Mouti, pocketing Bery's missile launch key.

*****

"That's funny," said Chief Yablonski. "I think I heard a bang

218

coming from the Marseilles."

"Trouble?" asked Thomas.

"I don't know," replied Yablonski.

"They are climbing and turning toward us, sir," said Moeller.

"An attack?" asked Hampton.

"As sure as if they were waving a sign," replied Thomas. "Their captain is reducing my options."

"Stand bye countermeasures," said Hampton.

"Sir, priority message from CINCLANT. Captains eyes only," said Smith.

"Give me a printout here and now, Mr. Smith,"

Smith handed over the message. Thomas read it silently and handed it to Hampton.

"Break off immediately and head for home? What the hell?" asked Hampton.

"Smith, hold off on the reply. We're busy right now. I want you to break out the code book and have the slowest midshipman on board decode it," said Thomas.

"Yes, sir," replied Smith.

"Fish in the water. One. Now two," cried Yablonski.

"Hard to starboard, ninety degrees, Mister Blanchard. Ahead full," said Thomas. "Launch countermeasures."

The countermeasures fell behind providing sound and motion to attract the torpedoes.

"The Marseilles is continuing to the surface," said Moeller. "Sir."

"Are they crazy? Stand bye all weapons, Mr Hampton," said Thomas.

*****

"Deploy the antenna, search for a signal, then dive immediately," said Mouti to the helmsman.

"Forty ..... thirty ..... twenty ..... antenna deployed."

"There is a signal," said Zehan.

The men waited silently.

"Got it!" cried Zehan.

"Take us down to one hundred meters," shouted Mouti as the boat was rocked by explosions.

Mouti looked up at the ceiling. "They missed. God is with us."

"It is a launch order, sir," said Zehan.

The surface explosions faded as they descended.

*****

"Mr. Hampton, we are going to have to do a lot better than that if we want to become admirals," said Thomas.

The men chuckled, breaking the tension.

"Two more fish in the water," said Yablonski.

"Hard to port, ninety degrees, Mr. Blanchard. Stand bye countermeasures," said Thomas. "Deploy now!"

Four barrels shot out into the water. Sonar, acoustic, and magnetic sensors would be confused. Two explosions sent water onto the men manning the depth charges.

"They are descending and changing course, sir," said Moeller.

"They started this and I mean to finish it. Depth charges, Mr. Hampton," said Thomas.

"Yes, sir," replied Hampton.

*****

The hull shook violently again. Mouti picked up his mic.

"How soon?" asked Mouti.

"The coordinates are entered. Fueling will take another ten minutes," replied the missile officer.

"We'll launch as soon as possible. Let me know when you are ready," said Mouti.

"Yes sir."

*****

"Somebody down there has a real talent for avoiding the depth charges," said Yablonski. "Course and depth changes as soon as he hears a splash. That boat has taken more of a pounding than I thought possible."

"Launch the ship killers. We no longer have the time to play fair," said Thomas.

"Aye, aye," replied Hampton. "Deploy ship killers."

"They are climbing again. This time steadily,"said Moeller.

The experimental guided torpedo splashed into the water.

"Control signal lost upon entry into the water," said weapons specialist Thurston.

"Send another," said Hampton.

"Torpedo running," replied Thurston.

The torpedo track showed on the console in front of Thurston and Moeller. A wire guided torpedo had special problems. The hydraulic drag on the wire usually broke it before it got to its end. Then the standard sonar and magnetic sensors kicked in. You just had to get it close enough.

*****

"I'll be ready to launch in thirty seconds," reported the missile officer.

"Climb to launch depth," said Mouti.

"Torpedo coming," said Danzai. "Straight for us."

"Counter measures?" asked Mouti.

"Ineffective," said Danzai.

They stared at the hull in silence. The torpedo noise was faint. Then louder. And louder still. Then it faded.

"God is truly with us. Zehan, take over while I fire the missile," said Mouti running for the missile deck.

*****

"What the hell went wrong!" said Thomas.

"It was me, sir. I tried to guide the torpedo right in to the kill," said Thurston quietly.

"How many left?" asked Thomas.

"One, sir," replied Thurston.

"Fire it immediately. This time just get close and let the automatics take over," said Thomas.

"Aye, sir," replied Thurston.

"If you don't get it right this time, we will be forced to try to intercept a nuclear tipped missile with our hull," said Thomas.

*****

"Seventy meters.... sixty ..... fifty ....."counted the Helmsman.

Mouti thumbed the mic.

"Stand by for missile launch," he said as he jammed his launch key into the fire control panel and turned it as the missile officer did the same.

The shock wave threw him to the deck.

"Launch! Launch now!" shouted Mouti to the missile officer.

A second explosion shook the boat and the communications system went dead followed by the lights on the missile control panel. Men around him were shouting.

"Allah Akbar!" shouted Mouti in the dim emergency lighting.

*****

The cheering on the bridge subsided.

"The Marseilles is sinking, sir. Sinking deep in two pieces," said Moeller.

"Good work, Thurston. You earned your pay," said Thomas.

"Code breaking is reporting in, sir. The signal was an order to launch somewhere in England," said Smith.

"Thank you Mr. Smith. I want you to delete everything related to that signal," said Thomas.

Smith looked back in surprise.

"Everyone listen up. This was a weapons exercise. Nothing more. We don't know where the Marseilles is. Am I clear?" asked Thomas looking around the bridge.

The crew nodded in assent.

"Mr. Smith, when you have completed your task, you will acknowledge the earlier signal and reply that we have broken off the search and are heading for home," said Thomas.

Yablonski sat silently listening to the sonar.

"Is something bothering you, Mr. Yablonski," asked Thomas

"I hear men yelling," replied Yablonski.

He switched on the overhead speaker. Faint shouts brought a chill to the room.

"Crush depth and still going down," said Hampton looking at Moeller's console.

A series of popping sounds were heard from the speakers.

"It's over," said Yablonski removing his headphones.

The rattle of keys in the lock brought Hansen to full alert. The lights came on and a squad of armed guards waited outside the door. Lieutenant Clayton put them in handcuffs and led them outside. It was cold and clear. A beautiful morning. Too bad it was going to be the last he would ever see. They were marched to the British army car and truck waiting just outside the gate.

"This looks familiar," said Tom.

"I was thinking the same," said Clarke.

A civilian was waiting for them.

"I am Inspector Giscard of Interpol, here to transport two prisoners," said Giscard to Clayton.

Clayton read over the papers Giscard held out.

"Everything looks in order Inspector. They are your problem now. But be very careful, especially with this one," said Clayton pointing to Hansen. "They've been on a murder spree."

"Yes, of course," said Giscard signaling the soldiers.

"See you in hell, gentlemen," said Clayton.

Clarke and Hansen were loaded into the back of the truck by masked soldiers. Six more covered them inside. The back was closed and they moved out.

Hansen was determined to go out fighting. The six guards and the handcuffs made that difficult. Clarke nodded off but Hansen watched and waited.

The truck stopped and started again. Moving slowly on uneven ground. That hadn't taken long. He kicked Clarke's leg. Clarke looked up. Hansen nodded toward the opening. They really didn't have much chance. The truck stopped. It was now or never.

Hansen dived out the moment the back opened. He hit on his shoulder, rolled, and started running for some nearby trees. There were soldiers standing around four armored vehicles staring at him curiously. He looked back as he ran into the forest. The soldiers hadn't moved. Hadn't done anything at all. He turned to see four more soldiers standing in the forest in front of him. They motioned with their weapons for him to return to the truck. It was over.

He walked back passing another civilian sitting on the ground in handcuffs.

"Nice day for executions," said Tom as he passed the man.

The man on the ground tried to shout through his gag and struggled with his bonds. Giscard was removing the handcuffs from Clarke.

"Merci, merci" said Clarke embracing Giscard and kissing both of his cheeks.

"That's the worst case of Stockholm syndrome I've ever seen," said Hansen sarcastically. "I'd like to go out with my hands free also. But I'm not going to kiss you, Giscard."

"It's OK. This isn't Giscard. That man over there is," said Clarke.

Hansen turned to look at the man on the ground. When they looked he again made noises through his gag.

"Then who are you?" asked Hansen.

"Chief Inspector Balleau of Interpol, at your service," replied Balleau.

"The Inspector is part of my network. I didn't recognize him because we've never met before," said Clarke. "Brent made it to Middlebourne just in time. The real Giscard was intercepted and here we are."

"Just so. I was at Middlebourne and volunteered. It was easy," said Giscard.

"And I and these men were the backup plan," said Sykes coming from the command vehicle.

"Career back on track?" asked Clarke noticing Sykes uniform.

"Yes, Major Sykes now," beamed Sykes slapping Clarke on the back.

"Now what?" asked Tom.

"You're off to Middlebourne Manor. Remember the war council? You've been missed Clarke. You too, Hansen," said Sykes.

*****

Middlebourne Manor was no longer an isolated country house. It was surrounded by soldiers, armored vehicles, anti-aircraft batteries, and all the paraphernalia of impending battle. They were ushered into a side room.

There were tears in Jane's eyes as she ran to Tom. She kissed him passionately and held him. Then she stood back.

"No more heroics from you, mister. I thought I was going to lose you and I don't want to go through that again. Ever!" she said alternating between tears of joy and anger.

Hansen held her close and said nothing.

"I've got to go," she said breaking away and hurrying from the room.

"What? Where?" asked Tom, surprised.

"Back to broadcast control," said Captain Waring walking in. "Come with me to the map room. Admiral Sommerville will fill you in before the broadcast."

"What broadcast?" asked Clarke.

"The King's first speech," replied Waring leading them into the large dining room.

"Did he say king?" asked Tom looking at Clarke.

"I haven't a clue," said Clarke puzzled.

A variety of officers and support staff filled the room. In the center was a large map of England spread out on the dining table. Sommerville nodded from across the table.

"Glad to have you both with us. When I reviewed Major Sykes' report, I realized how important your contributions have been," said Sommerville. "Colonel Mills, could you fill these gentlemen in on the latest events."

"Yes, sir. Yesterday, we were able to snatch the Archbishop of Canterbury out from his hiding place and brought him here. We requested the crown jewels be released to us for the occasion but the Tower Guard refused. No surprise there. Jane Hansen used the camera equipment left here to broadcast the coronation of the new king live last night," said Mills.

"She's our media director and doing a great job," said Sommerville. "Leading the fight against the stream of lies coming from London. Her experience is proving to be of great value."

"It's starting," said Waring motioning toward the monitors. Everyone turned to watch.

Parliament was packed and Prime Minister Alexander Smith faced the room.

"Good evening, I am speaking to you tonight about the crisis that Britain and much of Europe finds itself mired in. Rest assured that our security services at every level are doing their utmost to combat the criminal element responsible for mayhem and murder across our beloved country."

"Let me remind everyone that this Parliament, our Parliament, represents the will, and carries the authority, of the people. Since the signing of the Magna Carta in 1215, the power of English monarchs has been reduced steadily while the power of the

225

people has become supreme through this body."

"The people have long called for constitutional and structural changes for the benefit of all. In our peaceful land, change is slow to arrive, and long in deliberation. However, the recent crisis has called for immediate action to stave off the breakdown of law and order.

"Tonight I am announcing the completion of the long overdue constitution. First, the House of Lords has been abolished. A body that only serves to maintain the unfair advantage of the few at the expense of the many has no place in a just society. The house of commons will remain as the one true voice of all Scots, Welsh, and Englishmen! Second, we have added a new executive post similar to the presidency of France and America. An election for this office will be held after this crisis is over."

The room erupted in applause. Smith held up his hands to restore order.

"Now let me address the most recent events of the crisis. Last evening, many of you watched the sham coronation of the criminal leader, Edmund Bane. He calls himself king. Do not be fooled or persuaded that this man has any claim to the throne. He does not. Further, I have proof of his involvement in this vast criminal outrage that plagues our land and hangs over our futures. This known Nazi sympathizer, Edmund Bane, murdered the Royal Family to take the throne for himself. How else can he explain why they died on his property! He has since surrounded himself with a band of criminals and traitors. His intelligence director, Oliver Clarke, has spread racist propaganda for many years. His military adviser, Tom Hansen, led a recent attack against English troops in the west. Killing ninety loyal men, and destroying valuable equipment. If that is not enough, Interpol has named him a conspirator in the assassination of the Pope on Christmas eve!"

Catcalls filled parliament. Hansen turned to Clarke.

"Looks like I won't be traveling anywhere for a while."

"Assassins, murderers, racists, criminals, and a man leading them calling himself king. England has never seen such an outrage and we are taking steps tonight to see it never does again. We have voted unanimously to free ourselves from the yoke of feudalism that has burdened the common Englishman for more than a thousand years. We have abolished the throne of England and further declare it against the law for anyone to claim this title or any other. This means that we are no longer the United Kingdom of England, Scotland and Wales. We are now the Republic of Great Britain."

Applause broke out again.

"With the murder of the royal family we have no king. With these changes to government we need no king!"

A huge cheer broke out.

"We know who the enemy is. Edmond Bane and his traitors will be stopped! Under the leadership of General James Kaddour, the army will mobilize and defend our homeland!"

Further applause.

"So tonight I ask that everyone who believes in truth, justice, law, and order, support your parliament and join the fight for England's future. Goodnight," said Smith.

A cheer broke out as Smith's supporters rushed forward to congratulate him. Waring turned off the monitors.

"Well. Now we know where we stand. Smith has given us a declaration of war in so many words. The King and all of us against parliament and those loyal to Kaddour," said Sommerville.

"A no man's land is developing along a rough line from the Wash to Northampton, Oxford, and Portsmouth. We are gaining control of all the territory north and west. Those loyal to the Muslim Directorate are moving toward London. So far, they haven't stopped those loyal to us from moving north. That will soon change, I'm sure," said Mills pointing to the map.

A footman touched Hansen's arm. He motioned to Clarke as well.

"The king wishes to see both of you," he said.

They followed the footman down the corridor to a large empty room that was set up as a broadcast studio. Jane waved from the control area and turned back to Wisdom and Brent who were trying to straighten out a mess of cables. Bane sat with his feet on a desk in the far corner. He waved as they entered.

"Pretend you don't know," whispered Tom.

Clarke and Hansen strolled over.

"Looks like we get to meet the new king. Know much about him?" asked Tom.

"The king? Of course, no one knows him better. Let's see where do I start? I'd say he's a man of honor, hard working, smart too, no brilliant. A man of action, not a sit around type. Fearless in battle, immensely good looking, and devastating with the ladies," replied Bane.

"Sounds like a man after your own heart," said Tom.

"Precisely," replied Bane grinning as he leaned his chair back against the wall.

"The prime minister said we were on the king's staff. And a lot of other things that weren't true," said Clarke.

"Yes. They were mostly lies but not all. You are on the king's staff. Just between us, did you really shoot the pope? There are quite a few hours you never accounted for," said Bane looking serious.

"Wisdom was with me the whole time. I think we can blame Jane's old boss, William, for that one," said Tom. "I'm a wanted man everywhere around the world because of him."

"Too true. You're safe here, though," said Bane.

"Did you find your family?" asked Tom.

"Unfortunately, I did. All of them. I plan to bury them here at Middlebourne. State funeral for the royals. The others will be turned over to their relatives when we find them," said Bane wistfully.

Colonel Mills entered the room carrying a dress sword.

"Will this do, your majesty?" asked Mills offering the sword to Bane.

Bane took the sword and waved it about.

"Yes, it will. Everyone take your places. Clarke, Hansen, stand in front of the throne. That chair over there. Just temporary of course. First order of business. Kneel," said Bane.

Clarke and Hansen did as commanded. Bane tapped their shoulders with the sword.

"Arise Sir Thomas Hansen. Arise Sir Oliver Winston Clarke," said Bane.

Clarke and Hansen stood up.

"Nice work when you can get it. How did you get the job?" asked Tom.

"Process of elimination. Excuse the pun. I'm the only peer left in England. There wasn't anybody else to take the job. And we desperately needed something or someone to rally around in a hurry," said Bane. "You are both on my staff. Clarke, I want you to take over the intelligence office. You're the only man who seems to know what is going on. Hansen, I want you to be my personal military adviser. Anyone who can whip up a winning army in twenty four hours from scratch has the kind of talent I need."

"Very true. So why not make me a duke or an earl or at least a baron. After all, I saved your ass in Malta," said Tom.

"And almost got me killed by pirates," replied Bane.

"Don't forget Clarke and I saved you from execution only a few days ago," said Tom.

"And I saved you both just this morning. Can I tell you a secret?" asked Bane leaning close. "Giving out titles is the only real power I have. If I made you a duke every other officer would want the same. I have to ration these titles or I won't last very long."

"I was only messing with you. I will always be a commoner at heart, but thanks for the knighthood," said Tom sincerely.

"We're ready now," called Jane as Sommerville and his leading officers filed in and stood behind Bane's desk.

"Showtime," said Bane as Jane added a few final touches of makeup.

Bane sat at the desk with the Union Jack behind him and his officers to either side. Bane took a deep breath and gave Jane the thumbs up.

"Five, four, three, two..." said Jane moving her hand in time.

"My name is Edmund Arthur Bane, your newly crowned King. Most of you have never seen me before last night so I am using television to introduce myself. Before I discuss the future of our country, I must address recent events."

"Tonight you heard Prime Minister Smith say that I murdered the royal family to gain this throne. Not a word he said is true. Before the crisis began I was a serving officer aboard HMS Valient stationed in Malta. Due to my ship being sunk and the political turmoil there, it took me until January 5 to return to England. I was not in the country when these murders occurred. When I returned to my home here at Middlebourne Manor, I discovered the remains of the royal family and hundreds of others. With a small band of loyal men, I overpowered those responsible and dedicated myself to uncovering the truth about these crimes. We discovered a plot devised and carried out by those who now control parliament. They planned to seize this country by force, and rule it for their own benefit. My entire family was murdered here as well. I would not kill those that I loved to gain a title I never wanted. But now that history has taken this course, I embrace this road we are embarking upon with humility and the desire both to lead and to serve the loyal men and women of this United Kingdom."

"So tonight, as my first act, I claim my sovereign authority as king and defender of the faith, to declare parliament dissolved until such time as the traitors are arrested and a new government can be formed. Behind me are the leading military men of this nation, standing with me in this time of crisis. They are here with me now having seen the evidence that proves the truth of what I have shared with you. So I call upon all loyal Englishmen to join with us in the fight to remove the traitors from power and restore all that is good about our land. Good night and god bless you all," said Bane.

"We're off," shouted Jane.

Bane sat back in his chair and breathed a sigh of relief.

"I know what Bane said is true. But can we prove it?" asked Tom turning to Jane..

"Does it matter? Hearts and minds right? We have to get our story out or we're lost. Remember what we said before?" asked Jane.

"In the absence of other information, people believe the first thing they hear," replied Tom.

"So he who lies first wins," replied Jane. "Speaking of liars, my old boss, William, is directing the propaganda campaign from the BBC."

"How do you know?" asked Tom.

"I phoned some contacts over there and got all the gossip. It's a funny war we're in. We're two armed camps but I can call over there for information and could probably take a trip to London and back," said Jane.

"Not if William caught you. One rescue is free, the next one will cost you," said Tom pulling her close.

Nick Farrow approached the barricade in the pre-dawn darkness. His guide stopped to talk to the sentry. The sentry nodded and waved them past. They turned into a building where three men stood around a fire. Others were sleeping where they could.

"You're here for Gunther Kraus, yes? Good. Follow me," said Earnst Bloch. "I'll miss the old fool. Best shot here. He said he could kill a man at a thousand yards and he fucking could. He took out ten of the bastards in sixty seconds one day. I won the bettting pool on that one. He had good stories, too. Stories of what Vienna was like before the foreigners began to take over."

They stopped at the barricade. A human form lay under a blanket unmoving.

"Here he is," said Bloch.

Bloch picked up the blanket and handed it to Nick. Gunther looked frozen solid. Dying at his post. Fingers still wrapped around the Mauser. Block freed the weapon and the ammunition pouch. He handed them and the knapsack to Nick. Two other men lifted the body and carried it to a row of other dead men.

"How did he die?" asked Nick.

"I don't know. No sign of blood. I don't think he was shot. Just old age," said Bloch.

"Do you have a wagon so I can carry him home. Or to an undertaker for burial?" asked Nick.

"We didn't summon you here to take the body. You're here to replace him," replied Bloch firmly.

"This isn't my fight. I'm Australian. I would have left long ago if I could have. You people wouldn't let me out," said Nick.

"Your pathetic story means nothing here. Every able bodied man is needed for this fight. Do it for Gunther. Or consider yourself drafted. Either way you are now under my command. Are we clear?" asked Bloch.

"No fucking way," said Nick turning away.

Bloch's men raised their rifles. Nick froze.

"This isn't a debate. You are either with us or against us. If you disobey you will be shot. If you desert you will be shot. You can't run or hide so don't get any ideas. We know where Heidi Gunther lives. It won't be pretty," said Bloch.

Nick tried to think of a way out. He had to get back to Heidi. She would be alone, unprotected. He needed time.

"You win," said Nick.

"Good. Do you know how to use that thing?" asked Bloch.

"I did my military service," replied Nick.

"Take Gunther's spot. We expect an attack at dawn. Shoot anything that moves. We'll be at the fire. Carry on, private," said Bloch heading back.

Nick put a bullet in the chamber and studied his field of fire. He covered himself in the blanket as best he could and settled in. It was kill or be killed now. His own side was as unforgiving as the enemy. If this position was overrun and he survived it, he could make his way back to Heidi. But if this post was overrun it meant that the city had fallen. Then the real hell would begin.

*****

The big black BMW was very comfortable. Nothing like his tank. Colonel Ivan Borovich looked out at the frigid streets of Moscow. Prosperous and expensive. Once again the capitol of an empire. The car grew dark as it passed into the back entrance of the Lubyanka. Once headquarters of the Cheka, then the KGB, and now the Federal Security Service. So many had passed through this same entrance to an early grave. What was that joke? The Lubyanka is the tallest building in Moscow because you can see Siberia from the basement. It had always been a building that kept its secrets.

He was taken to the third floor office of the director. Foreign minister Volynsky sat in the high backed chair facing director Golovkin.

"Come in, Borovich. Good to see you. I have read your report about Bulgaria. You will be getting some kind of medal for that. So will all our brave field commanders who succeeded so well. You proved yourself down there. So now you get a new job. A special job. One that you have been very good at in the past," said Golovkin.

"Intelligence?" asked Borovich.

"Yes. And more. Minister?" said Golovkin.

"Have a seat, Borovich," said Volynsky pointing to the chair nearest him. "Did you hear the speech of the British prime minister?"

"No. But I did read about it on the internet," replied Borovich.

"So you saw the reference to the British King's intelligence man, Clarke," said Volynsky.

"I did. And I was surprised. He was a low level civil servant who had no chance of advancement in their class structure," said Ivan.

"Never the less, you mention him frequently in your reports. What is your relationship with this man?" asked Volynsky.

"A very good one. He knew I was the intelligence officer at the embassy. He shared everything he knew about the Muslim Directorate with me. He was a good source for us," said Ivan.

"It is confirmed that he is the director of intelligence for the new king," said Golovkin. "They are locked into a civil war with the Muslim Directorate. We expect years of bloody fighting."

"Our ambassador is still in London. We officially recognize parliament as the legitimate government of England," said Volynsky. "But if the king should get full control we will switch to him and we want to get in on the ground floor. You will leave for England immediately. Make your relationship with Clarke as strong as possible. Assess who will win this conflict. If the king has a chance of victory offer aid. We want the king's army to win. We have been allies with England in the past and we can be again. But not if it is controlled by the Muslim Directorate. We are meeting here to keep this meeting secret. You will be operating outside normal channels. You will be working directly for Golovkin and he will pass your reports directly to me."

"I understand, Minister," said Ivan.

"Let us toast to your success, Borovich," said Golovkin pouring the vodka.

"Do well with this project and doors will open for you. An uncertain world makes room at the top for competent men," said Volynsky.

"To Russia!" toasted Borovich enthusiastically.

*****

Hansen walked up to the second floor room that had become Clarke's intelligence office. Colonel Mills passed him walking stiffly, pale. Hansen knocked and entered.

"What's up with Mills? He looks like he's seen a ghost," said Tom.

"The worst possible news for him, I'm afraid. His family was killed. I have confirmation," replied Clarke.

"What?" asked Tom, shocked.

"Taken Hostage. You know the drill. Work for us or they get the chop. Half of the top officers are in the same boat. Families dead or missing. Leverage was applied. The leaks were coming right out of the war room," replied Clarke.

Bane sat at the desk by the window. "I've interviewed every officer here about their families. Required proof they weren't hostages. I feel like a catholic bishop taking confession," said Bane.

"What do we do with them?" asked Tom.

"I have them swear a loyalty oath to the crown and send them on their way," replied Bane.

"We're giving amnesty for all considering the circumstances. They are good men facing unbearable pressure. Those who have lost their families have more reason than ever to carry on this fight. The men whose families are missing are moved to less sensitive areas while I try to find out what happened to them," said Clarke.

"What's the word on when we attack?" asked Tom.

"I say attack now, but my advisers tell me to wait," said Bane.

"We're on hold until Hamadi's latest propaganda campaign plays out," said Clarke. "He's using photos of Middlebourne Manor to sell the idea that we are running a death camp. That we plan on gassing all people of color."

"So?" asked Tom.

"My preliminary data says that most of the young Muslim men are lining up for military service," said Clarke.

"That's not good," said Tom.

"The devoted are staying to fight. The moderates are looking for a way out. Families are fleeing to France in large numbers. At least two people leave for every new recruit who joins up. Who would choose to live in a war zone when peace and security lie a short distance across the channel? This drain of civilians around London will cause the infrastructure to collapse. Production of war materials, food, all services will slow to a crawl. Eventually all their supplies will have to come from France," said Clarke.

"Where they can be intercepted crossing the channel," said Bane.

"I predict that two thirds of the RAF and a third of the army will come over to our side by months end. And all of the navy, of course" said Clarke.

"Have you heard the news from parliament? They elected the president that Smith was promising last night. None other than Anwar Saidi, leader of the Muslim Directorate of England.

Unanimous vote of parliament got him in. Elections to follow never most likely. He's as likely to step down as the Grand Ayatollah of Iran is. Or me for that matter," said Bane.

"Don't put yourself in the same category as an Iranian Ayatollah. English kings since Henry VIII have been kings first and heads of the church second. This pretty much guarantees the secular tradition of our governments. The Ayatollah is an Islamic cleric first and supreme leader of the land second. Just about the opposite," said Tom.

"I like that," said Bane, smiling. "You can write my speeches from now on. I wanted to get serious about being defender of the faith in my speech but your Jane wouldn't let me. Something about negativity."

"Yes, she would. She grew up being told that tolerance was the greatest virtue. Tolerance at any cost," said Tom. "It's still ingrained in her thinking. It's also just as well. We don't want to start a theological congress right now. What we need is the widest possible support and all the allies we can find until England is united. Parliament is still recognized as the government by every nation out there."

"You both have a great understanding of the big picture. I appreciate that. And speaking of big pictures, I'm having some Hollywood films shown tonight in the banquet hall. Or should I organize a dance? We need a moral booster. All work and no play can't be good. We're done with these damned interviews aren't we?" asked Bane.

Clarke nodded.

"Good. I'll see you chaps later then," said Bane walking out.

Clarke threw his pencil at the door as Bane walked out then leaned back in his chair.

"I can't believe I'm doing this," said Clarke.

"What? Leading the intelligence office?" asked Tom.

"No. Doing everything I can to keep our new king in power. I was raised to be a republican. My mother's maiden name is Cromwell and I support what he stood for. I almost cheered last night after Smith's speech. I could have written it. Get rid of the House of Lords. End the monarchy and their feudal tyranny. Create the republic of Great Britain. But now, under the circumstances we find ourselves in, I have pledged my life to a new monarch. And every officer in that war room is expecting to get at least a knighthood and land out of this war. It makes me sick. It's back to the same old England. I'm tired of this war and it hasn't even started yet," said Clarke.

Hansen sat heavily on the chair that Bane had vacated.

235

"I need a vacation," said Hansen wearily.

They both chuckled.

"All I wanted was a little sailing trip. Now I can't go home because I'm a world wide fugitive. I never expected to walk right into the middle of a take over. Here I am a self proclaimed expert on demographic shifts and never saw this coming," said Tom.

"I for one am glad you made the trip. Otherwise I'd be in Norway hiding. Sykes would have got it simply for knowing me. Bane would have joined his family outside. And Sommerville would be isolated or dead. We're going to win. And someday your name will be cleared," said Clarke firmly.

"I shouldn't complain," said Tom. "I still have Jane. And the kids are almost grown up and safe in Australia. Plus I have a new and exciting career."

"Me too. And someday I'll figure out why they gambled on this coup. Their growing numbers would have given them the whole EU without a fight," said Clarke.

"Their average age is much lower than ours. The impatience of youth drove them on. Plus the multiculturalists. They supported the growth of separate nations within nations. They blocked attempts to require assimilation. They created the conditions for war in the name of peace. Minority groups either assimilate or fight for independence. The Igbo tribe tried to leave Nigeria and create Biafra. The Basque people tried to leave Spain. The Tamil Tigers tried to gain independence from the rest of Sri Lanki," said Tom.

"And they all failed," said Clarke.

"The other side had more guns and men. Slovakia and the Czech Republic split peacefully because they had no gripe with each other. But they still didn't want to share their countries with those who were different. When different cultures are mixed together, things can get really savage. Look at Bosnia, Rwanda, and Lebanon. Different tribes are coexisting peacefully until the day a real or perceived injustice occurs. Then boom. War starts. Bosnia was stopped by NATO but only after mass murders. Hezbollah is still attacking it's rivals in Lebanon decades after fighting started. And Rwanda was left to turn into a full blown genocide. The Muslim Directorate has concentrated themselves in one area. We face a straight fight for territory," said Tom.

"Can't we talk about something other than war?" asked Clark.

"Sorry. I'm a history professor. I don't know what hats were the rage in Rome back in 43BC, but I do know Octavian was victorious at Philippi that year. History is a continuous story of

236

border clashes, raids, assassinations, invasions, insurrections, revolutions, civil wars, world wars, and police actions. If that isn't enough you can throw in a genocide every now and again to spice things up. Plato said 'Only the dead have seen the end of war' twenty four hundred years ago. His words are just as true now as then. I don't understand why anyone is surprised when conflicts erupt. We're still the same human race that Plato referred to," said Tom.

"So the only sure path to security is to keep separate and stay that way," said Clarke. "Keep all who are us and keep out all who are them?"

"Muslims have been attacking Christian lands since Mohammad's day. Why should it stop now? Let Muslims live in their countries. Let us live in ours," replied Tom. "The question no one is asking is whether this people, this culture, this way of life is worth fighting for. If you think it is, we all face one choice. Join the fight or be swept into the dustbin of history."

"Isn't there any way to live together in peace?" asked Clarke.

"Yes there is," said Tom.

Clarke looked up in surprise.

"Embrace EU policy for the last generation. Surrender, capitulate, appease, and accept your enslavement. In a word, submission," said Tom.

*****

Mustapha Najid stood before the Douaumont Ossuaire and stared up at the tower. Lovely construction. Rain began to fall into his eyes. Rain was good. He entered the building and walked up to the large map mounted to the wall. His full staff filled the room.

"You all wonder why we are meeting here, yes?" asked Najid surveying the room. "Look around, enjoy the view while you can. Places like this will be fading from this land like the beliefs of the men who are buried outside. We are going to start the changes that we must make for the future of the sixth republic."

"First, we will begin by changing the curriculum of all schools this fall. Arabic and Islamic studies will be required for all students. Boys and girls will be separated. Youth will be redirected into the proper way of thinking. Over time the heritage of old France will be forgotten. Replaced by the new. The crucifix will be banned from all schools and all public places. The ban on the burqa and other Muslim symbols will be lifted."

"What about the churches? Should Christianity be outlawed?"

asked the minister of culture.

"No. Let the dhimmis find what comfort there that they can. They may keep their crosses for now but only inside the churches. Outdoor crosses must be removed. If they make trouble over this, show them no mercy," said Najid firmly.

"And the Jews?" asked the minister.

"The same rules apply. For ten years there has been a steady stream of Jews leaving Europe. Talk to the Rabbis. Encourage this. We cannot control the anger of our people at all times in all places. But put a cap on how much money they can take with them. We won't let them steal what belongs to us now."

"Second, national service is now required of all young men. Muslims into the military and all others into civil areas."

"Third, only the faithful can be trusted to have guns. In or out of the military. Private ownership of guns is banned for all infidels. There will be no counter revolution. Begin collecting them immediately."

The new police commissioner nodded.

"Fourth, there will be no Christian holiday celebrations outside of churches. Christmas and Easter will not be in any way supported by government or media. December 25 will now be called Liberation day and celebrated as our preeminent holiday."

"Fifth. Dhimmis will not be hired for any government jobs. Those currently holding lower and medium positions can retain their jobs until we replace them or they retire."

Najid stepped up to the map.

"Let us review the current situation. Turkey has gained control of Cyprus, Crete, Greece, Bulgaria, Albania, and Macedonia. We have gained control of Portugal, France, Italy, Austria, Bosnia, Slovenia, Croatia, Czech Republic, Belgium, Holland, Ireland, Denmark, Sweden, most of Spain, western Hungary, southern England, and Germany west of the the Rhine and south of the Main rivers."

The room broke out into applause. Mansour Hamdar stepped forward.

"This is a day for celebration. The Caliphate in Europe is now a reality. We have joined the faithful across these borders," said Hamdar.

More applause.

"It is not enough," said Najid.

"We did not liberate all of the EU members. But let us not forget how the Turks betrayed us," said Hamdar.

"So I thought, too. Now I see that they may have done more to hold back the Russians than any other factor. We are now living in the calm before the storm. We face German tanks along the Rhine, Russian tanks across the Danube, English tanks around London, and Spanish tanks in Galicia. Mark my words, our struggle is not over. We cannot show weakness lest we invite attack."

"Then attack now. We have a fuel advantage. That won't last when Russian oil refills their fuel reserves. Take the initiative before they do," said Hamdar.

"I agree. My sixth point is the removal of this thorn in our side down in Spain. The plan to capture Galicia is my military priority. General Salani, you will lead the attack as soon as the army is ready. We cannot allow this sore to fester long enough for the British to use it as a beach head against us. Without La Caruna, the Atlantic works for our defense as much as it does for the English."

"And Vienna?" asked General Salani.

"It is contained. They will surrender when they run out of food and ammunition," replied Najid. "Point seven. Saidi will fight for England. So long as England is fighting for its own land, they won't have resources to bother us elsewhere. If we are driven back, we shall leave a scorched earth that takes a generation to rebuild. This will keep them busy long enough for us to become secure and invulnerable in the rest of Europe."

"If we declare a Fatwah, the faithful from across the Muslim world will take up arms to fight for us in England," said Mullah Wahani.

"That option will be kept in reserve for when we need it most. Point eight. We must develop a detailed and effective mutual defensive strategy with our Muslim brothers in Turkey. Opportunities to expand in the east may present themselves in the future but now I am content to hold these borders without further fighting. Too much too soon would be a mistake. If the eastern front remains peaceful, we can move resources to England. Ambassador Aeule, you will work with General Marchiano on this," replied Najid.

"Point nine. You diplomats will get the American president over here for the NATO closing ceremony. We need to turn the page on NATO before an election changes American policy. We don't want them coming back to Europe in any way, shape, or form," said Najid.

"The agreed upon site at Fairford is in the hands of our enemies. Will we go there?" interrupted Ambassador Aeul.

"Of course not. Fairford was only chosen for security reasons. That's no longer a valid argument. It should have been in

Brussels all along. See to it, Auel," replied Najid.

Ambassador Aeul nodded.

"Item ten is something more pleasant. We will build a mosque. The largest and most beautiful mosque ever constructed," said Najid.

Hamdar looked pleased. "To celebrate our victory?"

"No, of course not. To celebrate the prophet, his name be praised, and to celebrate god. Everything we have achieved is god's will, not ours," said Najid.

"Do you have a place in mind?" asked Hamdar.

"Yes, the hill of Montmartre. From the heights it will dominate the city," said Najid.

"Tear down Sacre Coeur?" asked Hamdar.

"I think so. To modify it for our purposes would glorify the Christian past. Better to start from scratch. Reuse the stone if feasible. Call for design bids from across the Muslim world. Only Muslims will take part in this work," said Najid.

"What of the Christians?" asked Asim.

"Paris is full of churches. One less makes no difference. Don't think I am a savage, Hamdar. I was appalled by the destruction of the Banyan Bhuddas. World heritage sites will be protected. Notre Dame will be protected. But let them never forget that we are now the masters, they the dhimmis. Too much pride among the Christians will only lead to trouble in the future. We will make a clean break from the Christian past and cease to glorify it in any form. So I am also ordering the destruction of the Cathedral of Rheims. In addition, we will demolish monuments to the World Wars like this one. They serve no purpose now. They honor and remember a heritage that is now irrelevant. The Islamic Republic of France will not celebrate any history but that of the prophet and the struggle to form the Caliphate," said Najid.

"And the graves?" asked Hamdar.

"Leave them. The dead are no threat to us. Thank you all for coming, now get to work. Completion of theses ten points will secure the Caliphate and all our futures," said Najid moving to the door.

He shook hands and gave encouragement to all his staff members as they filed out. He motioned Hamdar and Asim to wait.

"Well?" asked Najid.

Asim tapped the map of Scotland.

"All the British missile submarines have left port. So have ours," said Asim.

"And the Marseilles?" asked Najid.

"I sent the recall order as you requested," replied Asim.

"And?" said Najid.

"Their fate is not known," said Asim.

Najid nodded.

"I have a secret mission for you, Hamdar. And you, Asim. One we will keep from the rest. I want you to go to England and meet with this new English king and his top man, Admiral Sommerville. Tell him that we won't use nuclear weapons against them if they will do the same. I don't want another Warsaw," said Najid.

He motioned for Hamdar to join him and headed outside. Out among the graves.

"Nineteen fourteen was the year the decline of Europe began. They were at their peak of wealth and influence. And hubris. Then they killed millions of their own people in this war for nothing. Afterward they started to lose faith in their way of life. Collapse was inevitable. Now they have lost everything."

Najid kneeled down and scooped up a handful of soil and held it out to Hamdar.

"This soil is alive, Hamdar. Black and moist and productive. The desert of our ancestors is a cruel place of heat and sand. It is a dead end for our people. Our numbers there are already more than our old lands can support. We can't grow there. We had no choice but to take this land from the dhimmis for ourselves. This green land is the paradise promised to us. Our children and grand children will prosper. We can live and thrive here for all time so long as we protect this earth. Clean water and food must be protected. Let's not lose it to nuclear poison. This land is too precious. When the oil is gone, good land will be the only thing that matters," said Najid.

Hamdar was surprised by Najid's emotions. They stood up. Najid became cold and serious again.

"You are the only one I can trust with this. Bypass Saidi. Get the British to agree. You must succeed or our victory will be meaningless," said Najid.

This is the BBC, Ali Ben Kasim reporting from London. After a week of fierce fighting in and around Brno, the invading army of Polish and German crusaders began retreating back to Poland. They were the last chance of rescue for the Christian extremists who had seized Vienna back in December and held out against security forces even as starvation gripped the city. As news of the retreat spread across Vienna, resistance crumbled and security forces moved quickly to restore order.

General Serif celebrated his victory with his men at the Schonbrunn Palace. He promised to build a monument to the struggle. One that would remember the faithful who had fallen during this siege of Vienna, as well as those who had fallen during the previous Muslim invasions of 1529 and 1683.

*****

William studied the ceiling of the great gallery. In his eyes, the Schonbrunn Palace, on the outskirts of Vienna, was the most beautiful in all of Europe. General Serif had made the palace his headquarters. Desks and staff members filled the space and at the end, like a Hapsburg Emperor, stood the general. Victor at Brno and conqueror of Vienna. William left his production team to follow the general's aide.

Serif watched his visitor approach. Sizing him up. William Hamadi was now a powerful man. Not just because has had Najid's ear. Hamadi was now director of all media in the Caliphate. That meant he could make or break almost anyone. A clever edit here or a new camera angle there could make a genius look like a fool and visa versa. Serif was an ambitious man. He needed friends like Hamadi. That is why he had so diligently tried to fulfill the request asked of him.

"I am pleased to meet you at last, general," said William shaking his hand. "Congratulations on your victory at Brno. Najid was impressed. We all were."

"We each have our talents. Mine is commanding an army in battle. I wouldn't trade it for any other. Not even yours," said Serif smiling knowingly.

"I am interested in all your opinions general. My team is ready to start interviewing you at your soonest convenience. Strike while the iron is hot as they say. And right now you and your victory are the hottest story of all. We're going to give it all we have. Every struggle needs heroes. You will be the first along with who ever you designate to share a small piece of your glory," said William.

"You are most kind. I appreciate what you are doing for me. I want you to know that you can count on me now and in the future," said Serif.

"I know I can. Now to the other matter. Did you ...? asked William.

"Here is all I found," said Serif motioning to his aide.

The aide stepped forward with a large envelope. Serif dumped the contents on his desk. William picked through the debris. A wallet with Nick's drivers license. A union card. A bracelet that had Nick engraved on it. He studied the passport photo. It was dirty and torn. One corner was covered in dried blood.

"I had my best men scour the city. These items were located at a place of execution. The prisoners belongings were taken before they were thrown into a mass grave. My best guess is that Nick Farrow was shot and lies with the others. Maybe he joined them or maybe it was a case of wrong place wrong time," said Serif.

"And the girl?" asked William.

"No sign of her. Things happened too quickly for me to do anything. I had only just routed the enemy at Brno when word arrived that resistance in Vienna was crumbling. The traffickers were here waiting for their chance and came in just behind the army. There is no way to know now what happened to Heidi Kraus. Or any other unprotected young woman in a city being sacked. I'm sorry," said Serif sincerely.

Sorry that he couldn't deliver a favor that would have put him solidly in Hamadi's good graces.

Hamadi scooped up the items and returned them to the envelope and tucked them into his coat pocket.

"I appreciate your diligence, general. Please consider me your friend, now and in the future," said William.

Serif shook his hand again, very pleased at this outcome.

*****

Doctor Ranjit Amapurti sat in his office at the end of the hospital ward. He had learned to ignore the sound of artillery fire in the distance. He had also learned to ignore the moans of pain from the casualties of battle. The staff was overworked. Some had stopped coming in. He didn't know what had happened to them. But he had the sense that they were deserting a sinking ship. Otherwise, it had been quiet. Only one stoning and two beheadings in front of the hospital today. He opened his journal and began to write.

'We live in unbelievable conditions of the most dreadful despotism, exercised by ignorant, vulgar, and corrupt elements. Of justice, nobody thinks. The war has annulled and canceled community, truth, honor, and self-respect, exchanging them for mischief, rape, and robbery stopping at nothing. The aim excuses the means. Of other morality, there is none. All industry has stopped. We are now struggling to find food.'

He pulled his bedroll from the top of the filing cabinet. He was either working or on call twenty four hours a day now. It made sense to live at the hospital. The streets were no longer safe.

*****

"Tom Hansen has given you such a glowing recommendation how could I say no?" said Dawayne Jackson cheerfully. "But when this trouble in England is sorted out, I would like you to present your teaching credentials as soon as possible. Now follow me."

Wisdom Achebe stood, straightened his new tailored suit, and followed the history chairman.

"We'll start you on the history of western civilization this quarter. See how things go. You'll need time to adjust to living in America I'm sure," said Dawayne stopping before the lecture hall door.

"There is always room for another African American on my staff. Or do you consider yourself an African?" asked Dawayne.

Wisdom thought about the question for a moment. He had left Africa behind for good.

"I think of myself as an American. That is what I want to be considered," said Wisdom.

"Uh, fine. Stop by if you need anything," said Dawayne.

"Thank you, I will," replied Wisdom shaking his hand again.

Wisdom stood at the front of the classroom, watching it fill up nervously. How could he teach a college class without experience or training or education? Captain Tom had assured him that he had more to offer young impressionable minds than most of the professors he knew. And Wisdom had studied the textbook that Captain Tom had picked out for him. He went to the chalk board and wrote his name.

"My name is Wisdom Achebe. I was born in Chad and after many years, I have arrived in America ready to share my perspective on history. This class is entitled the History of Western Civilization. If this is not your class please leave now," said Wisdom.

No one left the room. He began to feel more comfortable.

"Western civilization has much to offer the world. We will start with the development of the idea that the common man should have some political rights. Cleisthenes is credited with putting this idea into practice in Athens around the year 508 B.C. Fifty years later, Pericles is remembered for pushing this idea further, saying that the common man should have the same political rights as the wealthy aristocracy. Of course, this great idea was lost as the world became dominated by princes, kings, and emperors, who took absolute power into their own hands. Later we will examine the period known as the age of reason, where the aspirations of the common man re-emerge as political reality. The best example is the war of independence from England. The American founding fathers brought forth a great nation where rich and poor were politically equal if not in any other way. So you will see how the ideas of ancient times have affected the values of America today," said Wisdom.

"Hold on, hold on. I'll cut you some slack cause you're new here, but you can't be glorifying the founding fathers. They were a bunch of no good slave owners and that alone cancels out anything else you could say about them," said Andre Davis.

This was the class monitor from the African American student union that Captain Tom had warned him about. Next to him sat members of the other student unions who wanted to control the education process. Wisdom studied the young man. Sizing him up instinctively as years of jungle fighting had taught him. He was soft.

"Stand up," said Wisdom calmly.

"I'm in charge here, bro. I don't have to do shit for you," said Andre slouching.

"Stand up!" said Wisdom sharply.

Andre was surprised by Wisdom's tone. He stood reluctantly.

"Name?" said Wisdom.

"That's none of your business," said Andre.

"Name!" commanded Wisdom.

245

"I am Andre Davis, class monitor from the African American Student Union," he replied.

Wisdom ignored him as he looked through the class list.

"You do not belong here, Mr. Davis. Please leave now," said Wisdom firmly.

"I'm staying to do my job. I'm standing up for justice in America," said Andre.

Wisdom looked him in the eye and shook his head. "To know about justice, you must first know about injustice. Otherwise it is empty talk like your talk."

"Hold on there, Mr. Chadian. You can't talk to me like that if you know what is good for you," said Andre.

"You are wrong. I know exactly what is good for me. You must leave my classroom and never come back if you know what is good for you," said Wisdom.

"Like hell I will. You can't make me," said Andre.

"Yes I can," said Wisdom. "I was driven from my village and later made a slave. When I escaped I was forced into an army and made into a killer of men. Then a slave again. Then a soldier again. Never a free man until I came to America."

"Yeah, right. What ever you say, Mr. Chadian," replied Andre cynically, sitting down again.

"You have come to my class uninvited and give me orders. You try to impose your will upon me. When I left Africa I swore that I would never kneel again. I have killed twenty seven men. You will become number twenty eight if you do not leave immediately!" said Wisdom walking slowly up the steps to the back of the lecture hall.

Andre Davis was taken by surprise. No one had challenged him before. He watched with increasing fear as Wisdom climbed each step. He couldn't mean what he just said, could he?

"I'll get you for this," shouted Andre as he went out the back way.

Wisdom stared hard at the other trouble makers who avoided eye contact with him. When they had all left the hall, he returned to the podium and straightened his tie. He went to the blackboard and began to write.

"Lesson number one. The common man has gained and lost his freedom many times over the centuries. But one thing is always true. People who will not fight, lose everything!"

*****

General Salazar finished his cigar and threw the stub over the side of HMS Dauntless. He could see the lights of La Caruna on the horizon as the destroyer cruised back and forth along the Spanish coast.

He had accepted that he couldn't save Spain early on. Then he had realized that he would lose the fight for Galicia. He would get no reinforcements from England. Or America. Even the Russian pilots and dock workers couldn't change the slow attrition that guaranteed defeat. While the enemy rotated fresh troops in and out, his men could never leave the front. Airstrikes and artillery fire never ended. Homes were burned, farmers strafed. This fight would end with everyone who supported him killed on the battle field or after surrendering.

Then a way out presented itself in the form of a cease fire arranged by Tom Hansen and Khalil Asim. He didn't know what brought them together. They were a very odd pairing. Over the last two days of negotiation they had both referred to 'the deal' or 'the bigger picture' when they hit an impasse. They didn't reply when he asked about it. They would look at each other and nod. Clearly some secret he would not be told. He returned to the captain's cabin.

Hansen's assistant brought in the finished document.

"OK, I'll read the final draft and then we can all sign," said Hansen.

Salazar and Asim nodded.

"One. The ceasefire will continue while all points of this agreement are satisfied. Two. All combatants and their families will be loaded on transport ships to be provided by Mr. Asim. Non combatants and their families will not be allowed to leave. Non combatants will not be punished in any way. Three. The transports will travel directly from La Caruna to Buenos Aires with no stops in between. No soldiers will be allowed to travel to England. Now or in the future. Four. Soldiers will be allowed to take one automatic rifle of caliber 7.62 millimeters or less and one hundred rounds of ammunition each. No other weapons or weapons systems will be removed. Brazilian observers will inspect all cargo for compliance. Five. Ships will disembark no later than seventy two hours after loading begins. Five. HMS Dauntless will escort the transport ships to Buenos Aires, with Khalil Asim, Tom Hansen, and General Salazar aboard, to guarantee compliance. Six. Violation of any of these points will void this agreement. Seven. General Salazar is granted immunity from prosecution for all acts committed from the outbreak of the Canary Island rioting to his arrival in Buenos Aries. And finally. General Salazar will be allowed to take his yacht, the Santa Ana, to Argentina on the condition neither he nor his yacht ever return to Europe."

Hansen paused.

"If we sign now, we can begin tomorrow morning at oh eight hundred. Are we agreed?" he asked looking at Salazar.

It was the end. He would go ashore once more then never see his beloved Spain again in his lifetime. He would meet his family in Argentina and live the rest of his days in exile, wondering what more he could have done to change this outcome. He had tried his best. No one had supported him. Now it was over. He sighed with resignation.

"Yes, I agree," said Salazar raising his pen.

*****

Jane surveyed her broadcast empire. She was the face of the news just like before. Only now she was the boss. Of everything. The King's minister of information. Locked into a battle with her old boss, William Hamadi, for the soul of England.

"This is the BBC. Jane Hansen reporting from Edinburgh. After days of fierce fighting, the royal army has captured Reading. While the army has slowly advanced toward London from three sides, Admiral Sommerville has stated that no moves into the city can begin until the heavily fortified Parliamentarian Army at Aldershot is neutralized."

"Outside of Cambridge today, the King made a surprise visit to a forward artillery position and helped fire the guns until return fire required him to seek cover with the other men. He continues to tour the front lines to bolster moral."

"Liverpool harbor is busier now than at any time since World War II. Ships from the navies of the new Caliphate of Europe continue to mutiny and head to ports in Britain. Admiral Sommerville has stated that naval ships of all nations not at war with Britain are welcome to visit for as long as they like. When asked for comment, a spokesman for the new Caliphate denied that any ships had mutinied."

"From London comes the story that the contents of the British Museum are being packed up for transport to Paris. A parliamentarian spokesman said this is being done to protect the world's best collection of antiquities from looters or war damage. The contents will be moved even though the King has guaranteed that hospitals and other sites of historical and cultural significance will not be bombed. The spokesman also stated that the crown jewels have been removed from the Tower of London.

When asked specifically, he promised that the jewels would not be removed from England and that this was only being done for security reasons."

"On the international front, the Spanish army was stopped outside of Lugo four days ago after a strong counter attack by the rebel Christian army led by General Salazar. A spokesman for the Spanish army stated that the victory was achieved by the air superiority of new MIG fighter jets from Russia. General Salazar has denied any kind of military alliance with Russia. An unnamed source in Madrid claims that the MIGs were not only given to the rebels, but that they were being flown by Russian pilots. A cease fire has been in effect since the battle while both sides seek an answer to this bloody conflict."

"As fighting rages across Europe, the President of the United States spoke to the press today in Atlanta. He said that America had no interest in European wars any longer. He supported the Jeffersonian idea of no foreign entanglements in Europe. At the same time, he reaffirmed his support of the Monroe doctrine with respect to the new world. The doctrine in which the United States gives itself the power to intervene unilaterally in any country of central or south America."

"The president of Venezuela responded to this speech by reminding the President that the Organization of American States, meeting in Caracas last month, voted to reject the Monroe doctrine as an unacceptable and outdated example of American imperialism."

Jane paused as a staff member put a sheet of paper in front her. She scanned it quickly and covered the microphone.

"Are you sure about this?" she asked her producer.

The producer gave her a firm thumbs up.

"We turn to a breaking story coming to us from Venezuela. There are widespread reports of gun fire outside of Caracas. All normal communications have ceased with that country. Our only reliable source is saying that American marines have landed on the coast in two places in support of airborne troops who have parachuted into the country to secure the Venezuelan oil fields. We'll have more on this developing story as it becomes available."

"This is Jane Hansen reporting from Edinburgh, goodnight."

www.ingramcontent.com/pod-product-compliance
Lightning Source LLC
Chambersburg PA
CBHW031316040426
42443CB00005B/93